THE ULTIMATE COCKTAIL BOOK II

© Foley Publishing Corp

Cover by LeRoy Neiman

Printed in the United States of America

First Printing August 1998

10 9 8 7 6 5 4 3 2 1

© Copyright 1998 by Raymond Peter Foley

Published by Foley Publishing Corp.

ISBN 0-9617655-5-0

DEDICATION

To LeRoy Neiman for his contribution

and acknowledgment of Bartenders

in his Art and Heart!

To the 145,000 plus readers

of BARTENDER Magazine

and the thousands of bartenders

who sent us recipes via our website.

www.bartender.com

And especially to

Jaclyn Marie and Ryan Peter Foley

© Foley Publishing Corp

INTRODUCTION

As a Bartender for over 20 years and publisher of *BARTENDER Magazine* for 19 years, I now have the honor of presenting *The Ultimate Cocktail Book*.

I started collecting cocktail recipe books over 20 years ago and my collection now consists of over 750 different books from 1862 to the present day. Many new products and cocktails have been created since 1862. With the influx of new products in the 90s, many new cocktails have become as popular as the old standards. We have included in this guide the old standards as well as the more popular cocktails of the 90s and into the millennium.

I have also selected the finest ingredients to be represented in *The Ultimate Cocktail Book*. After all, when preparing a great steak, you must start with a great piece of meat. Likewise, by using the best liquor you create the ultimate cocktail. The proof is in the taste. Use premium brands at all times. They represent your cocktail, your establishment, and you.

We have not included drink recipes with items you'll have difficulty finding (i.e., Italian blue olives, Chinese sesame syrup, New Zealand kumquat mix, etc.).

Drinks are listed alphabetically by Liquor in the Table of Contents and by Name in the Index.

Enjoy *The Ultimate Cocktail Book*. But, please remember not to drink in excess. Moderation is the key word. Good judgment for yourself and your guests is most important to any successful party. Drinking and driving do not mix! The cocktail recipes herein are for your pleasure. Enjoy in moderation.

CHEERS,

Raymond P. Foley

Ray Foley is the publisher of the critically acclaimed BARTENDER Magazine and has been a professional bartender for more than 20 years. He is the author of Bartending for Dummies*, The Ultimate Little Shooter Book, Advice from Anonymous, The Book of X-Rated Drinks, and Spirits of Ireland.

*Bartending for Dummies is a registered trademark under exclusive license to IDG Books Worldwide, Inc. from International Data Group, Inc.

© Foley Publishing Corp

ACKNOWLEDGMENT

TO THE BRAND MANAGERS, PUBLIC RELATIONS FIRMS, AGENCIES AND SUPPLIERS WHO MADE THIS *THE ULTIMATE COCKTAIL BOOK*

I would like to personally thank the following who have made this *The Ultimate Cocktail Book:*

The Alden Group Public Relations, with special thanks to Laura Baddish.

Anheuser-Busch, Inc., with special thanks to Diane Burnell and also Michael McNeal of Busch Media Group, Inc.

Bensur Advertising, with special thanks to Michelle Leone.

Bacardi-Martini, U.S.A. Inc., with special thanks to Celio Romanach, Carlos Ribas and Carol Lloyd.

C&C International, with special thanks to Alan Lewis.

Charles Jacquin, et Cie., Inc., with special thanks to Norton J. Cooper, Patricia Bornmann and Kevin O'Brien.

Fleishman-Hillard, Inc., with special thanks to Sandy Schenck.

Heublein Inc., with special thanks to Jason Madrak.

Hiram Walker & Sons, Inc., with special thanks to Marshall Dawson, Guido Goldkuhle, Eric Larsen, Charles Metzger, Janine Paley, Mike Seguin and Dave Waluk.

IDV North America, with special thanks to Merry Hampton, Kay Olsen and Alan Weber.

Libbey Glass, Inc., with special thanks to David Pett.

Lorraine Hale, Marketing Manager, Kobrand Corporation, New York, NY

Manning Selvage & Lee, with special thanks to Danielle Brown and Andi Spolan.

Milton Samuels Advertising, with special thanks to Keith Klein.

MSA Promotions Group, with special thanks to Dana Smith.

Neiman Studios, with special thanks to LeRoy Neiman and Lynn Quayle.

Niche Marketing Corp., with special thanks to Peter Nelson, Michelle C. Krause, and Brian Winarsky.

Seagram Americas, with special thanks to Bob Bernstein, Drew DeSarno and Carl Horton.

The Redwing Company, Inc., with special thanks to Troy Woodrow.

UDV North America, with special thanks to Helaine Harte.

Gary Clayton and Onute Miller of Domecq Importers, Inc.

And to all those who posted recipes on our website at www.bartender.com and e-mailed us at barmag@aol.com.

ACKNOWLEDGMENT
ABOUT THE ARTIST
LeROY NEIMAN

The art of LeRoy Neiman vividly chronicles the vitality, depth, and emotion of the art of Bartending. The very principle we urge all of you to reflect in the way you work—the fact that Bartending is an art as well as a profession to be treated with respect, dignity, and pride—Neiman reflects in his art with consummate skill, insight and sensitivity.

To refer to him as the most popular artist in America today is almost an understatement. Over the years, LeRoy Neiman has firmly established himself as the artist of and for the people. He renders the excitement, color, movement and emotion of people and places popular enough for all to relate to and identify with.

Throughout the 1950s, Neiman was living in Chicago's near North Side in the Night Club Belt where he drew on the activities of its people for his material. Critics at the time referred to his work as a revival of the historically popular saloon painting, capturing the sights and emotions of this universal and timeless relaxation of man.

His work, The Chicago Key Club, was exhibited at the Corcoran American Exhibition of Oil Painting, 25th Biennial, Washington, DC, in 1957. Also in 1957, his oil painting The Pump Room won the popular prize from out of the 3,000 works exhibited in the Chicago Artist Show at the Navy Pier, voted on by some 25,000 visitors. In 1958, Neiman's painting The Bartender won the Municipal Art Award in the Chicago Artist Show.

Also in 1958, Neiman began his feature, Man at His Leisure, in *PLAYBOY MAGAZINE* with The Pump Room. The 15 ensuing years the feature ran allowed Neiman to expand his interest in capturing Man at His Leisure from the popular saloons of Chicago traveling internationally to the world's most expensive and glamorous social and sporting events.

It is not simply coincidence that caused Neiman to focus his early work on bartenders. Growing up in St. Paul, Minnesota, Neiman recalls that during the depression there was little else for the fathers to do than to spend time in neighborhood bars. Amid all of this stood the Bartender, a distinctive figure and neighborhood hero. In contrast to his customers, the Bartender was always cleanly dressed in his pressed white shirt, wearing his Sunday finest every day of the week. He maintained his dignity and a sense of style and class by not drinking and being in control throughout his customers' downhearted imbibing and stimulated revelry.

We once again would like to thank LeRoy Neiman for sharing his talent and generosity with *BARTENDER Magazine, The Ultimate Cocktail Book* and its readers.

Photo by Paul Chapnick

© Foley Publishing Corp

CONTENTS AT A GLANCE

ABSOLUT VODKA

ABSOLUT CITRON VODKA

ABSOLUT KURANT VODKA

ABSOLUT PEPPAR VODKA

ALIZÉ

BEEFEATER DRY GIN

CANADIAN CLUB

CHAMBORD

CUERVO (JOSE)

CUTTY SARK

DRAMBUIE

GOLDWASSER (DER LACHS)

HIRAM WALKER LIQUEURS

IRISH PRODUCTS: CAROLANS

IRISH MIST

28

MARTINI & ROSSI

MOZART CHOCOLATE LIQUEUR

SINGLE MALTS

ANHEUSER-BUSCH, INC

SIGNATURE DRINKS

POUSSE-CAFES

© Foley Publishing Corp

FACTS ON LIQUOR AND PROOF

THE MEANING OF PROOF

Proof spirit, underproof, and overproof are terms difficult to explain in easy language since they are arbitrary standards set up by governments for collection of revenue.

Proof spirit is defined by law to be spirit which at 51°F. weighs $^{12}/_{13}$ of an equal measure of distilled water. At 51°F. it has a specific gravity of .92308. It is a mixture of about 57% pure alcohol and 43% water.

An underproof mixture of alcohol and water contains less than 100% of the mixture called proof spirit. So in 100 gallons of 20 underproof whiskey there is 80 gallons at proof strength and 20 extra gallons of water.

Overproof whiskey contains more alcohol and less water than proof spirit.

This proof chart shows these differences.

Britian & Canada		American		Alcohol by % Vol.
	75.25	200	Proof	100.0%
	Overproof			
50	Overproof	172	Proof	86.0%
30	Overproof	149	74.5%	
	Proof	114.2	Proof	57.1%
12.5	Underproof	100	Proof	50.0%
30	Underproof	80	Proof	40.0%
50	Underproof	57	Proof	28.5%
100	Underproof	0	Proof	0.0%

CHARTS & MEASURES

MEASUREMENTS

	Metric	Standard
1 Dash	0.9 ml	$\frac{1}{32}$ ounce
1 Teaspoon	3.7 ml	$\frac{1}{8}$ ounce
1 Tablespoon	11.1 ml	$\frac{3}{8}$ ounce
1 Pony	29.5 ml.	1 ounce
1 Jigger	44.5 ml.	1-$\frac{1}{2}$ ounces
1 Wineglass	119.0 ml.	4 ounces
1 Split	177.0 ml.	6 ounces
1 Miniature (nip)	59.2 ml.	2 ounces
1 Half Pint	257.0 ml.	8 ounces
1 Tenth	378.88 ml.	12.8 ounces
1 Pint	472.0 ml.	16.0 ounces
1 Fifth	755.2 ml.	25.6 ounces
1 Quart	944.0 ml.	32.0 ounces
1 Imperial Quart	1.137 Liter	38.4 ounces
1 Half Gallon	1.894 Liter	64.0 ounces
1 Gallon	3.789 Liter	128.0 ounces

Dry Wine and Champagne

	Metric	Standard
Split ($\frac{1}{4}$ bottle)	177.0 ml	6 ounces
Pint ($\frac{1}{2}$ bottle)	375.2 ml.	12 ounces
Quart (l bottle)	739.0 ml.	25 ounces
Magnum (2 bottles)	1.534 Liter	52 ounces
Jeroboam (4 bottles)	3.078 Liter	104 ounces
Tappit-hen	3.788 Liter	128 ounces
Rehoboam (6 bottles)	4.434 Liter	
Methuselah (8 bottles)	5.912 Liter	
Salmanazar (12 bottles)	8.868 Liter	
Balthazar (16 bottles)	11.829 Liter	
Nebuchadnezzar (20 bottles)	14.780 Liter	
Demijohn (4.9 gallons)	18.66 Liter	

DEPARTMENT OF THE TREASURY
BUREAU OF ALCOHOL, TOBACCO AND FIREARMS
DISTILLED SPIRITS

Bottle Size	Equivalent Fluid oz.	Bottles/ Per Case	Liters/ Per Case	U.S. Gallons Per Case	Corresponds To
1.75 Liters	59.2	6	10.50	2.773806	½ Gallon
1.00 Liters	33.8	12	12.00	3.170064	1 Quart
750 ml.	25.4	12	9.00	2.377548	⅘ Quart
500 ml.	16.9	24	12.00	3.170064	1 Pint
200 ml.	6.8	48	9.60	2.536051	½ Pint
50 ml.	1.7	120	6.00	1.585032	1, 1.6, 2 oz.

DEPARTMENT OF THE TREASURY
BUREAU OF ALCOHOL, TOBACCO AND FIREARMS
WINE

Bottle Size	Equivalent Fluid oz.	Bottles/ Per Case	Liters/ Per Case	U.S. Gallons/ Per Case	Corresponds To
4 Liters	135				1 Gallon
3 Liters	101	4	12.00	3.17004	⅘ Gallon
1.5 Liters	50.7	6	9.00	2.37753	⅖ Gallon
1 Liter	33.8	12	12.00	3.17004	1 Quart
750 ml.	25.4	12	9.00	2.37763	⅘ Quart
375 ml.	12.7	24	9.00	2.37753	⅘ Pint
187 ml.	6.3	48	8.976	2.37119	⅖ Pint
100 ml.	3.4	60	6.00	1.58502	2, 3, 4 oz.

CALORIES & CARBOHYDRATES

	Calories	Carbo-hydrates
Ale	72	
Beer (12 oz. bottle or can)	144	11.7
Light Beer	110	6.9
Bourbon		
80 proof, distilled	65	trace
86 proof, distilled	70	trace
90 proof, distilled	74	trace
94 proof, distilled	77	trace
100 proof, distilled	83	trace
Brandy		
80 proof, distilled	65	trace
86 proof, distilled	70	trace
90 proof, distilled	74	trace
94 proof, distilled	77	trace
100 proof, distilled	83	trace
Champagne		
Brut (4 fl. oz.)	92	2.1
Extra Dry	97	2.1
Pink	98	3.7
Coffee Liqueur		
53 proof	117	16.3
63 proof	107	11.2
Creme de Menthe, 72 proof	125	14.0
Gin		
80 proof (1 oz.)	65	0.0
86 proof (1 oz.)	70	0.0
90 proof (1 oz.)	74	0.0
94 proof (1 oz.)	77	0.0
100 proof (1 oz.)	83	0.0
Rum		
80 proof (1 oz.)	65	0.0
86 proof (1 oz.)	70	0.0
90 proof (1 oz.)	74	0.0
94 proof (1 oz.)	77	0.0
100 proof (1 oz.)	83	0.0

	Calories	Carbo-hydrates
Scotch		
80 proof, distilled	65	trace
86 proof, distilled	70	trace
90 proof, distilled	74	trace
94 proof, distilled	77	trace
100 proof, distilled	83	trace
Tequila		
80 proof, distilled	64	0.0
86 proof, distilled	69	0.0
90 proof, distilled	73	0.0
94 proof, distilled	76	0.0
100 proof, distilled	82	0.0
Vodka		
80 proof (1 oz.)	65	0.0
86 proof (1 oz.)	70	0.0
90 proof (1 oz.)	74	0.0
94 proof (1 oz.)	77	0.0
100 proof (1 oz.)	83	0.0
Whiskey		
80 proof (1 oz.)	65	0.0
86 proof (1 oz.)	70	0.0
90 proof (1 oz.)	74	0.0
94 proof (1 oz.)	77	0.0
100 proof (1 oz.)	83	0.0
Wine		
Aperitif (1 oz.)	41	2.3
Port (1 oz.)	41	2.3
Sherry (1 oz.)	41	2.3
White or red table (1 oz.)	29	1.2
Non-Alcoholic		
Club soda (1 oz.)	0	0.0
Cola (1 oz.)	12	3.1
Cream soda (1 oz.)	13	3.4
Fruit-flavored soda (1 oz.)	13	3.7
Ginger ale (1 oz.)	9	2.4
Root beer (1 oz.)	13	3.2
Tonic water (1 oz.)	9	2.4

© Foley Publishing Corp

HOME BAR RECOMMENDATIONS & TIPS

Location

Choosing the proper location is essential. Select an open area that is easily accessible. A kitchen counter or a sturdy table near the kitchen counter is well suited. It should be convenient to the refrigerator and sink. The kitchen also becomes a gathering point for many partiers. Cleaning up water and spills is a lot easier on your kitchen floor, than your carpet.

If your kitchen is too small, a location near your kitchen on a sturdy table and, if you're worried about your carpet, spread a small rug beneath.

When setting up for a party of 25 or more, it's best to use the diagram below known as the "Diamond Plan."

The "Diamond Plan" gives the best guest flow and has two focal points: food and liquor.

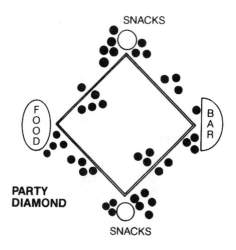

SNACKS

FOOD

BAR

PARTY DIAMOND

SNACKS

41

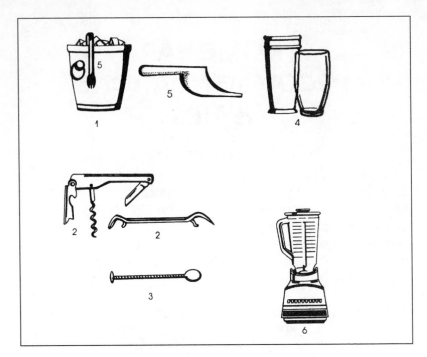

Bar Tools

The following should be displayed
on your bar top (or table):

1. Ice Bucket. Try to find one with a vacuum seal, and large enough to hold at least three (3) trays of ice.

2. Wine/Bottle Opener. A good wine opener or waiter type Church key or bottle opener that can open cans as well as snap off bottle tops.

3. Bar Spoon. One long spoon for stirring drinks or pitchers of drinks.

4. Cocktail Shaker and Mixing Glass. Mixing glass for use in stirring drinks. Shaker fits over glass to shake drinks.

5. Ice Scoop/Tongs. Use to pick up ice cubes from an ice bucket and place in glass. A must for every home bar. Never use your hands. If necessary, a large mouth spoon can be used.

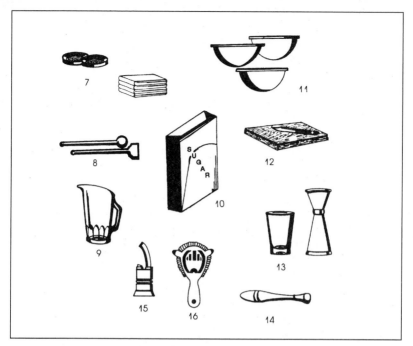

6. Blender. Blending Margaritas, Piña Coladas, and Daiquiris. Can also be used for crushing ice and making three or more drinks at once.

7. Napkins/Coasters. To place drink on or hold drink.

8. Stirrers/Straws. For mixing and sipping drinks.

9. Pitcher of Water. A large pitcher for water only.

10. One Box of "Superfine" Sugar.

11. Three Large Bowls. One for cut fruit, two for garnish (olives, onions, etc.)

12. Knife and Cutting Board. Use to cut more fruit.

13. Jigger/Measuring Glass. All drinks should be made with a measuring glass or jigger. Drinks on the rocks or mixed drinks should not contain more than 2 oz. of alcohol. Doubles should not be served.

14. Muddler. To muddle your fruit.

15. Pourer.

16. Strainer.

Stocking The Bar For Home

The traditional bartender's formula for setting up a simple home bar is:

— Something white *(Vodka, Gin, Rum or Tequila)*

— Something brown *(Scotch, Canadian Whiskey or Bourbon)*

— Something sweet *(a Liqueur)*

— Wine and/or Vermouth if you want an aperitif or plan on making martinis.

In stocking your home bar for the first time, don't attempt to buy all types of exotic liquors and liqueurs. *Your inventory should be based on items you and your friends will use most. Keep in mind that people will bring their favorite brands as gifts.*

We're into the 90s and premium liquor is the call. Folks might be drinking less, but they're drinking the best. Buy the best. It's only pennies more and saves a lot of excuses and embarrassment. Treat yourself and your guests to the best!!

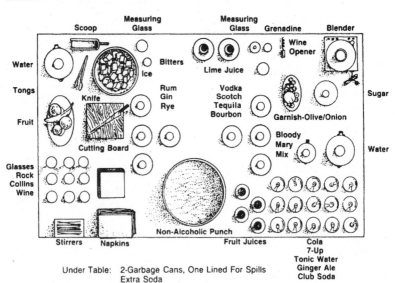

BASIC BAR STOCK AND PARTY TABLE

Product	Basic Stock (Quantities in Liters)	Number of Guests			
		10/30	30/40	40/60	60/100
White Wine					
Domestic (750 ml.)	2	4	4	6	8
Imported (750 ml.)	1	2	2	2	3
Red Wine					
Domestic (750 ml.)	2	1	2	3	3
Imported (750 ml.)	1	1	1	2	2
Blush Wine	1	1	2	2	2
Champagne					
Domestic (750 ml.)	1	2	3	4	4
Imported (750 ml.)	1	2	2	2	2
Vermouth					
Extra Dry (750 ml.)	1	1	1	2	2
Rosso (Sweet) (750 ml.)	1	1	1	1	1
Liquors					
Vodka (choice of imported/ domestic	1	2	3	3	4
Rum	1	1	2	2	2
Gin (choice of imported/ domestic	1	1	2	2	3
Scotch	1	1	2	2	3
Whiskey (choice of American/Canadian)	1	1	1	2	2
Bourbon	1	1	1	1	1
Irish Whiskey	1	1	1	1	2
Tequila	1	2	2	2	3
Brandy/Cognac	1	1	2	2	3
Beer (12 oz. bottles)	6	48	72	72	96
Others					
Aperitifs: (choice of 1)					
Campari	750 ml.	1	1	2	2
Dubonnet					
Red	750 ml.	1	1	1	2
Blonde	750 ml.	1	1	1	2
Lillet	750 ml.	1	1	1	2

BASIC BAR STOCK AND PARTY TABLE

Product	Basic Stock (Quantities in Liters)	Number of Guests			
		10/30	30/40	40/60	60/100
Cordials/Specials (choice of 3)					
Alizé	750 ml.	1	2	2	2
Grand Marnier	750 ml.	1	1	1	1
Creme de Menthe					
White or	750 ml.	1	1	1	1
Green	750 ml.	1	1	1	1
Peach Schnapps	750 ml.	1	1	1	1
Kahlua	750 ml.	1	1	1	1
Creme de Cacao					
White or	750 ml.	1	1	1	1
Dark	750 ml.	1	1	1	1
Irish Cream	750 ml.	1	2	3	3
Romana Sambuca	750 ml.	1	2	3	3
Amaretto	750 ml.	1	2	2	2

Total Cost (approximate): $250-300

Number of Guests:	10/30	30/40	40/60	60/100
Cost:	$300-400	$400-550	$550-700	$700-800

1. This chart is based on 1¾ oz. per drink; this is a basic.

2. Product will vary on age (usually the younger the crowd, 21-35, the more beer and mixed drinks); so increase by one-half the amount of vodka, rum, tequila, and beer.

3. Geographical location is also important in selecting and cost of your liquor stock for your guests. Consult your local bartender or liquor clerk to find the most popular products in your area.

4. The time of the year or season should also be considered—in fall/winter less beer; spring serve more beer, vodka, gin and tequila.

Other Supplies

Product	Basic Stock (Quantities in Liters)	Number of Guests			
		10/30	30/40	40/60	60/100
Soda (2 Liters):					
Club/Seltzer	1	3	3	4	5
Ginger Ale	1	2	2	2	3
Cola	1	3	3	3	4
Diet Cola	1	3	3	3	4
7-Up	1	2	3	3	4
Tonic	1	2	2	3	3
Juice (Quart):					
Tomato	1	2	2	3	3
Grapefruit	1	2	2	3	3
Orange	1	2	2	3	3
Cranberry	1	2	2	3	3
Miscellaneous:					
Ice (trays)	2	10	15	20	30
Napkins (dozen)	1	4	4	6	8
Stirrers (1,000/box)	1	1	1	1	1
Major Peters' Bloody Mary Mix	1	2	2	3	3
Major Peters' Grenadine	1	1	1	1	2
Superfine Sugar (box)	1	1	1	1	1

Other Miscellaneous:

1 Quart Milk

2 Large Bottles Mineral Water

2 Bottles Major Peters' Lime Juice

1 Bottle Angostura Bitters

1 Bottle Worcestershire Sauce

1 Bottle McIlhenny Tabasco sauce

1 Small Jar Horseradish for Bloody Marys

1 Can Coco Lopez Cream of Coconut

CUTTING FRUIT

Different kinds of fruit are used to garnish different kinds of drinks. REMEMBER to wash all fruit and vegetables before cutting.

Lemon Twist
1. Cut off both ends. 2. Using a sharp knife or spoon, insert between rind and meat carefully separating. 3. Cut skin into ¼" strips.

Pineapple
1. Cut off top and bottom. 2. Cut pineapple in half. 3. Cut in half again. 4. Cut ½" slices. 5. Cut wedges.

Celery
1. Cut off bottom of celery, also, you may cut off top. 2. If leaf is fresh, you may use this as garnish. 3. Cut celery stalk in half.

Oranges
1. Cut oranges in half. 2. Slice orange into half moon cuts. 3. Half moon cut.

Limes
1. Cut ends of lime. 2. Slice lime into half. 3. Cut in half moons.

Wedges (Lemon/Limes)
1. Slice lime in half. 2. Cut halves flat down and half again. 3. Cut to ¼" to ½" wedges.

© Foley Publishing Corp

LIBBEY GLASS

There has been a lot written—and even more said—in professional circles about the importance of using the right glass for the right drink. Just how important is adherence to the classic standards of usage? What are the best glasses to have on hand if you can't afford, or don't have the space, to inventory them all? What are the hot looks in contemporary glassware and how can you use them to justify higher tariffs in your establishment? This chapter will answer these and many other questions about the selection and usage of glassware today.

Q: What will happen if you serve a straight-up Martini in a water glass?

A: Nothing will happen to the Martini. If you mixed it right, it will have the clear color and taste of a Martini, especially if you throw in an olive or a twist. It might even be chilled to perfection. The problem is it won't look like a Martini to many of your customers.

Over the years a number of our most popular cocktails—the Martini, Manhattan, Old-Fashioned, Whiskey Sour, Tom Collins and Margarita to name a few—have become synonymous with the glasses in which they are traditionally served. The right glass for the right drink.

How important is it for you, a professional bartender, to adhere to these presentations today? After all, the 1920s and 30s—when these standards were established—are long gone.

The answer to that question depends largely on the preferences and expectations of your clientele. If you tend bar in a private country club that caters to a mature and upscale crowd, chances are it is very important that a traditional cocktail, or wine or beer selection for that matter, be offered to the customer in the "right" glass. On the other hand, if your establishment is populated by a young college crowd, you might be able to bend the rules a little.

The important thing to remember is that any bar patron—young or mature, white collar or blue, male or female—appreciates and *will pay a higher tariff* for a well prepared and attractively presented beverage. The little touches—a sparkling clean glass, fresh garnishes, a napkin—do make a difference.

Bear in mind that anyone can purchase a bartender's guide, stop by the neighborhood liquor store, mix up a cocktail in the kitchen and serve it in "whatever's handy." Once that same person becomes a *customer* at your establishment, however, his standards and expectations change considerably. Why? Because, he's *paying* you for a professional product and professional service.

If The Drink Fits Pour It

There are reasons—other than good looks—why straight-up Martinis and Manhattans are served in 3 to 6 ounce stemmed cocktail glasses. For one, the stems keep hands from warming the drink. But, perhaps even more important, is the fact that those drinks *fit* into those glasses without spilling over—from a glass that's too small—or looking lost—in a glass that's too large. A good rule of thumb: A drink should almost fill its glass. No patron feels good about paying top dollar for a drink that looks skimpy—even if it isn't—because it's served in a glass that's too big. On the other hand, putting a customer in the position of having to artfully gulp off the first ounce or two, rather than run the risk of dribbling the concoction onto a silk tie or "dry clean only" dress, is equally unappreciated.

Martinis, Manhattans and Stingers fit nicely into stemmed cocktail glasses. Highballs fit nicely into highball glasses; Tom Collins into collins glasses; Whiskey Sours into sour glasses...and that alone makes a good case for sticking to the traditional glass. If you can't resist the urge to be creative OR if your customers expect you to be (tulip-garnished Martinis, on-the-rocks, served in little flower pot-shaped glasses), just make certain that the drink fits the glass.

To Stem or Not To Stem

The guideline for stem usage is a simple one, but one that should be kept in mind: *Use stems for chilled cocktails (or wines) that are served straight-up (without ice).* The stem keeps the hands off the bowl and prevents the drink from warming too quickly. Other than that one rule, stems can be used in any number of creative presentations, especially to dress up a drink (or even a premium beer, "designer" water or iced tea) and give it a more upscale appearance. Remember: the use of stemware in unexpected or creative contexts can translate to higher tariffs. One of the most versatile of all stems is the 8½ to 14 ounce round wine glass.

Citation
Red Wine Glass
#8414

Citation
All Purpose
Wine Glass
#8470

Embassy Martini
Cocktail Glass
#3779

Designed for red wine service, it can be used for almost anything from cocktails to brandy to beer. And it looks spectacular!

Another must-have stem is the all-purpose 8 ounce wine glass which can be used to fine effect for red or white wine to Bloody Marys to Daiquiris and Piña Coladas to beer and beyond.

Other stems we recommend to round out your service:

Cocktail glass. Solid stems are not just for show; they keep hands from warming the drinks. Available in 3 to 6 ounce capacities, the 4½ ounce size is good for classic straight-up Martini,

Manhattan and Stinger service.

Sour glass. A short-stemmed glass traditionally used to serve sours, these can also hold Daiquiris and be used interchangeably with cocktail glasses in a pinch. The $4\frac{1}{2}$ ounce version is the most popular.

White wine glass. The stem of a wine glass is used to maintain the product at the proper room temperature. The most popular sizes are from $6\frac{1}{2}$ to 10 ounces. These can also be used for frozen Daiquiris and other specialty drinks.

Red Wine Glass. These have wider bowls—rounder to permit the red wine, usually served at room temperature to breathe—and to keep the aroma trapped.

Flute or tulip champagne glass. The most popular sizes are small—from $4\frac{1}{2}$ to 6 ounces. The major advantage—aside from a decidedly upscale appearance—are tapered bowls which help prevent the bubbles from escaping too quickly. For any sparkling service, including ducks and ciders.

Saucer champagne glass. The traditional choice for champagne and sparkling service. It can also be used to enhance ice cream drink and ice cream dessert presentations. Avoid the hollow stemmed varieties which

Embassy
Sour Glass
#3775

Bristol Valley
White Wine Glass
#8564SR

Bristol Valley
Red Wine Glass
#8541SR

Citation
Flute
#8477

Bristol Valley
Flute
Champagne Glass
#8595SR

Embassy
Saucer
Champagne
Glass
#3777

are difficult to clean and can be unsanitary.

Sherry glass. Serve sherry, port and aperitifs in these small, 2 to 3½ ounce, stems. Cordials, at 1 ounce, and 2 ounce brandy glasses are also available.

Brandy snifters. Brandy snifters range in size from 5½ to 22 ounces and larger. Small sizes can also be used for serving Cognac, liqueurs, and premium whiskeys whose bouquets deserve the special treatment. The larger sizes provide the maximum possible "noseful" desired by serious brandy drinkers. All snifters feature large bowls on short stems, designed to be cupped by the hand to warm the liquid.

Rocks Glasses and Tumblers

Rocks, highball glasses and other tumblers are primarily designed for serving medium to large capacity drinks on ice. We recommend that you start with the following:

Highball glass. These versatile glasses, available in a wide variety of capacities, are used for more drinks than any other glasses (for Gin and tonics, Scotch and waters, Rum and colas, etc.). Most are clear and fairly tall. The most popular sizes range from 8 to 12 ounces.

Embassy
Sherry Glass
#3788

Embassy
Brandy Snifters
7½ oz.
#3708

Embassy
Brandy Snifters
5½ oz.
#3702

Lexington
Tall Hi-Ball Glass
#2310

Heavy Base
Hi-Ball Glass
#132

Collins glass. These are really just taller, often frosted, versions of the highball glass. They are traditionally used for collins service and also lend a cool, tropical look to Sloe Gin Fizzes, Singapore Slings, Sunrises, and other fruity concoctions.

Heavy Base Collins Glass #126

Rocks glasses. These are also known as old-fashioned glasses. The most popular sizes hold from 6 to 10 ounces and are used exclusively for on-the-rocks presentations. Larger double rocks sizes range between 12 to 15 ounces.

Heavy Base Finedge Double Rocks Glasses #816CD

Coolers. These taller and some-what larger capacity tumblers have been gaining popularity in recent years for extra volume highballs and non-alcoholic beverages. They hold a lot of ice and can accommodate fair-ly large treatments.

Heavy Base Finedge Rocks Glasses #916CD

Hurricane glasses. Use these large (usually 16 to 23½ ounces) tall, curved, footed glasses for Bloody Marys and tropical fruit drinks.

Heavy Base Finedge Coolers #817CD

Beer Service "Heads" For Variety

Up until a few years ago, beer service was pretty cut and dried: Simply pour into a mug or hourglass pilsner and set 'em up. Those days are gone. The growing popularity of premium beers—both domestic and imported—means that beer drinkers are not only more sophisticated

Specialty Hurricane Glasses #3616

about what kind of beer, ale or stout they drink, but also about what they drink it from. The traditional pilsner and mug are still fine for tap service, as well as for many non-premium domestic brands. But, if your establishment caters to the growing number of beer connoisseurs, here are some new shapes in beer service you might want to pick up on:

Stems. Traditional beer goblets are very stout and European looking. For a more contemporary, lighter look try serving premium brands in sheer rim 10 or 12 ounce wine stems or in balloon wines.

Flare pilsners. These sophisticated pilsners—minus the hourglass shape—flare up from the bottoms in 10 to 12 ounce sizes. Perfect for premium domestic brands.

Footed pilsners. The short stems and foot on these flare-shaped pilsners give them a decidedly upscale and continental appearance. They are well-suited to premium imports.

Footed ales. Available in 10 and 12 ounce sizes, these attractive glasses feature a very heavy base and a unique bowed-out shape well-suited to the full-bodied flavor of imported ales and stouts.

Napa
Stemmed
Beers
#8730

Flare
Pilsners
#19

Clubhouse
Collection
Footed
Pilsners
#3633

Specialty
Footed
Beers
#3810

For Special Drinks:
Specialty Glasses

The classic aside, there is more latitude for creativity behind the bar today than ever before. There has also never been such an exciting selection of domestically-produced and widely available specialty glasses from which to choose.

Glasses in the shapes of owls, cowboy boots, flower pots, snowmen, and so on can fuel your imagination from one season of the year to the next. There is no end to the number of tasty and creative concoctions you can dream up and serve in specialty glasses to the delight of both your customers and your management. Remember: *Well-dressed drinks served in spectacular or whimsical glasses can command higher check averages.*

Must-have specialty glasses? We can think of a few:

Irish-coffee glass/cup. In most parts of the country the fall and winter months are made for merchandising hot beverages—Irish coffee and other coffee drinks, spiked or unspiked apple ciders, chocolates and toddies. Some of these items are available "heat-treated" for maximum durability.

Parfait glasses. These 7½ to 8

Specialty Glasses Napoli #1619

Specialty Mugs Jackpot #97336

Specialty Glasses Dollar Sign #3635

Catalina #3821

Specialty Mugs Golfbag #97067

ounce footed glasses are used for drinks and desserts containing fruit or ice cream. They can also be used for Bloody Marys and highballs.

Crested glasses. Consider having a house glass or specialty glass crested (printed) with the logo, name and address of your establishment. For special occasions or promotions, give them away to your customers (you can work in their cost to the price of a specialty drink) as a form of take-away advertising.

Best Bets in Glassware for the Home Bar

The popularity of entertaining at home has grown dramatically in recent years and many of today's hosts are no longer content to serve cocktails and other beverages in "whatever's handy." On the other hand, few people have the space to store all of the different kinds of glasses they might like to have. This section will help you separate the "must haves" from the "nice to haves" for the home bar.

Perhaps the easiest way to stock a home bar with the most popular shapes and sizes of glassware is to invest in an entertainment set of domestically manufactured and packaged barware. Typical sets, widely available and affordably prices, will usually consist of 18, 24 or 32 pieces

Specialty Glasses Hoffman House #5210

Specialty Glasses Cactus Margarita #3619JS

Irish Coffee Glass #5295

Catalina Flute #3822

Crested Beer Mugs #52061

Your Logo Here

Lifestyles

and include beverage/highball glasses, tumbler/cooler glasses, and on-the-rocks/old-fashioned glasses. Such a set will easily handle most of your iced beverage service needs and should be considered "must haves."

The only other thing you'll need is an 8 to 10 ounce all-purpose wine stem. This versatile addition to the home bar can be used for serving red or white wine—even sparkling wines—as well as a wide range of straight-up and chilled cocktails (Martinis, Manhattans, Sours, Daiquiris, etc.) liqueurs, and brandies. Consider it a "must have."

If the selection recommended above is still too much glassware for your cramped quarters or pragmatic disposition, consider the 8½ to 14 ounce stemmed balloon wine glass for all of your serving needs. This spectacular looking and versatile glass can be used for everything from red or white wine to beer to cocktails and brandy.

If space permits, you might wish to consider the following list of "nice to haves" to round out your selection of home barware:

Double rocks/old-fashioned glass. Also known as English highball glasses, these are the glasses of choice for on-the-rocks doubles.

Home & Hearth

Stemmed Cocktail #3170

Cordial #3790

Because of their large capacity—usually about 13 ounces—they can also be used for most highballs as well as for Bloody Marys and other voluminous garnished cocktails.

Champagne flutes. The perfect choice for all festive occasions; made for sparkling service. The tall profile and small mouths of these stems keep the bubbles from evaporating too quickly.

Brandy snifters. Available in a wide range of sizes, these glasses feature large bowls and short stems designed to be cupped in the hand to warm the liquor. They are also fine for Cognac and premium whiskey service.

Beer pilsners or mugs. Cordial or liqueur glasses. There you have it! Our best for home bar glassware. No matter what selection or "mix" you finally decide on, remember that all of your glassware should be sparkling clean and in perfect condition when you use it. Your guests will often overlook your choice of glasses, but not unsightly chips, spots or lint.

Champagne
Flute
#3795

Brandy Snifter
#3702

Beer Mug
#5309

© Foley Publishing Corp

COCKTAIL — WHERE DID IT COME FROM?

Cocktail. According to *Jack's Manual* by J. A. Grohuska, 1933, the word cocktail first appeared in *The Balance*, an American periodical, under date of May 13, 1806. It read: "Cocktail is a stimulating liquor composed of spirits of any kind, sugar, water, and bitters—it is vulgarly called 'bitter sling' and is supposed to be an excellent electioneering potion."

The above is the first time the word cocktail can be traced in print. However, our search does not stop there. Listed below are the stories and their sources of just where the word cocktail originated.

So read on...The stories of where the word cocktail first originated will go on forever. Which do you believe?

1. From *Jack's Manual* by J. A. Grohuska, Alfred A. Knoff, New York, 1933:

Linguists have been misled by the word 'cocktail' into imagining that it was once in some way connected with the plumage of the domestic rooster. But this is not so. The true and incontrovertible story of the origin of the cocktail is as follows:

Somewhere about the beginning of the last century, there had been for some time very considerable friction between the American Army of the Southern States and King Axolotl VIII of Mexico. Several skirmishes and one or two battles had taken place, but eventually a truce was called and the King agreed to meet the American general to discuss terms of peace with him.

The place chosen for the meeting was the King's pavilion,

and thither the American general repaired, and was accommodated with a seat on the bench, as it were, next to King A, himself. Before opening negotiations, however, His Majesty asked the general, as one man to another, if he would like a drink and being an American, he of course said yes. The King gave a command, and in a few moments there appeared a lady of entrancing and over-whelming beauty, bearing in her slender fingers a gold cup encrusted with rubies and containing a strange potion of her own brewing. Immediately an awed and ominous hush fell upon the assembly, for the same thought struck everyone; namely, that as there was only one cup, either the King or the general would have to drink from it first, and the other would be bound to feel insulted. The situation was growing tense and the cup bearer seemed also to realize the difficulty, for, with a sweet smile, she bowed her shapely head in reverence to the assembly and drank the drink herself. Everything was saved and the conference came to a satisfactory ending; but before leaving, the general asked if he might know the name of the lady who had shown such tact, "That," proudly said the King, who had never seen the lady before, "is my daughter Coctel."

"Your Majesty," replied the general, "I will see that her name is honored forevermore by my Army."

Coctel, of course, became cocktail, and there you are! There exists definite, unquestionable proof the truth of this story, but no correspondence upon the subject can in any circumstances be entertained.

2. *The Cocktail Book*, A Sideboard Manual for Gentlemen, L. C. Page and Company, Boston, 1913, "The Real Tale of the Cock's Tail:"

In a famous old tavern not far from the Philipse Manor House, the site of what is now Yonkers on the Hudson, and the very centre of the most popular sport of the times, was blended the first delightful cocktail. If the descendants of William Van Eyck, its jolly host, may be believed, no better place could be found along the length of the river, for William's stories were as good as the liquor that washed them down, and his liquors as honest and true and as sparkling withal as his daughter, Mistress Peggy, who gave them forth with such demure grace as made their serving doubly welcome to the thirsty gallants who thronged the bar and taproom.

Now Master Van Eyck loved but three things well—his daughter, his cellar, and his old Lightening, his great fighting bird, the acknowledged champion from New York to Albany. Indeed 'twere hard to tell which loved he the most, though his daughter was truly the idol of his heart.'

Mistress Peggy's lovers were many, and many were the strong potions quaffed, even when the driest throats were long since drowned in good liquor, because of her bewitching beauty, which gave added flavour and bouquet to the concoctions for which the bar was famous. But so well did she justify her father's confidence and her own good name that, though the gay bucks from town quarreled and even fought for her favour, the most fortunate could not boast of the lightest thing to her discredit. On especial occasions she was wont to make for her father, and certain good friends of hers and old Lightening's a most delicious beverage, the composition of which was secret, but which was so popular that it lacked naught but appropriate naming to give it more than local fame.

Young Master Appleton, mate of the clipper-ship Ranger, had long been Mistress Peggy's ardent lover, and had even gone so far as to obtain mine host's reluctant consent that, when he could boast of a command, his daughter should be his and she would. Now Peggy, when she admitted to her coquettish self that she had a heart, knew that eventually she would be forced, in order to still its clamourings, to surrender it unconditionally into the keeping of the certain bold sailor; but womanlike put off capitulating as long as she might. The time came, however, when the knowledge of his promotion gave Master Appleton the courage he had lacked to force the citadel which his coquetry had heretofore so jealously guarded; and, when of a sudden Peggy's heart refused longer to be maligned by her mouth, and spoke eloquently from out of bright eyes grown almost serious—before she could summon her and to the fray—she was conquered, and, close embraced, was calling him dear whom, but the day before, she had flouted with reckless audacity.

Except when in training for a main, Van Eyck's champion game-cock held his court in an apartment built for him and adapted to his Majesty's special wants. None found favour in his master's eyes, nor forsooth in the eyes of Mistress Peggy, who failed in admiring and respectful homage to old Lightening. Worshipful attendance upon his pampered hero of many bloody victories, together with honest admiration for the daughter of his host, was looked upon as the surest way of gaining Master Van Eyck's personal approval and the first step in advancing from favoured customer to friend.

It was here that Peggy surrendered to her lover. And here it was that after a proper and reasonable time spent in the sweet dalliance due to such occasions, she mixed for him this most delightful of all drinks in order that he might face with proper spirit her bluff old father's temporary ire at the loss of his daughter. Just as the right proportions of bitters, root wine, and mellowest of old whiskey had been put to cook in a glass half-full of bits of purest ice, an interruption occurred, and the clarion voice of the brave old warrior bird was heard as if in celebration of the momentous event which had happened under his very eyes. As he plumed and shook himself after his effort, one of his royal tail feathers floated gently down toward his mistress.

"Lightening names the drink!" she cried, as she seized the feather and with it deftly stirred the glass's contents. And, again, with a sweeping curtsy, holding the glass aloft:

"Drink this Cocktail, sir, to your success with my father, and as a pledge to our future happiness!"

Thus was the drink named. And, in after days, when Master Appleton kept the tavern, its sign was the sign of the Cock's Tail, which ever proved an emblem of good fortune to him and his good wife, their children and their children's children.

3. *The Bon Vivant's Companion or How to Mix Drinks,* compiled for his friends by George A. Zabriskie, Armond Beach, Florida, 1948 (not to be confused with Jerry Thomas, 1928, Bon Vivant's Companion); "Where Cocktails Came From:"

A Frenchman, Dr. Tardieu, declares that in the course of certain scientific investigations he discovered that cocktails, generally considered of American origin, are really the ancient French coquetele, popular for several centuries in regions of Bordeaux. Dr. Tardieu will be expected by Americans to produce evidence profoundly convincing. No mere ipse dixit will suffice. It is not the first time that foreigners have impugned the American beginning of the cocktail. Robert Keable declared that the mixings were invented by the court physician of the festive Roman Emperor Commodus. None will deny that Commodus would have drunk cocktails if he had 'em, but Mr. Keable's statement is not supported by Gibbon or any other dignified authority.

The most persistent American tradition regarding the cocktail fixes its birth in 1779 in Betsy Flanagan's Inn on the road between Tarrytown and White Plains, (NY) where American soldiers with gin, and French soldiers with vermouth, blended these beverages in token of brotherhood, stirring the resultant mess with the tail feathers of Mrs. Flanagan's rooster. Yet it may be that all of this happened in Peggy Van Eyck's Cock's Tail Tavern in Yonkers, as another story runs. The grave antiquarian, Issac Markens, preferred to believe that the decoction first saw light as early as 1652 in the Tavern of Peter Cock, which stood where No. 1 Broadway is now.

Another delver into things historic, Appleton Morgan, rejected these theories and insisted that the name "cocktail" was applied to a mixed drink because of the color and shape of the arch formed when expert bartenders tossed the liquors from one tumbler to another.

Whatever the truth, the name of the drink was established early enough for its use by Hawthorne in "The Blithedale Romance," by Fenimore Cooper in "The Spy," by Hughes in "Tom Brown," and by Thackeray in "The Newcomers."

Dr. Tardieu may be right, but let him prove it. And if he is wrong he has at least brought once more to the forum of the world a great question. Before the origin of the cocktail vanishes in the "twilight of fable, let the truth be captured."

4. *What'll You Have,* compiled and edited by Julien J. Roskauer, A. L. Burt Company, Chicago, 1933; more on Betsy Flanagan's Inn; "How the Cocktail Got Its Name!":

In revolutionary days there was a famous roadhouse in what is now known as Westchester County, called "Betsy's Tavern," which later became known as "The Bracer Tavern." Here the American and French officers came for their liquor, ale, lager and rum, not to mention fine fowl.

One day the American officers raided a British Commissary and stole several male birds. Then as now, this fowl was known as a "cock." At the wild boisterous party which followed, Betsy poured many kinds of liquor into wine glasses and stirred it with the tail of a cock pheasant. The drinks were delicious.

A toast to Betsy and the new mixed drink was: "Here's to the divine liquor which is as delicious to the palate, as the cock's tails are beautiful to the eye."

Hardly had this toast ended, when one of the French officers cried out: "Vive le cocktail!"

And that's how "cocktail" came into the world's vocabulary."

5. *The Mexican Story*

A visiting sailor drank local punches at Campeche, Gulf of Mexico, stirring them with wooden spoons. One bartender substituted a local root known as "Cola de gallo" — translated, "Cocktail."

6. *The English Stories*

From John Doxat, Mixologist and Author (who found the word "mocktail," a non-alcoholic drink).

A. English Story Number 1: An Englishman, Dr. Johnson, introduced to a wine from a friend named Boswell, told that this wine was mixed with gin replied "to add spirits to wine smacks of our alcoholic hyperbole. It would be a veritable cocktail of a drink."

"What is a cocktail?" asked Bosell.

"In parts of the country, it is a custom to dock the tails of certain horses of mint, yet which one not of entirely pure stock. Such animals of mixed province are known as cocktails."

B. English Story Number II: The cocktail was named in honor of "The Officer of the Second Regiment of Royal Sussex Fusileers, in the British Army. The men of this regiment wore plumes resembling rooster feathers in their caps, were commonly called "the Cocktails" by the men of other regiments."

7. *The Mississippi Stories*

A. Winning gamblers abroad river-steamers made a drink with a selection of every liquor in the bar. They drank this drink out of glasses shaped like a cock's breast, and the stirrer had a resemblance of a tail feather. There also was an illustration to a ballad published in 1871 called An American Cocktail of this event.

B. Mississippi River men challenged one another to become "The Cock of The Walk," meaning the strongest, meanest and best wrestler on the river. The winner earns the right to wear a bright red rooster feather in his hat. He could proclaim to all he could out drink and out fight all. Cock of the Walk plus tail = Cocktail.

8. *The Horse Trainer Story. (Another horse's tale)*

Horse trainers would give their horses a strong mixture of spirits that would make the horses "cock their tails" and run faster.

9. *The Fighting-Cock's Story*

More mixtures (cock-ale) but this time to fighting cocks. Plus a toast to the winner with as many different spirits as feathers on the winning bird (could these men also be Mississippi gamblers?)!

10. *New Orleans Story*

A French physician served a drink to his friends using a double-ended, gallic-style egg cup, coquetiers. His friends called them, you guessed it, Cocktails!

11. *The H. L. Mencken Story*, published in The Sunday Sun, December 13, 1908, Editor, H. L. Mencken.

The cocktail was invented on April 17, 1846, at 8:15 a.m. by John Welby Henderson of North Carolina at the Old Palo Alto Hotel in Bladensburg, Maryland. The first cocktail was served to John A. Hopkins of Fairfax, Virginia. The story goes on that it was served to Mr. Hopkins, to have his nerves restored after a duel.

This could be one of H. L. Mencken's many hoaxes.

And there you have it. Eleven versions of how the word cocktail originated. Which do you believe?

This mystery will go on forever. We will never know why this word became associated with America's favorite past time.

© Foley Publishing Corp

NAMES & ORIGINS

Alabama Slammer
A cocktail popularized at the University of Alabama made with sloe gin, amaretto, Southern Comfort, and orange juice.

Alizé
Evocative of the gentle tropical tradewinds of the French Caribbean islands for which it is named, Alizé de France is a totally unique product in a new category of its own creation.

Ambrosia
A cocktail reputedly first concocted at Arnaud's restaurant in New Orleans immediately following the end of Prohibition.

Bacardi Cocktail
A cocktail made with lime juice, sugar, grenadine, and Bacardi Light Rum. The name dates back to 1934 and was associated with the firm Bacardi Imports, Inc., of Miami, Florida. In 1936, a New York State Supreme Court ruled that to be authentic, a "Bacardi Cocktail" had to be made with Bacardi Rum, since the name Bacardi was a registered trademark.

Bamboo Cocktail
A cocktail said to have been invented about 1910 by bartender Charlie Mahoney of the Hoffman House in New York.

Drink is made with a dash of orange bitters, 1 oz. sherry and 1 oz. dry vermouth, stirred with ice, strained, and served in a wine glass with a lemon peel.

Bellini
Invented at Harry's Bar in Venice, Italy, around 1943.

Black Russian

By Bartender Gus Tops at the Hotel Metropoli in Brussels. Gus also dispensed scarfs with his silhouette and recipe of his cocktail.

Black Velvet

Also known as Bismarck or Champagne Velvet. Created in 1861 at Brooks's Club, London.

Blue Lagoon

Created around 1960 at Harry's Bar, Paris, by Harry's son, Andy MacElhone.

Bloody Mary

Invented by Pete Petiot at Harry's Bar, 5 Rue Daunou, Paris, France, in 1921; he later became Captain of Bars at the St. Regis Hotel, New York, NY.

Bobby Burns

Named after Robert Burns (1759-96), the Scottish poet and song writer best known for 'Auld Lang Syne.'

Bronx

By Johnny Solon of the Waldorf Bar in New York's Waldorf Astoria. Johnny created it the day after a trip to the Bronx Zoo.

Cuba Libre

This drink is a political statement as well as a cocktail. It translates to "Free Cuba," a status the country enjoyed in 1898 at the end of the Spanish-American war. Cuban/American relations were friendly around the turn of the century, when a US Army lieutenant in Havana mixed some light native rum with a new-fangled American soft drink called Coca Cola and braced the libation with a lime.

Daiquiri

Connived by workers from Bethlehem Steel during a malaria epidemic in the Village of Daiquiri, near Santiago, Cuba.

French 75

If one requests this drink, you might receive a mix of gin and champagne. In the French trenches of World War I, however, gin was scarce but cognac and champagne were not. American doughboys soon discovered that a combination of the two produced an effect similar to getting zapped by an artillery piece known as a French 75.

Gibson

Named after New York artist, Charles Dana Gibson, by his Bartender, Charles Connoly, of the Players Club in New York. Another version credits Billie Gibson, a fight promoter.

Gin Rickey

By a Bartender at Shoemaker's in Washington, DC, for his customer, "Colonel Jim" Rickey, a Lobbyist.

Harvey Wallbanger

Created by Bill Doner at Newport Beach, CA. The Harvey Wallbanger started as a fad by Bill and was first served at a bar called The Office. Bill was last seen as Vice President of Marketing at Caesars Palace in Las Vegas. Before that, he ran a fleet of fishing boats in Cabo San Lucas, Mexico. Thank you Bill for a great drink and legend...wherever you are.

Irish Coffee

Was originated at the Buena Vista Cafe in San Francisco, where the late Chronicle columnist and travel writer, Stanton Delaplane, often frequented. On a trip to Ireland during the early fifties, Delaplane noted the custom of bolstering airport coffee with whiskey. Intending to elaborate on these crude airport toddies, he and his cronies at the Buena Vista settled on the perfect recipe: three sugar cubes, an ounce and a half of Irish whiskey, coffee, and a float of quickly agitated whipped cream.

Kioki Coffee

Created by George Bullington, founder of Southern California's Bully's restaurant chain. During the sixties, Kahlua-based coffee drinks were popular at his LaJolla location. Perhaps to defray costs, Bullington made a drink with a one-half jigger of Kahlua, one-half jigger of the less expensive but similar-tasting dark creme de cacao and a float of brandy and whipped cream. Bullington's Hawaiian customers started referring to the drink as a Coffee Kioki— "Kioki" meaning "George" in Hawaiian.

Kir

After the Mayor of DiJon (Major Kir) to increase sales of Cassis.

Long Island Iced Tea

Hails from Long Island, specifically the Oak Beach Inn in Hampton Bays. Spirits writer John Mariani credits Bartender Robert "Rosebud" Butt as the inventor, whose original recipe calling for an ounce each of clear liquors (vodka, gin, tequila, light rum), a half ounce of triple sec, lemon juice and a splash of cola is still popular with young drinkers. (Though not with those who have to get up early the next day).

Mai Tai

Invented by Vic Bergeron in 1944 at his Polynesian-style Oakland bar. He did not want fruit juices detracting from the two ounces of J. Wray Nephew Jamaican Rum he poured as the base for his creation. He merely added a half ounce of French orgeat (an almond-flavored syrup), a half ounce of orange curacao, a quarter ounce of rock candy syrup and the juice of one lime. Customer Carrie Wright of Tahiti was the first to taste the concoction, to which she responded, "Mai tai...roe ae," (Tahitian for "Out of this world...the best"). The Mai Tai became famous, and conflicting stories about its origins aggravated Bergeron so much that he elicited a sworn statement from Mrs. Wright in 1970, testifying to his authorship of the cocktail.

Margarita

One story tells of a bartender in Pueblo, Mexico, named Daniel Negrete who had a girlfriend named Margarita. She took a dab of salt with everything she drank. To please her, Negrete created a drink of ice, Cointreau, tequila and lime juice and put salt around the rim of the glass.

Another legend says that Margarita Sames of San Antonio, Texas, was a frequent visitor to Acapulco and a patron of the bar at the Flamingo Hotel. She had a special passion for tequila and encouraged the bartenders to create variations using the Mexican liquor. Her special favorite was a combination of tequila, Cointreau and lime juice.

And then there's the tale of the ship that lost most of its provisions during a violent storm. All was lost save a supply of Cointreau, tequila and limes. An imaginative ship's mate combined the ingredients, was delighted with the result, and named the mixture after his beloved—you guessed it—Margarita!

Mimosa

Created around 1925 at the Ritz Hotel Bar, Paris. It took its name from the mimosa flowering plant, whose color it resembled.

Manhattan

The recipe was created around 1874 at the Manhattan Club, New York, for Lady Randolph Churchill, Winston's mother, on the occasion of her banquet in honor of the lawyer and politician Samuel J. Tilden.

Martini

1. By Bartender Professor Jerry Thomas of San Francisco from a stranger on his way to Martinez. Made with Gin, Vermouth, Bitters, Dash of Maraschino.
2. By a Bartender in Martinez, California, for a gold miner who struck it rich. The miner ordered champagne for the house. But there was none. The Bartender offered something better, a "Martinez Special," some (Sauterne) and Gin. The rich miner spread the word ordering throughout California a "Martinez Special."
3. After the British army rifle: The Martini and Henry. The rifle was known for its kick, like the first sip of Gin and "it" ("it" being Vermouth).
4. After Martini and Rossi Vermouth, because it was first used in the drink, Gin an It, with ½ Gin and ½ Martini and Rossi Vermouth.
5. At the Knickerbocker Hotel in the early 1900s, a Bartender named Martini di Arma Tiggia mixed a Martini using only a dry Gin and only dry Vermouth.

Moscow Mule

Unveiled at Hollywood's Cock N' Bull by owner Jack Morgan and one Jack Martin in 1946 to rid himself of an overstock of ginger beer.

Negroni

It seems that a certain Count Negroni of Florence once requested a drink that would stand apart from all the Americanos ordered at his favorite neighborhood cafe. The Bartender answered his request with a cocktail composed of equal parts gin, sweet vermouth and Campari, and he garnished the result with a tell-tale orange slice. Unfortunately for the Count, the drink became as popular as the Americano.

Old Fashioned

Originated by a Bartender at the Louisville Pendennis Club in Kentucky for Colonel James E. Pepper, a distiller of Bourbon Whiskey.

Piña Colada

Two stories, take your pick. On a plaque at 104 Forales Street, once the Barrchina Bar and now a perfumery, reads: "The house where in 1963 the Piña Colada was created by Don Ramon Portas Mingat." Across town at the Caribe Hilton, Bartender Ramon (Monchito) Marrero says he created the Piña Colada in 1954...

Planters Punch

To a Bartender at Planters Hotel in St. Louis; also credited to a Jamaican planter's wife offering a drink one part sour, two parts sweet, three parts strong and four parts weak to cool off from the Jamaican sun.

Ramos Fizz

By the proprietor of the Old Stagg Saloon in New Orleans' French Quarter, called Ramos, of course. Stories say it took eight to ten waitresses to shake this drink.

Rob Roy

From Robert MacGregor, Scotland's Robin Hood. Roy being the Scottish nickname for a man with red hair.

Screwdriver

By Texas oil rig workers who stirred vodka and orange juice with their screwdrivers.

Side Car

Harry's New York Bar in Paris, according to owner at that time, Harry MacElhone, after a motorcycle sidecar in which a customer was driving into the bar.

Silk Panties

Created by Sandra Gutierrez of Chicago, IL, and winner of BARTENDER Magazine's 1986 Schnapps contest.

Singapore Sling

By Bartender at the Long Bar in Singapore's Raffles Hotel around 1915.

Tom Collins

By John Collins, a waiter at Lipmmer's Old House, Coduit Street, Hanover Square in England. "Tom" was used instead of John from the use of Old Tom Gin. Today a "John Collins" would use whiskey.

Tom and Jerry

Created by Jerry Thomas around 1852 at the Planters' House Bar, St. Louis, MO.

The Ward Eight

From Boston's Ward Eight, a dominant political subdivision of the community, known for it's bloody political elections. A Whiskey Sour with a splash of grenadine. Locke-O'Ber's in Boston is a great place to try one.

Zombie

Inventor Don Beaches was an innovator of the Polynesian-style, umbrella-bedded fufu drink. Real Polynesians never drank such things, but the tropical atmosphere at Beaches's Los Angeles restaurant inspired him. Don the Beachcomber, made Scorpions, Beachcombers and Zombies seem as island-indigenous as poi. He invented the Zombie back in the thirties as a mix of three different rums, papaya juice, orange juice, pineapple juice, lemon juice, grenadine, orgeat, Pernod and curacao. What has survived is the 151 float. That and the effect its name suggests.

© Foley Publishing Corp

ABSOLUT VODKA

The name "Absolut Vodka" conjures visions of wit and humor, art and fashion. It also represents a premium product born of high standards and cutting-edge innovation. Every drop of Absolut Vodka consumed in the world is made solely from grain grown in the rich fields of southern Sweden and water from a single source—a specially-designated well near the distillery in Ahus.

From its clarity and magnificent smooth character to its unique bottle and legendary advertising campaign, Absolut has always stood above the crowd.

An Overnight Success—Since 1879

Although the people of Sweden had been distilling with vodka since the 15th century, the "Absolut Story" truly begins in 1879, when a new heat distillation process was invented under the brilliant leadership of an innovator named Lars Olsson Smith. This revolutionary new "selective distillation" process produced the cleanest and smoothest vodka to date. And in 1979, after 100 years of perfecting "Absolut Rent Brannvin" (Absolutely Pure Vodka), Smith's tradition of innovation and risk-taking continued, when Vin & Sprit AB (V&S), the producer of Absolut, introduced the product to America as Absolut Vodka.

Absolut Breakthrough

Before shipping Absolut into the U.S.—the world's most competitive vodka market—V&S set to work creating the image and packaging that would truly reflect the brand. The challenge was to design a bottle that would project the quality and tradition associated with the Absolut heritage. The solution was inspired by a traditional Swedish medicine bottle—a distinctive shape that is elegant, unique and absolutely Swedish.

To convey the contemporary appeal of the spirit and to emphasize its clarity, labeling was avoided. Instead, text was printed directly on the bottle with blue and black lettering to suggest the clean and natural taste. And as a tribute to the man who had been known as Sweden's "King of Vodka," a portrait of L. O. Smith was featured on a medallion near the neck of the bottle.

Absolut Advertising

From the moment the decision was made to export Absolut, V&S felt strongly that creative marketing was required to communicate the uniqueness and quality of the product.

The result? A whole new type of advertising that challenged the boundaries between advertising and art. Each ad is a witty variation on the same simple theme: a picture of the Absolut Vodka bottle with a two to three word caption starting with the work Absolut.

The first ad, "Absolut Perfection" with a halo circling above the bottle, appeared in 1980 with a distinctive wit that redefined alcohol advertising. Just as Bach composed many beautiful variations on the same melody, the original ad has spawned hundreds of variations.

Absolut Artistry

"I love the packaging, I love the feeling of it, I want to do something..." so said Andy Warhol when asked what he thought of the Absolut Vodka bottle. Absolut has become known for its support of artists since 1985, when Warhol, the godfather of pop art, famous for his interpretations of soup cans and Marilyn Monroe, was commissioned to do a painting of the Absolut Vodka bottle. Warhol's graceful image of the Absolut bottle was the cornerstone of what has grown into Absolut's successful partnership with the arts. When the painting appeared as an ad, it garnered immediate worldwide media attention.

Warhol later recommended to Absolut one of his young proteges, Keith Haring, who had risen to fame with his anonymous paintings on the New York subway. Works then followed from Kenny Scharf, Stephen Sprouse, Edward Ruscha, Armand Arman and other leading American artists.

Absolut's approach to art has been one of a global art gallery. Instead of simply donating money to artists, the brand promotes talent by bringing it into the national spotlight in a time of declining support for arts programs across the U.S. The artists are given complete artistic freedom, the only stipulation being that the Absolut bottle must be visible in the work. While some of the commissioned artists are established talents whose work is widely known, many are young or emerging in the national art scene. To date, over 300 artists have been commissioned.

Over the years, Absolut has commissioned not only painters, but artists in all disciplines: sculptors like Arman; crystal designers like Bertil Vallien; musicians like Dizzy Gillespie; fashion designers like David Cameron.

Sometimes, Absolut sponsorships take art to new heights—take, for example, the 11 meter high ice sculpture of the Absolut bottle done in the Swiss Alps. Absolut artists work in all fields, including an eastern Kansas wheat field sown in the shape of an Absolut bottle. This unique piece of "agro-art" was the size of 12 football fields and visible only from the air.

Absolut Style

Absolut Vodka entered the fashion world in a big way with a small dress. "Absolut Cameron" was the caption that accompanied a photo of model Rachel Williams in a one-of-a-kind dress creation. The commission was a much noticed one, and since then, Absolut has been intensively involved in the fashion world. Absolut has worked with both established and emerging designers to create everything from dresses to ties.

Absolut fashions are often worth their weight in gold. One example is Anthony Ferrara's solid gold dress, made entirely out of 18K gold—16 pounds of it to be exact. Value? $530,000.

Absolut Quality

Every drop of Absolut Vodka consumed around the world comes from the same place: a distillery near Ahus in southern Sweden, for centuries a region famous for its vodka. Built in 1906, the Ahus distillery combines the best of old, local distilling tradition with the best of modern technology. Theoretically, vodka can be made from almost any fermentable organic material, from whey to molasses. Absolut Vodka, however, is made solely from grain, which more than 400 years of tradition has proven to produce the smoothest vodka possible.

And to this very day, this small town of barely 10,000 inhabitants not only produces, but packs and ships all the tens of millions of liters of Absolut Vodka consumed around the world. That translates to total quality control over the entire production process. Every bottle, every day.

ABSOLUT VODKA MARTINI

1½ oz.   Absolut Vodka

dash   Martini & Rossi Extra Dry Vermouth

Stir in cocktail glass with ice. Strain and serve straight up or on the rocks with some ice in cocktail glass. Add lemon twist or olive, OR: Shake and strain and serve up or on the rocks with some ice.

ALIZE:	Replace Martini & Rossi Vermouth with Alizé
ALIZE PASSIONATE:	Replace Martini & Rossi Vermouth with Alizé and dash of cranberry juice
CORNET:	Replace Martini & Rossi Vermouth with Port Wine
DILLATINI:	Dilly Bean (try and find one)
FASCINATOR:	Add dash Pernod and sprig mint
GIBSON:	Add onion

GIMLET:	Replace Martini & Rossi Vermouth with Major Peters' Lime Juice, garnish with Lime
GYPSY:	Add cherry
HOMESTEAD:	Add orange slice
ITALIAN:	Replace Martini & Rossi Vermouth with Hiram Walker Amaretto
JACKSON:	Replace Martini & Rossi Vermouth with Dubonnet and dash of bitters
LONE TREE:	Add dash lemon juice
MICKEY FINN:	Add splash of Hiram Walker White Creme de Menthe, garnish with mint
NAKED MARTINI:	Just Absolut Vodka
NAVAL COCKTAIL:	Replace Martini & Rossi Extra Dry with Martini & Rossi Rosso Vermouth; add onion and twist
ORANGETINI:	Add splash of Hiram Walker Triple Sec and orange peel
PERFECTION:	Replace Martini & Rossi Extra Dry Vermouth with Martini & Rossi Rosso Vermouth
QUEEN ELIZABETH:	Add splash Benedictine
RED PASSION MARTINI	Replace Vermouth with Alizé Red Passion
RICHMOND:	Replace Martini & Rossi Vermouth with Lillet, add twist of lemon
ROSA:	Add Hiram Walker Cherry Flavored Brandy
ROSALIN RUSSELL:	Replace Martini & Rossi Vermouth with Aquavit
ROSELYN:	Add Major Peters' Grenadine and lemon twist
SAKITINI:	Replace Martini & Rossi Vermouth with Sake
SILVER BULLET	Float Cutty Sark on top
SMOKY MARTINI:	Replace Martini & Rossi Vermouth with The Glenlivet®
SOUR KISSES:	Add egg white, SHAKE
TRINITY aka TRIO PLAZA:	Replace Martini & Rossi Extra Dry Vermouth with half Martini & Rossi Rosso and half Extra Dry. Equal parts of Vermouth and Absolut Vodka
VELOCITY:	Add orange slice and shake
WALLICK:	Add dash of Hiram Walker Curacao
WARDEN:	Add dash of Pernod

ABSOLUT AND TONIC

1¼ oz. ABSOLUT VODKA
Tonic

Pour Absolut Vodka over ice in a tall glass. Fill with tonic. Add a squeeze of lime.

ABSOLUT BRAVO

1 oz. ABSOLUT VODKA

½ oz. Campari

Pour Absolut Vodka and Campari over ice in a tall glass. Top with tonic. Garnish with a slice of lemon and a slice of lime.

ABSOLUT COLLINS

1¼ oz. ABSOLUT VODKA

¾ oz. Sweetened
Lemon Mix
Club Soda

Shake with ice and pour in tall glass with ice. Fill with club soda.

ABSOLUT COOLER

1¼ oz. ABSOLUT VODKA

½ tsp. Powdered Sugar
Ginger Ale or
Carbonated Water

Stir powdered sugar with 2 oz. carbonated water. Fill glass with ice and add vodka. Fill with carbonated water or ginger ale and stir again. Insert a spiral of orange or lemon peel (or both), dangle over rim.

ABSOLUT GIMLET

1¼ oz. ABSOLUT VODKA

½ oz. Fresh Lime Juice

Mix Absolut Vodka and lime juice in a glass with ice. Strain and serve in cocktail glass. Garnish with a twist of lime.

ABSOLUT MADRAS

1½ oz. ABSOLUT VODKA
Orange Juice
Cranberry Juice

In a tall glass with ice, fill with half orange juice, half cranberry juice.

ABSOLUT NUT

1 oz. ABSOLUT VODKA

1 oz. Frangelico

Stir. Strain into glass filled with ice.

ABSOLUT SALTY DOG

1½ oz. ABSOLUT VODKA

¾ oz. Grapefruit Juice

¼ tsp. Salt

Coat rim of glass with salt. Mix and pour on the rocks.

ABSOLUT SEABREEZE

1¼ oz. ABSOLUT VODKA

Cranberry Juice

Grapefruit Juice

Pour Absolut Vodka over ice in a tall glass. Fill half way with grapefruit juice and top it off with cranberry juice.

ABSOLUT SMOKY MARTINI

1¼ oz. ABSOLUT VODKA

dash Glenlivet Single Malt Scotch

Pour Absolut Vodka and the Glenlivet over ice. Shake or stir well. Strain and serve in a cocktail glass straight-up or over ice. Garnish with a twist.

ABSOLUT TESTAROSSA

1 oz. ABSOLUT VODKA

½ oz. Campari

Pour Absolut Vodka and Campari over ice in a tall glass. Top with tonic. Garnish with a slice of lemon and a slice of lime.

ABSOLUT TRANSFUSION

1¼ oz. ABSOLUT VODKA

Grape Juice

In a tall glass with ice, fill with grape juice. Can top with club soda.

ABSOLUT WHITE RUSSIAN

1 oz. ABSOLUT VODKA

½ oz. Godiva Liqueur

Heavy Cream

Pour Absolut Vodka, Godiva Liqueur and cream over ice in a rocks glass. Shake and serve.

ABSOLUTION

1 part ABSOLUT VODKA

5 parts Mumm Champagne

In a fluted champagne glass cut a lemon peel in the form of a ring to represent a halo. The lemon peel can be either wrapped around the top of the glass or float on top of the champagne.

ALMOND LEMONADE

1¼ oz. ABSOLUT VODKA

¼ oz. Hiram Walker Creme de Almond

Lemonade

Pour over ice in a tall glass. Garnish with lemon slice.

AQUEDUCT

¾ oz. ABSOLUT VODKA

¼ oz. Hiram Walker
Triple Sec

¼ oz. Hiram Walker Brandy

½ Tbs. Major Peters' Lime
Juice

*Combine with ice in a shaker.
Strain into chilled cocktail
glass.*

BANANA BOOMER

1½ oz. ABSOLUT VODKA

½ oz. Hiram Walker Creme
de Banana

*Shake. Serve up or on the
rocks.*

BERRY LEMONADE

1 oz. ABSOLUT VODKA

¼ oz. Hiram Walker
Strawberry Liqueur

Lemonade

*Pour over ice in a tall glass.
Garnish with fresh strawberry.*

BLACK EYE

1½ oz. ABSOLUT VODKA

½ oz. Hiram Walker
Blackberry Brandy

Stir. Serve up or on the rocks.

BLACK RUSSIAN

1 oz. ABSOLUT VODKA

¼ oz. Kahlua

Serve up with a twist of lemon peel.

BLIZZARD

1¼ oz. ABSOLUT VODKA

Fresca

*In a tall glass with ice. Garnish
with twist of lemon.*

BLOODY BULL

1¼ oz. ABSOLUT VODKA

Tomato Juice

1½ oz. Beef Bouillon

1-2 tsp. Lemon Juice

dash Worcestershire Sauce

dash Tabasco Sauce

Pepper

*Combine with ice in shaker.
Strain into old-fashioned glass,
pepper to taste.*

BLOODY MARY

1½ oz. ABSOLUT VODKA

Tomato Juice

1-2 tsp. Lemon Juice

dash Tabasco

dash Worcestershire Sauce

Pepper

*Combine in shaker. Strain into
chilled old-fashioned glass,
pepper to taste.*

BLUE LAGOON

1 oz. ABSOLUT VODKA

¼ oz. Hiram Walker Blue Curacao

½ oz. Pineapple Juice

Bitters

Combine in shaker with ice. Strain into chilled cocktail glass. Twist lemon peel over drink and add.

BLUE MONDAY

1 oz. ABSOLUT VODKA

¼ oz. Hiram Walker Triple Sec

dash Hiram Walker Blue Curacao

Combine with ice in shaker. Strain into chilled cocktail glass.

BOCCI BALL

1¼ oz. ABSOLUT VODKA

¾ oz. Hiram Walker Amaretto

1 oz. Orange Juice

Serve up or on the rocks.

BROWN DERBY

1¼ oz. ABSOLUT VODKA

Cola

In a tall glass with ice, fill with cola.

CAPE CODDER

1¼ oz. ABSOLUT VODKA

3 oz. Cranberry Juice

dash Major Peters' Lime Juice

Combine in a chilled cocktail glass over ice.

CHI CHI

1½ oz. ABSOLUT VODKA

¾ oz. Pineapple Juice

1½ oz. Cream of Coconut

Blend with ice to slush. Add cherry.

CLAMDIGGER

1¼ oz. ABSOLUT VODKA

3 oz. Mott's Clamato Juice

dash Tabasco Sauce

dash Worcestershire Sauce

Combine in mixing glass, stir well. Add ice and strain into chilled old-fashioned glass. Twist lemon peel and add.

CLOUDY NIGHT

1 part ABSOLUT VODKA

1 part Tia Maria

Stir on the rocks.

COOPERHEAD

1¼ oz. ABSOLUT VODKA

Ginger Ale

In a tall glass filled with ice, add a squeeze of lime and garnish with lime wedge.

DARK EYES

1 oz. ABSOLUT VODKA

¼ oz. Hiram Walker Blackberry Brandy

½ tsp. Major Peters' Lime Juice

Combine with ice in shaker. Strain into brandy snifter. Garnish with lime slice or mint sprig.

DUBLIN DELIGHT

¾ oz. ABSOLUT VODKA

½ oz. Midori

Combine with ice in shaker. Strain into old-fashioned glass half filled with crushed ice. Garnish with green maraschino cherry.

FIRE FLY

1¼ oz. ABSOLUT VODKA

Grapefruit Juice

Major Peters' Grenadine

Combine ABSOLUT and grapefruit juice in tall glass over ice. Add grenadine.

FUZZY NAVEL

1 oz. ABSOLUT VODKA

1 oz. Hiram Walker Peach Schnapps

4 oz. Tropicana Orange Juice

Pour into a highball glass filled with ice. Stir.

GODMOTHER

1 oz. ABSOLUT VODKA

¼ oz. Hiram Walker Amaretto

Serve in rocks glass over ice.

GORKY PARK

1¼ oz. ABSOLUT VODKA

1 tsp. Major Peters' Grenadine

dash Orange Bitters

Combine in shaker with crushed ice, or blend. Strain into chilled cocktail glass. Garnish with ½ strawberry.

GREYHOUND

1¼ oz. ABSOLUT VODKA

Grapefruit Juice

In a tall glass with ice, fill with grapefruit juice.

HARVEY WALLBANGER

1½ oz. ABSOLUT VODKA

4 oz. Orange Juice

½ oz. Galliano

In a highball glass filled with ice, combine Absolut and orange juice. Stir. Float the Galliano on top.

HOP-SKIP-AND-GO-NAKED

1 oz. ABSOLUT VODKA

1 oz. Beefeater Dry Gin

Juice of ½ Lime

In a mug; serve over ice. Fill with Budweiser.

HORSESHOT

1¼ oz. ABSOLUT VODKA

4 oz. Tomato Juice

1¼ tsp. Horseradish

Over ice in a cocktail glass. Garnish with celery stalk.

ICE PICK

1¼ oz. ABSOLUT VODKA

Lemon-flavored Iced Tea

Pour over ice in a tall glass. Garnish with a slice of lemon.

IMPERIAL CZAR

¼ oz. ABSOLUT VODKA

¼ oz. Hiram Walker Triple Sec

¾ oz. Dry Sparkling Wine

dash Major Peters' Lime Juice

dash Orange Bitters

Combine in shaker, except wine. Strain into chilled wine glass. Add wine, stir.

KAMAKAZI

1 oz. ABSOLUT VODKA

splash Hiram Walker Triple Sec

splash Major Peters' Lime Juice

Combine and shake well with ice. Strain into shot glass or on the rocks.

KREMLIN COLONEL

1¼ oz. ABSOLUT VODKA

2 Tbs. Sugar Syrup

Combine in shaker with ice. Strain into cocktail glass. Garnish with 3 to 4 mint leaves torn in half.

MIDNIGHT MARTINI

1 oz. ABSOLUT VODKA

¼ oz. Kahlua

Serve up with a twist of lemon peel.

NEGRONI

1 part ABSOLUT VODKA

2 parts Punt E Mes

Stir on the rocks. Garnish with an orange slice.

PANZER

1 part ABSOLUT VODKA

1 part Beefeater Dry Gin

1 part Hiram Walker
         Triple Sec

Combine in shaker with ice. Strain into chilled cocktail glass.

PINEAPPLE LEMONADE

1¼ oz. ABSOLUT VODKA

2 oz. Pineapple Juice

4 oz. Lemonade

Pour over ice in a tall glass. Garnish with pineapple spear.

PINK MINK

¾ oz. ABSOLUT VODKA

¼ oz. Bacardi Rum

¼ oz. Hiram Walker
        Strawberry Liqueur

Combine with ice in shaker. Strain into a cocktail glass with rim moistened with strawberry liqueur and sugar-frosted. Garnish with ½ strawberry.

PRAIRIE OYSTER

1¼ oz. ABSOLUT VODKA

2 oz. Tomato Juice

dash Worcestershire Sauce

1 Egg Yolk

Drop unbroken egg yolk in bottom of chilled wine glass. In separate mixing glass, combine other ingredients; mix well. Pour over egg yolk. Salt and pepper to taste.

PURPLE PASSION

1¼ oz. ABSOLUT VODKA

2 oz. Grapefruit Juice

2 oz. Grape Juice

Chill, stir, add sugar to taste, and serve in a collins glass.

SALT LICK

1¼ oz. ABSOLUT VODKA

2 oz. Bitter Lemon Soda

2 oz. Grapefruit Juice

Pour over ice in salt-rimmed wine glass.

SCREWDRIVER

1¼ oz. ABSOLUT VODKA

Orange Juice

In a tall glass with ice, fill with orange juice.

SEX ON THE BEACH

1 oz. ABSOLUT VODKA

1 oz. Hiram Walker Peach Schnapps

2 oz. Orange Juice

2 oz. Cranberry Juice

Stir. Serve up or on the rocks.

SILVER BULLET

2 oz. ABSOLUT VODKA

¼ oz. Martini & Rossi Dry Vermouth

¼ oz. Cutty Sark

Stir on the rocks. Float ¼ oz. Scotch on the surface.

SLALOM

1 part ABSOLUT VODKA

1 part Hiram Walker White Creme de Cacao

1 part Romana Sambuca

1 tsp. Heavy Cream

Combine in blender with ice. Strain into chilled cocktail glass.

SLIM JIM

1¼ oz. ABSOLUT VODKA

Diet Soda

In a highball glass with ice, fill with diet soda. Garnish with lemon or lime slice.

SPOTTED DOG

¼ oz. ABSOLUT VODKA

¾ oz. Hiram Walker Amaretto

¼ oz. Hiram Walker White Creme de Cacao

Vanilla Ice Cream

Mix all ingredients in a blender until smooth. Pour into cocktail glass and serve.

SUN STROKE

1¼ oz. ABSOLUT VODKA

dash Hiram Walker
Triple Sec

Tropicana Grapefruit
Juice

*Serve in a rocks glass over ice.
Add dash of Triple Sec.*

SUNBURST

1¼ oz. ABSOLUT VODKA

dash Hiram Walker
Triple Sec

Grapefruit Juice

*Serve in rocks glass over ice.
Add dash of Triple Sec.*

SWEDISH BEAR

¾ oz. ABSOLUT VODKA

½ oz. Godiva

1 Tbs. Heavy Cream

*Pour over ice in chilled old-
fashioned glass, and stir.*

SWEDISH COCKTAIL

¾ oz. ABSOLUT VODKA

¼ oz. Beefeater Gin

¼ oz. Hiram Walker White
Creme de Cacao

*Combine in shaker with ice.
Strain into chilled cocktail
glass.*

SWEDISH LADY

1 oz. ABSOLUT VODKA

¼ oz. Hiram Walker
Strawberry Liqueur

1 oz. Lemon Juice

1 oz. Sugar Syrup

½ oz. Heavy Cream

*Combine in shaker with ice.
Strain into chilled whiskey sour
glass.*

THE TWIST

¾ oz. ABSOLUT VODKA

½ oz. Hiram Walker White
Creme de Menthe

Orange Sherbert

*Blend. Pour into a champagne
glass.*

WHITE ELEPHANT

1 oz. ABSOLUT VODKA

¼ oz. Hiram Walker White
Creme de Cacao

Milk

In a tall glass with ice.

WHITE RUSSIAN

1½ oz. ABSOLUT VODKA

½ oz. Kahlua

½ oz. Cream

Shake and serve over ice.

WHITE SPIDER

2 parts ABSOLUT VODKA

1 part Hiram Walker White
Creme de Menthe

Stir on the rocks.

WOO WOO

¾ oz. ABSOLUT VODKA

¾ oz. Hiram Walker
Peppermint
Schnapps

In a tall glass with ice.

Add your favorite Absolut recipes here.

© Foley Publishing Corp

ABSOLUT CITRON VODKA

Absolut Citron, the true essence of citrus fruits, is a flavored vodka predominantly tasting of lemon with notes of lime, mandarin orange and grapefruit. This spirit adds a zesty "twist" to your favorite vodka drinks, from the Absolut Lemondrop (chilled Citron served with a sugar-coated lemon wedge) to Absolut Appeal (Citron mixed with lemonade and club soda).

Introduced in selected U.S. markets in 1988, Absolut Citron was imported from Sweden as an extension of the increasingly popular Absolut product line. Absolut Citron, which keeps the Absolut tradition of being absolutely clear, is packaged in a frosty bottle with bold yellow lettering to reflect the citrus flavor of the product.

Flavored vodkas, a long tradition in Europe, are increasingly popular in this country. Since early times in Sweden, where Absolut is produced using the finest grain grown in the rich fields of Southern Sweden, vodka has been flavored with a variety of fruits and berries. It has been traditionally enjoyed served chilled, straight-up.

For additional recipes on Absolut Citron, please visit our website at http://www.absolutvodka.com

ABSOLUT APPEAL

1¼ oz. ABSOLUT CITRON

Lemonade

Club Soda

Pour Absolut Citron over ice in a tall glass. Fill most of the way with lemonade. Top with a splash of club soda. Garnish with lemon wedge.

ABSOLUT CITRON & TONIC

2 oz. ABSOLUT CITRON

Tonic

In a tall glass with ice, fill with tonic. Add squeeze of lemon.

ABSOLUT CITRON BREEZE

1¼ oz. ABSOLUT CITRON

5 oz. Grapefruit Juice

3 oz. Cranberry Juice

Mix in chilled collins glass with ice cubes. Garnish with lime slice.

ABSOLUT CITRON COLLINS

1¼ oz. ABSOLUT CITRON

1 oz. Lemon Juice

½ oz. Sugar Syrup

Club Soda

Mix ingredients in a collins glass. Stir well, add ice, garnish with fruit, top with club soda.

ABSOLUT CITRON GODMOTHER

1¼ oz. ABSOLUT CITRON

¾ oz. Hiram Walker Amaretto

Serve in rocks glass over ice.

ABSOLUT CITRON RICKEY

1¼ oz. ABSOLUT CITRON

Club Soda

In a tall glass with ice, fill with club soda. Add squeeze of fresh lime.

ABSOLUT CITRON SOUR

1¼ oz. ABSOLUT CITRON

¼ oz. Lemon Juice

1 tsp. Sugar Syrup

Mix in a shaker. Strain into chilled glass and garnish with cherry.

ABSOLUT LEMONADE

1¼ oz. ABSOLUT CITRON

¼ oz. Hiram Walker Triple Sec

½ Sweet & Sour Mix

½ 7-Up

In a tall glass with ice put Absolut Citron and Triple Sec, fill with ½ sweet & sour and ½ 7-Up. Mix, do not shake. Garnish with a lemon wheel.

ABSOLUT MONTAUK CITRON BREEZE

1¼ oz. ABSOLUT CITRON
5 oz. Grapefruit Juice
3 oz. Cranberry Juice

Mix in chilled collins glass with ice cubes. Garnish with lime slice.

ABSOLUT SQUEEZE

1¼ oz. ABSOLUT CITRON
2 oz. Orange Juice
3 oz. Pineapple Juice
splash Chambord

Pour Absolut Citron, orange juice and pineapple juice over ice in a tall glass. Top with Chambord. Garnish with a lemon wedge, or try a whole strawberry.

B.C.

1 part ABSOLUT CITRON
1 part Godiva

Stir on the rocks.

BEACH BALL COOLER

1¼ oz. ABSOLUT CITRON
½ oz. Hiram Walker Creme de Cassis
1 tsp. Lime Juice
Ginger Ale

Mix in a collins glass with ice. Fill with ginger ale. Garnish with lemon and cherry.

BLUE LEMONADE

1¼ oz. ABSOLUT CITRON
splash Hiram Walker Blue Curacao

Pour over ice in a tall glass.

CILVER CITRON

1¼ oz. ABSOLUT CITRON
½ oz. Mumm Champagne

Serve up.

CITRON AND SODA

1¼ oz. ABSOLUT CITRON
Club Soda

Pour Absolut Citron over ice in a tall glass. Fill with club soda. Garnish with a lemon twist.

CITRON CELEBRATION

1¼ oz. ABSOLUT CITRON

Serve on the rocks and celebrate.

CITRON CODDER

1½ oz. ABSOLUT CITRON
Cranberry Juice

In a tall glass with ice, fill with cranberry juice.

CITRON COOLER

1¼ oz. ABSOLUT CITRON
½ oz. Lime Juice
Tonic Water

Mix with ice cubes in a chilled collins glass and fill with cold tonic water. Garnish with a lime wedge.

CITRON KAMIKAZI

¾ oz. ABSOLUT CITRON
¾ oz. Hiram Walker Triple Sec
¾ oz. Lime Juice

Pour Absolut Citron, Triple Sec and lime juice over ice in a glass. Shake well and strain into a cocktail glass. Serve straight-up or on the rocks. Garnish with a wedge of lime.

CITRON MADRAS

1¼ oz. ABSOLUT CITRON
Orange Juice
Cranberry Juice

In a tall glass with ice, fill with half orange and half cranberry juice.

CITRON MARTINI

1¼ oz. ABSOLUT CITRON
dash Extra Dry Vermouth

Pour Absolut Citron and vermouth over ice. Shake or stir well. Strain and serve in a cocktail glass straight-up or over ice. Garnish with a twist or an olive.

COOL CITRON

1 oz. ABSOLUT CITRON
½ oz. Hiram Walker White Creme de Menthe

Stir on the rocks.

FLORIDA JOY

1¼ oz. ABSOLUT CITRON
½ oz. Hiram Walker Triple Sec

Mix with cracked ice in a shaker or blender and pour into a chilled highball glass. Garnish with lemon slice.

GOLFER

1 oz. ABSOLUT CITRON
½ oz. Beefeater Dry Gin
¼ oz. Martini & Rossi Extra Dry Vermouth

Serve on the rocks with a twist of lemon peel.

LEMONDROP

1¼ oz. ABSOLUT CITRON

Serve with a wedge of lemon coated with sugar. Shoot the Absolut Citron, then suck the lemon.

PAR 19

1½ oz. ABSOLUT CITRON

Grape Juice

Ginger Ale

In a tall glass with ice, fill with half ginger ale and half grape juice.

PILOT HOUSE FIZZ

1 oz. ABSOLUT CITRON

1 oz. Hiram Walker Triple Sec

dash Major Peters' Lime Juice

dash Orange Bitters

Mix all except champagne with ice in a shaker. Strain into a chilled wine goblet. Fill with champagne.

PINK BABY

1¼ oz. ABSOLUT CITRON

½ oz. Chambord

½ oz. Lemon Juice

Mix with cracked ice in a shaker or blender and strain into a chilled cocktail glass.

PINK LEMONADE

1¼ oz. ABSOLUT CITRON

splash Major Peters' Grenadine

Pour over ice in a tall glass.

RAINBOW

1¼ oz. ABSOLUT CITRON

Grapefruit Juice

Grape Juice

In a tall glass with ice, fill with half grapefruit and half grape juice.

REATHA'S RELAXER

1½ oz. ABSOLUT CITRON

½ oz. Hiram Walker Triple Sec

½ oz. Cognac

2 oz. Half & Half

Shake. Serve up.

SALTY GROG

1¼ oz. ABSOLUT CITRON

4 oz. Grapefruit Juice

pinch Salt

dash Raspberry Syrup or
Major Peters'
Grenadine

Mix with ice in a large, chilled wine goblet.

SUPER LEMON COOLER

1½ oz. ABSOLUT CITRON

3 oz. Tonic Water

3 oz. Bitter Lemon Soda

Mix with ice in a chilled collins glass and garnish with a lemon slice.

SWEDISH BLACKBERRY

1½ oz. ABSOLUT CITRON

½ oz. Hiram Walker
Blackberry Flavored
Brandy

½ oz. Lemon Juice or
Major Peters' Lime
Juice

Mix in shaker and strain into chilled glass. Garnish with lemon slice.

THE RIGHT IDEA

1½ oz. ABSOLUT CITRON

½ oz. Hiram Walker
Triple Sec

½ oz. Lemon Juice or
Major Peters' Lime
Juice

Mix in a shaker and strain into chilled cocktail glass. Garnish with orange slice.

TROPICAL ORCHARD

1¼ oz. ABSOLUT CITRON

½ oz. Hiram Walker
Triple Sec

4 oz. Tropicana Orange
Juice

½ oz. Major Peters' Lime
Juice

½ oz. Grapefruit Juice

Mix with cracked ice in a shaker and pour into chilled double old-fashioned glass.

TWISTED BULL

1 oz. ABSOLUT CITRON

4 oz. Beef Broth (Bouillion)

Serve over rocks. Garnish with lime.

TWISTED TEARDROP

1½ oz. ABSOLUT CITRON

½ oz. Hiram Walker
       Triple Sec

Mix with cracked ice in shaker or blender and pour into chilled highball glass. Garnish with lemon slice.

WHITE CITRON

1½ oz. ABSOLUT CITRON

½ oz. Kahlua

2 oz. Half & Half

Shake with ice and pour over ice.

Add your favorite Absolut Citron recipes here.

© Foley Publishing Corp

ABSOLUT KURANT VODKA

Absolut Kurant reveals an aromatic blend of the tart fresh taste of black currant berries within the smooth character of Absolut Vodka. Savor Absolut Kurant's subtle berry flavor in a refreshingly different Cosmopolitan. And for a fruitful alternative to a traditional favorite, try it in place of tequila for your first-but-surely-not-your-last Kurant Margarita.

Flavoring vodka with berries is an age-old Swedish tradition. Absolut Kurant, made from Northern Europe's exotic black currant berries, which grow North of the Arctic Circle, was introduced in 1992. Its name is derived from the Swedish work for "premium," which sounds like the American name for the berry: Kurant.

The unusual combination of light, temperature and moisture found in northern climates gives these currants a tart, berry taste. It took years of development to find the particular strain of black currants that would successfully match the quality and mixability of Absolut. A year of consumer testing proved the long search was worth it.

Like all the Absolut products already on the market, Absolut Kurant is crystal clear. The bottle, however, differs from the more familiar Absolut bottle in two respects: The name of the product appears in purple letters, suggestive of Black Currant berries, and a pattern of berries and leaves appears to be etched into the clear glass.

For additional recipes on Absolut Kurant, visit our website at http://www.absolutvodka.com

ABSOLUT CHOCOLATE MARTINI

1¼ oz. ABSOLUT KURANT

dash Hiram Walker Light Creme de Cacao

Pour Absolut Kurant and Creme de Cacao over ice. Shake or stir well. Strain and serve in a chocolate-rimmed cocktail glass straight-up or over ice. Garnish with an orange peel. (Hint: to rim the glass, first rub a piece of orange around the top of the glass, then gently place the glass upside-down in a plate of unsweetened chocolate powder.)

ABSOLUT KURANT BREEZE

1¼ oz. ABSOLUT KURANT

Grapefruit Juice

Cranberry Juice

In a tall glass with ice fill with half grapefruit and half cranberry.

ABSOLUT KURANT RICKEY

1¼ oz. ABSOLUT KURANT

Lemon-Lime Soda

Pour Absolut Kurant over ice in a tall glass. Fill with lemon-lime soda. Garnish with a slice of lemon and a slice of lime.

ABSOLUT MARGARITA

1 oz. ABSOLUT KURANT

½ oz. Hiram Walker Triple Sec

Juice of small lime

Mix Absolut Kurant, Triple Sec and lime juice with ice. Strain and serve in a cocktail glass. Garnish with a slice of lime.

ABSOLUT NOIR

1 oz. ABSOLUT KURANT

½ oz. Godiva Liqueur

Combine Absolut Kurant and Godiva Liqueur in a brandy snifter.

AU KURANT

1¼ oz. ABSOLUT KURANT

Major Peters' Lime Juice

Major Peters' Grenadine

Pour chilled Absolut Kurant into a cocktail glass. Add a splash of grenadine and splash of lime juice.

BERRY PATCH

1 oz. ABSOLUT KURANT

¼ oz. Hiram Walker Blackberry Brandy

Major Peters' Lime Juice

Shake with ice and serve.

GOLDEN BERRY

1¼ oz. ABSOLUT KURANT
Ginger Ale

In a tall glass with ice.

KURANT AFFAIR

1¼ oz. ABSOLUT KURANT
Cranberry Juice
Club Soda

Pour Absolut Kurant over ice in a tall glass. Fill most of the way with cranberry juice. Top off with a splash of soda. Garnish with a wedge of lime.

KURANT COSMOPOLITAN

1¼ oz. ABSOLUT KURANT
Cranberry Juice
Major Peters'
Lime Juice

Pour chilled Absolut Kurant into a cocktail glass. Add a splash of cranberry juice and splash of lime juice.

KURANT MADRAS

1¼ oz. ABSOLUT KURANT
Orange Juice
Cranberry Juice

In a tall glass with ice. Fill with half orange and half cranberry juice.

KURANT MARTINI

1¼ oz. ABSOLUT KURANT
dash Extra Dry Vermouth

Pour Absolut Kurant and vermouth over ice. Shake or stir well. Strain and serve in a cocktail glass straight-up or over ice. Garnish with a twist or an olive.

KURANT SUNBEAM

1¼ oz. ABSOLUT KURANT
Orange Juice

In a tall glass with ice. May use a slice of orange in place of orange juice.

SUMMER AFTERNOON

1¼ oz. ABSOLUT KURANT
Grapefruit Juice
Major Peters'
Grenadine

In a tall glass with ice.

SUNDAY BRUNCH

1¼ oz. ABSOLUT KURANT
½ oz. Mumm Champagne

Serve up in a champagne glass.

VICTORIA'S SECRET

1½ oz. ABSOLUT KURANT
¼ oz. Chambord
splash Major Peters'
Sweet & Sour Mix

Served on the rocks.

© Foley Publishing Corp

ABSOLUT PEPPAR VODKA

Absolut Peppar is a robust-tasting, crystal-clear vodka flavored with the glowing warmth and crisp taste of jalapeño pepper and paprika. Absolut Peppar adds the spice of variety to many popular cocktails, giving the Peppar Bloody Mary a lively edge in taste and the Cajun Martini a spirited difference.

In keeping with the Absolut tradition, Absolut Peppar is absolutely clear. The super premium brand offers a robust yet mellow flavor—with a subtle warm note of jalapeño.

Absolut introduced this feisty flavor in the heat of summer in 1986. Although packaged in the familiar clear bottle, Absolut Peppar is inscribed in black and red lettering—a colorful way to suggest the bold flavor of its contents.

For additional recipes on Absolut Peppar, visit our website at http://www.absolutvodka.com

ABSOHOT

½ shot ABSOLUT PEPPAR

dash Hot Sauce

Serve with Budweiser chaser.

ABSOLUT HOLY HAIL MARY

1¼ oz. ABSOLUT PEPPAR

5 dashes Tabasco Sauce

splash Tomato Juice

Mix the tabasco, tomato and Peppar and strain into a chilled rocks or shot glass.

ABSOLUT PEPPAR BULL SHOT

1¼ oz. ABSOLUT PEPPAR

5 oz. Beef Consomme

5 dashes Worcestershire Sauce

1 tsp. Lemon Juice

pinch Celery Salt or Seed

Mix ingredients with ice in a 14 oz. double old-fashioned glass.

ABSOLUT PEPPARMINT

1¼ oz. ABSOLUT PEPPAR

¼ oz. Hiram Walker Peppermint Schnapps

In a shot glass.

ABSOLUT SALT AND PEPPER

1¼ oz. ABSOLUT PEPPAR

Pour chilled Absolut Peppar into a salt-rimmed cocktail glass. Garnish with a cucumber spear.

AFTERBURNER

½ oz. ABSOLUT PEPPAR

½ oz. Kahlua

½ oz. Hiram Walker Cinnamon Schnapps

Serve in 2 oz. sherry glass.

BLACK PEPPAR

1¼ oz. ABSOLUT PEPPAR

¼ oz. Hiram Walker Blackberry Flavored Brandy

In a shot glass.

BLOODY BURNS

1 oz. ABSOLUT PEPPAR

1 oz. Fernet Branca

4 oz. Tomato Juice

1 Large Clove Garlic

dash Celery Salt

½ oz. Worcestershire Sauce

2 dashes Tabasco

Score the garlic with a knife and rim a 12-14 oz. tumbler. Fill with ice and add ingredients, top with Fernet. Garnish with cucumber slice.

COOL PEPPAR

1¼ oz. ABSOLUT PEPPAR
         Wedge of Lime

Pour freezer-cold Absolut Peppar into a shot glass. Squeeze the juice of the wedge of lime into the glass.

CAJUN MARY

1¼ oz. ABSOLUT PEPPAR
4 oz.   Tomato Juice
        Juice of ½ Lemon
2 dashes Worcestershire Sauce
½ tsp. Horseradish
dash   Salt
dash   Celery Salt

Combine all ingredients. Fill an 8-oz. glass with ice and pour in mixture. Place celery stalk in drinks as stirrer.

DOYLE'S MULLIGAN

1 oz.   ABSOLUT PEPPAR
4 oz.   Budweiser

Shoot Absolut Peppar while drinking beer.

DRAGON FIRE

1 oz.   ABSOLUT PEPPAR
¼ oz.   Hiram Walker Green
        Creme de Menthe

In a rocks glass over ice.

FIREBIRD

1¼ oz. ABSOLUT PEPPAR
4 oz.   Cranberry Juice

Serve on the rocks.

GARBO

1¼ oz. ABSOLUT PEPPAR
5 oz.   Clear Borscht

Mix over ice in 14 oz. double old-fashioned glass.

HOT LAVA

1¼ oz. ABSOLUT PEPPAR
¼ oz.   Hiram Walker
        Amaretto

Serve on the rocks.

HOT PANTS

¼ oz.   ABSOLUT PEPPAR
1 oz.   Hiram Walker Peach
        Schnapps

Serve on the rocks.

LONG ISLAND HOT TEA

¼ oz. ABSOLUT PEPPAR

¼ oz. Tequila

¼ oz. Bacardi Rum

¼ oz. Beefeater Dry Gin

   Major Peters'
   Sweet & Sour Mix

   Cola

In a tall glass with ice, shake. Top with cola.

PEPPAR BAYOU MARTINI

1¼ oz. ABSOLUT PEPPAR

¼ oz. Martini & Rossi Extra Dry Vermouth

1 small Pickled Jalapeño

Place four ice cubes in a small pitcher and add PEPPAR and vermouth. Stir briskly. Serve in chilled martini glass. Add pickled jalapeño.

PEPPAR SOMBRERO

1 oz. ABSOLUT PEPPAR

½ oz. Kahlua

1 Tbs. Heavy Cream

Combine PEPPAR and Kahlua. Pour over ice in a 4-oz. goblet. Float cream on top.

PEPPAR SOUTHSIDE

1 oz. ABSOLUT PEPPAR

2 Tbs. Major Peters' Lime Juice

2 tsp. Sugar

½ tsp. Fresh Mint Leaves, torn

Place all ingredients in a blender. Blend until smooth. Pour into chilled 4-oz. glass. Place lime on rim of glass.

PEPPAR TODDY

1 oz. ABSOLUT PEPPAR

4 oz. Cranberry Juice

½ Cinnamon Stick

2 Allspice Berries

   Orange Peel

1 tsp. Sugar

2 tsp. Lemon Juice

Combine all ingredients, except PEPPAR in saucepan. Boil two minutes, add PEPPAR.

RAGIN' CAJUN

1¼ oz. ABSOLUT PEPPAR

4 oz. Tomato Juice

2 dashes Salt

   dash Cayenne Pepper

In a tall glass with ice.

SCORPION'S STING

1¼ oz. ABSOLUT PEPPAR

¼ oz. Hiram Walker White Creme de Menthe

In a rocks glass over ice.

SEA & SOL

1¼ oz. ABSOLUT PEPPAR

4-6 oz. Clamato Juice

4-6 dshs. Bloody Mary Maker

Build over ice in highball or collins glass. Garnish with scallion spear, pepperoncini pepper and lime wedge.

SPARKS

1 oz. ABSOLUT PEPPAR

3 oz. Mumm Champagne

In a champagne glass.

SWEDISH BULL

1¼ oz. ABSOLUT PEPPAR

4 oz. Beef Broth (Bouillon)

Serve over rocks. Garnish with lime.

SWEET RED PEPPAR

1¼ oz. ABSOLUT PEPPAR

½ oz. Major Peters' Lime Juice

3 oz. Orange Juice

4 oz. Major Peters' Bloody Mary Mix

Combine all ingredients in a 16 oz. glass, filled with ice. Garnish with an orange wheel.

TEAR DROP

1¼ oz. ABSOLUT PEPPAR

¼ oz. Hiram Walker Triple Sec

In a shot glass, drop a cherry in.

THE ABSOLUT PEPPAR CAJUN MARTINI

1¼ oz. ABSOLUT PEPPAR

dash Martini & Rossi Extra Dry Vermouth (to taste)

Mix with ice in a mixing glass. Strain and pour on the rocks or serve in a chilled cocktail glass.

THE ABSOLUT PEPPAR EXPERIENCE

1¼ oz. ABSOLUT PEPPAR

Pour over ice in a chilled glass. Serious vodka drinkers may prefer it neat in a shot glass, poured from a freezer-cold bottle.

THE FLAME

1¼ oz. ABSOLUT PEPPAR

¼ oz. Chambord

Serve on the rocks.

ULTIMATE SHOOTER

A raw oyster or clam in a shot glass with ABSOLUT PEPPAR topped with a spoonful of cocktail sauce or a dash of horseradish and a squeeze of lemon. SHOOT IT DOWN.

VODKA STEAMER

1 oz. ABSOLUT PEPPAR

3 oz. Clam Juice

2 oz. Tomato Juice

Combine clam and tomato juice in a small saucepan. Heat only until warmed through and pour over vodka in a mug. Garnish with lemon slice.

VOLCANO

1¼ oz. ABSOLUT PEPPAR

dash Major Peters' Grenadine

In a shot glass.

Add your favorite Absolut Peppar recipes here.

For additional recipes on Absolut Peppar, visit our website at
http://www.absolutvodka.com

© Foley Publishing Corp

ALIZÉ & ALIZÉ RED PASSION

Alizé is an intriguing and infinitely mixable beverage—an inspired blend of fine French cognac and passion fruit juice of the tropics—that has almost singlehandedly revolutionized the Specialty Spirits category. Alizé is not heavy or sweet like traditional liqueurs, but light and refreshing, with a memorable aroma and tangy taste reminiscent of mango, pineapple and honey. The product is 84% passion fruit and 16% cognac (16% alcohol by volume—32 proof).

Passion fruit, which is an oval-shaped, egg-sized fruit, offers a tart-sweet flavor that suggests a blend of mango, pineapple and honey. It's quickly become an uncommonly flavorful addition cropping up in everything from food and beverages on the grocer's shelf and to recipes from the world's leading chefs. Here are some facts about this exotic newcomer:

Passion fruit was originally discovered in the tropics of Brazil. It is now cultivated in tropical, subtropical and temperate regions in Southeast Africa, Fiji, New Zealand, Hawaii and Florida. In favorable climates, the plant can flourish year-round, bearing mature fruits, buds and flowers. It is cultivated along rack-like trellises of posts and wires.

Passion fruit was so named by early Spanish Jesuit missionaries in the South American wilderness who saw in the parts of its flower what appeared to suggest Christ's crucifixion: the crown of thorns, hammer, the three nails, five wounds and 12 apostles.

Though there are many varieties of passion fruit, "Passion Flora Edulis Forma Edulis," also called Purple Passion, is the most popular. It can be identified by its leathery, blackish-purple skin. It's found in such places as Kenya, Angola, South Africa and New Zealand.

Another variety of passion fruit is "Passiflora Edulis Forma Flavicarpa." Also known as Yellow Passion Fruit, it can be identified by its wild, spicy taste. It is grown in Florida, Fiji, South America and Ceylon.

Because of the many seeds and ochre-colored pulp contained within, the passion fruit is also called "granadilla," a Spanish word meaning "little pomegranate."

The passion fruit's magnificent white, gold and purple flower is considered one of the most beautiful of all fruit blossoms. It emits an intense, musky fragrance.

One passion fruit yields about one heaping tablespoon of intensely flavored pulp. The pulp of two or three of these small fruits is often enough to endow a fish with the flavor and aroma of the tropics.

Passion fruit juice contains high levels of vitamins A and C, and three and a half ounces—a large amount—contains about 90 calories. It takes about 25 fruits to yield an eight ounce glass of juice.

Passion fruit is one of the key ingredients fueling a recent trend in French and American cooking, the most significant new taste since the arrival of the kiwi fruit on the culinary scene two decades ago.

Cognac...it's the warmth-giving, amber essence that more and more status-conscious consumers are enjoying in the afterglow of a fine meal, or along with spirited conversation. Often called the "King of Brandies," Cognac is a spirit distilled from wines made of white grapes grown only within the Cognac region of France, an area located about 200 miles southwest of Paris. The word "brandy" comes from the Dutch word "brandewijn," meaning "burned wine."

This is what this enticing, velvety beverage was called in the 16th Century, with the launch of the brandy trade between France and Holland.

Cognac's superior quality is due to a special, government-supervised, distillation process, along with the unique qualities and combinations of soil, climate and grape varieties.

The grapes used in Cognac are harvested, pressed and fermented with the skins and pips, which helps impart character to the beverage. The distilling season begins each November and must be completed by April 30th of the next year according to law.

Cognac is aged in hand-crafted oak casks which gives it a mellow taste and amber color. The alcohol content is reduced to 80 proof with the addition of demineralized water as the cognac ages.

Cognac must age at least two and a half years in wood before it can go on market shelves. Special reserve blends can improve in wood for longer than fifty years. Once the Cognac is bottled, however, it ceases to age.

With Alizé's introduction in 1986, Kobrand singlehandedly created both a dazzling, new product success story and whole new category for the spirits industry, one that capitalized on consumers' tastes for exotic flavors, prestige spirits and drinks with a moderate alcohol content.

In 1998, Alizé was joined by Alizé Red Passion. This product adds the enticing flavor of cranberry and a hint of peach to Alizé's already winning blend of fine French cognac and passion fruit juices.

Imported from France and packaged in the same distinctive, frosted bottle as the original, Alizé Red Passion offers a refreshing taste experience that is 16% cognac and 84% passion fruit, cranberry and peach juices. At only 32 proof, ruby-colored Alizé Red Passion is as infinitely versatile and mixable as the original—perfect served chilled, over ice, or mixed with juices, soda and other spirits to add a new twist to classic cocktails like the Martini.

Pronunciation: Ah-lee-zay

ALI-CAT

2 oz. ALIZÉ

1½ oz. Grapefruit Juice

splash Club Soda

Pour all ingredients over ice into highball glass. Garnish with a lime wheel.

ALI-COLADA

2 oz. ALIZÉ

dash Bacardi® Rum

Colada Mix

Mix Alizé, rum, piña colada mix in a blender with ice. Blend until smooth. Pour into piña colada glass. Garnish with a pineapple wedge.

ALI-MOSA

2 oz. ALIZÉ, chilled

2-3 oz. Sparkling Wine, chilled

Pour sparkling wine into champagne flute. Add Alizé. Garnish with a strawberry.

ALI-ROCKS

Pour 2 oz. Alizé, delicious just as it is, on the rocks.

ALIZÉ CARIBBEAN MARTINI

2 oz. ALIZÉ

½ oz. Bacardi® Limón

Fill shaker with ice, add above ingredients, cover martini shaker, shake. Strain "ice cold" into a martini glass. Garnish with a slice of lemon.

ALIZÉ COCKTAIL

1½ oz. ALIZÉ

½ oz. Hiram Walker Apricot Brandy

¾ oz. Fresh Lemon Juice

Shake all ingredients with ice and strain into chilled cocktail glass. Garnish with cherry.

ALIZÉ CRANBERRY PUNCH

1 oz. ALIZÉ RED PASSION

4 oz. Cranberry Juice

1 oz. Orange Juice, chilled

¼ tsp. Orange Extract

12 oz. 7-Up, chilled

1 pt. Raspberry Sherbert slightly softened

Mix the cranberry juice, orange juice and orange flavoring. Just before serving, add the 7-Up. Pour mixture into individual serving glasses and top with tablespoon sherbert.

ALIZÉ DREAMSICLE

1½ oz. ALIZÉ

½ oz. Absolut Vodka

2 oz. Pineapple Juice

2 oz. Orange Juice

½ oz. Coco Lopez

1 Tbs. Major Peters'
Grenadine

Blend with ice.

ALIZÉ MANGO TANGO

¾ oz. ALIZÉ

¾ oz. Mango Liqueur

2 oz. Mango Puree

1 oz. Coco Lopez

2 oz. Pineapple Juice

*Blend with ice until smooth,
splash ½ oz. raspberry puree
on the bottom of the glass
before pouring into Viva
Grande glass. Garnish with
pineapple and orange.*

ALIZÉ MARGARITA

2 oz. ALIZÉ

½ oz. Cuervo "White"
Tequila

splash Hiram Walker Triple Sec

*Fill shaker with ice. Add above
ingredients, cover martini shaker, shake. Strain "ice cold" into
a salted martini glass. Garnish
with a thin slice of lime.*

ALIZÉ MARTINI

½ oz. ALIZÉ

1½ oz. Absolut Vodka

*Fill shaker with ice, add above
ingredients, cover martini shaker, shake. Strain "ice cold" into
a martini glass. Garnish with a
thin slice of lemon.*

ALIZÉ MENAGE A TROIS

¾ oz. ALIZÉ

¾ oz. ALIZÉ RED PASSION

¾ oz. Orange-flavored
Vodka

1½ oz. Orange Juice

1½ oz. Cranberry Juice

*Pour Alizé, Red Passion and
vodka. Add cranberry and
orange juice. Garnish with
orange slice. Serve chilled in
martini glass.*

ALIZÉ PASSIONATE
MARGARITA

2 oz. ALIZÉ

½ oz. Cuervo "White"
Tequila

1 oz. Cranberry Juice

splash Hiram Walker Triple Sec

*Fill shaker with ice. Add above
ingredients, cover martini shaker, shake. Strain "ice cold" into
a salted martini glass. Garnish
with a thin slice of lime.*

ALIZÉ RASPBERRY BERET

1 oz. ALIZÉ

½ oz. Chambord

1 oz. Pineapple Juice

Chill over ice and strain into Martini glass. Garnish with a cherry.

ALIZÉ RED PASSION LEMONADE

2 oz. ALIZÉ RED PASSION

3 oz. Lemonade

Mix Alizé Red Passion and lemonade, shake and pour over ice in a tall glass. Garnish with a lemon twist.

ALIZÉ RED PASSION ROYALE

2 oz. ALIZÉ RED PASSION

3 oz. Absolut Vodka

Pour Champagne into fluted glass. Add Alizé Red Passion.

ALIZÉ SUNRISE

1 oz. ALIZÉ

1 oz. ALIZÉ RED PASSION

Shaken together in a martini shaker and pour over ice. Pour into a rocks glass with a slice of orange as a garnish.

ALIZÉ TROPICAL MARTINI

2 oz. ALIZÉ

½ oz. Malibu

Fill shaker with ice, add above ingredients, cover martini shaker, shake. Strain "ice cold" into a martini glass. Garnish with a maraschino cherry.

BRAIN FREEZE

1½ oz. ALIZÉ

½ oz. Absolut Citron

1 oz. Cranberry Juice

¼ oz. Fresh Lemon Juice

Shake all ingredients with ice and strain into an ice-filled goblet.

CAPARINHA ALIZÉ

1½ oz. ALIZÉ

½ oz. Cachaca (or Bacardi® white rum)

2 Tbs. Freshly Squeezed Lime Juice

1 Tbs. Superfine Sugar

Mix Alizé, Cachaca (or white rum), lime juice and sugar in a glass. Stir well. Add ice.

COSMALIZÉ

1½ oz. ALIZÉ

½ oz. Absolut Citron

1 oz. Cranberry Juice

¼ oz. Fresh Lemon Juice

Shake all ingredients with ice and strain into a chilled cocktail glass. Garnish with lemon peel.

EXOTIC COOLER

1 oz. ALIZÉ

1 oz. Hiram Walker Creme de Banana

½ oz. Major Peters' Grenadine

4 oz. Ocean Spray Paradise Passion

Shake with ice. Garnish with pineapple wedge and cherry speared.

FRENCH ALP

1½ oz. ALIZÉ

¼ oz. Hiram Walker Dark Creme de Cacao

2 oz. Pineapple Juice

3 oz. Whipped Cream

Shake all but whipped cream and creme de cacao. Top with whipped cream. Float dark creme de cacao. Garnish with ¼ orange wheel and 2 large straws.

FRENCH BREEZE

2 oz. ALIZÉ

2 oz. Cranberry Juice

splash Club Soda

Combine Alizé and cranberry juice in tall glass over ice. Add a splash of soda. Garnish with a lime wheel.

FRENCH MARGARITA

2 oz. ALIZÉ

½ oz. Cuervo

juice of 2 Fresh Limes

kiss of Hiram Walker Triple Sec

juice of 1 Lemon

Shaken, not stirred. Salt on rim optional.

FRUIT COCKTAIL

1 oz. ALIZÉ

1 oz. Midori

4 oz. Ocean Spray Kiwi/Strawberry

Shake with ice. Add squeeze of lime and garnish with fresh strawberry.

ISLAND ALIZÉ

2 oz. ALIZÉ

4 dashes Angostura Bitters

4 oz. Ginger Beer

Prepare like a highball. Garnish with a lime wedge.

ISLAND HIDEAWAY

1 oz. ALIZÉ

1 oz. Bacardi® Rum

2 oz. Orange Juice

2 oz. Pineapple Juice

Shake with ice. Garnish with pineapple wedge and cherry speared.

JAIL BAIT

1 oz. ALIZÉ

1 oz. Bacardi® Spice

1 oz. Orange Juice

3 oz. Cranberry Juice

Shake with ice. Garnish with orange wedge and cherry speared.

KIR-ALI

1 part ALIZÉ, chilled

2 parts Crisp Dry White Wine

Serve in wine glass.

KISS MY MONKEY

1½ oz. ALIZÉ

½ oz. Absolut Vodka

3 oz. Cranberry Juice

Serve in tall glass with ice.

MARIACHI-LOCO

1 oz. ALIZÉ

½ oz. Cuervo 1800 Tequila

2 oz. Cranberry Juice

1½ oz. Major Peters' Sweet & Sour Mix

Mix all ingredients. Fill 6 oz. rocks glass with ice and pour. Garnish with lime slice and cherry.

MIAMI ICE

2 oz. ALIZÉ

2 oz. Cranberry Juice

Pour ingredients over crushed ice or mix with ice in blender. Serve in martini glass. Garnish with a lime wheel.

MONEALIZÉ

½ oz. ALIZÉ

½ oz. Southern Comfort

1 oz. Pineapple Juice

1 oz. Orange Juice

Highball glass, shaken not stirred. Garnish with orange and cherry.

MONSOON

1 oz. ALIZÉ
1 oz. Schoenauer Apfel
       Schnapps
1 oz. Pineapple Juice
3 oz. Cranberry Juice

Shake with ice. Garnish with pineapple wedge and cherry speared.

P'DIDDY ALIZÉ SPECIAL

(Sean Puff Daddy Combs' drink of choice at his restaurant, Justin's)

1 oz. ALIZÉ RED PASSION
½ oz. Absolut Citron
¼ oz. Major Peters'
       Lime Juice
¼ oz. Hiram Walker
       Triple Sec
¼ oz. Chambord
1 oz. Major Peters'
       Sweet & Sour Mix

Chill martini glass. Pour all ingredients together then shake and strain in the martini glass. Garnish with either a lemon twist or lime. Serve chilled.

PARADISE IS CALLING

1 oz. ALIZÉ
1 oz. Bacardi® Limón
4 oz. Ocean Spray
       Mango Mango

Shake with ice. Garnish with pineapple wedge and cherry speared.

PASSION FLOWER

1 oz. ALIZÉ, chilled
2½ oz. Sparkling Wine,
       chilled
1½ oz. Cranberry Juice,
       chilled

Pour all ingredients into champagne flute. Garnish with an orange slice.

PASSION FREEZE

2 oz. ALIZÉ
1½ oz. Orange Juice
1½ oz. Cream
1½ oz. Simple Syrup or
       2 tsp. bar sugar

Blend all ingredients with crushed ice and serve in a large goblet. Garnish with fresh fruit.

PASSION PUNCH

2 oz. ALIZÉ

2 oz. Orange Juice

2 oz. Pineapple Juice

2 dashes Major Peters'
Grenadine

1 dash Angostura Bitters

Shake all ingredients with ice and strain into an ice-filled goblet. Garnish with fresh fruits.

PASSIONATE SUNSET

1 oz. ALIZÉ

½ oz. Cuervo Gold

splash Orange Juice

½ oz. Major Peters'
Grenadine

Mix Alizé, Cuervo Gold and orange juice. Shake well then layer over grenadine and ice. Pour into a martini glass. Garnish with orange slice dipped in sugar.

RAZZLE DAZZLE ALIZÉ LEMONADE

2 oz. ALIZÉ RED PASSION

6 oz. Cranberry Juice

6 oz. Lemonade

2 oz. Raspberry Juice

Mint Leaves
to garnish

Pour into a 16-ounce glass with ice. Garnish with mint leaves.

RED PASSION MARTINI

1½ oz. ALIZÉ

½ oz. Campari

Stir well and serve like a martini. Garnish with an orange peel.

ROCK LOBSTER ALIZÉ

1½ oz. ALIZÉ RED PASSION

½ oz. Chambord

balance Cranberry Juice

Shake together over ice until well chilled. Pour into shot glass. Garnish with lime.

SMILE MAKER

1 oz. ALIZÉ

1 oz. Hiram Walker
Amaretto

1 oz. Orange Juice

3 oz. Major Peters'
Sweet & Sour Mix

Shake with ice. Garnish with orange wedge and cherry speared.

STRAWBERRY DAIQUIRI ALIZÉ

2 oz.   ALIZÉ
½ cup   Crushed Ice
½ cup   Frozen Strawberries
1 Tbs. Freshly Squeezed
        Lemon Juice
        Superfine Sugar

Blend until smooth. Pour into martini glass.

SWEET TART ALIZÉ

½ oz.   ALIZÉ RED
        PASSION
¼ oz.   Vanilla-flavored
        Vodka
¼ oz.   Raspberry-flavored
        Vodka
balance Cranberry Juice

Shake together over ice until well chilled. Coat rim with sugar and pour into shot glasses.

TASTE OF PARADISE

1 oz.   ALIZÉ
1 oz.   Bacardi® Rum
2 oz.   Strawberry Puree
1½ oz. Ocean Spray
        Paradise Passion

Blend. Garnish with pineapple wedge and cherry speared.

TROPIC TWISTER

¾ oz.   ALIZÉ
¾ oz.   Southern Comfort
¾ oz.   Midori
2 oz.   Pineapple Juice
2 oz.   Orange Juice

Shake with ice or blend. Garnish with pineapple wedge and cherry speared.

TROPICAL PASSION

1 oz.   ALIZÉ

1 oz.   Midori

3 oz.   Pineapple

1 oz.   Orange Juice

Blend. Garnish with pineapple wedge and cherry speared.

TROPICAL SUNSET

2 oz.   ALIZÉ

2 oz.   Orange Juice

1 Tbs. Freshly Squeezed
        Lemon Juice

2 Tbs. Major Peters'
        Grenadine

Combine Alizé, orange juice and lemon juice in a tall glass over ice. Pour grenadine down the side of the glass.

Add your favorite Alizé recipes here.

BACARDI® RUM

How is it that BACARDI® rum is the most popular spirit in the world today? Unique taste. Outstanding quality. Unequaled mixability. And a natural complement to so many great foods. It's a rum as rich in taste as in its own history.

In the 19th century, when spirits were consumed straight, rum was little more than a harsh, fiery drink favored mostly by sailors who sailed the seven seas. Neither its reputation nor its taste were suited to the elegance of 19th century drawing rooms. However, a successful wine merchant in Santiago de Cuba, named Don Facundo Bacardi®, felt that with the right care, distillation, and mellowing, rum could be quite civilized. So, Don Facundo created a recipe and distillation formula around his ideas. And in 1862, BACARDI® rum was born—a light dry taste and mellow smoothness that forever changed the way people thought of rum.

And because the rum bore his proud family name, to this day the quality of BACARDI® rum has never been allowed to falter.

Soon, the taste of BACARDI® rum began winning awards for excellence all over the world, including the title of Purveyors to the Royal Household, bestowed upon Bacardi® by Queen Maria Cristina of Spain. Hence, the Spanish royal coat of arms proudly displayed on the label.

Toward the close of the 19th century, when people began experimenting with mixed drinks, BACARDI® rum became a natural favorite for a whole range of exciting new concoctions. The famous BAT symbol—the emblem of mystical power and good fortune that appears on every BACARDI® label today—was stamped on each bottle of BACARDI® rum right from the start.

THE HISTORY OF THE CLASSIC DAIQUIRI

A few years after the end of the Spanish-American War in 1898, an American in Cuba was inspired to new heights of refreshment.

Jennings S. Cox led a team of American engineers in a mining operation near the little town of Daiquiri. Workdays under the blazing Caribbean sun were hot and sweaty. Comforts were few.

To keep the men motivated in this hardship assignment, management gave them high salaries, free housing, free cigars, and every month, a gallon of Cuba's finest rum, BACARDI® rum.

One night, Cox showed his fellow engineers how to take fresh lime juice, sugar, ice and BACARDI® rum, shake them to perfection and serve them cool and frosty. The drink was an instant success.

A few weeks later while at the bar at the Venus Hotel in the nearby city of Santiago de Cuba, the engineers asked Cox to think of a name for this popular new drink. Cox thought about their life in Daiquiri. He thought about the beautiful island nation enjoying its newly won indepen-dence. In the war, American troops had made an important landing on the beach at Daiquiri.

So, for his men, for Cuba, for the rest of the world to remember, he called the drink "Daiquiri."

THE HISTORY OF THE CUBA LIBRE

After victory in the Spanish-American War in 1898, a group of off-duty soldiers from the U.S. Signal Corps were gathered in a bar in Old Havana.

A captain came in and ordered BACARDI® and Coke® on ice with a wedge of lime. The captain drank the concoction with such pleasure, it sparked the interest of the soldiers around him. They had the bartender prepare a round for them. The drink was an instant hit.

When they ordered another round, one soldier suggested that this great drink deserved a name. The room fell silent. All eyes were on the captain. He thought for a moment, raised his glass and sang out the battlecry that had inspired the victorious soldiers in Cuba's War of independence.

"Cuba Libre!" (Spanish for "Free Cuba"), he shouted, "Cuba Libre!". The response from the crowd was unanimous. To a man, they raised their glasses in a toast to a free Cuba, happiness, and the good fellowship they had discovered in this delicious new pleasure. The year 1998 marks the 100th anniversary of this classic cocktail, which is America's most popular drink.

BACARDI® rum, America's favorite distilled spirit, is also one of the most mixable. It can be used with all mixes and juices and is a great product to use when creating your own special drink.

The following BACARDI® rums are available:

BACARDI® LIGHT-DRY RUM is the original and most mixable of all BACARDI® rums. A subtle, delicate rum that is clear in color, light in body, and dry in flavor.

BACARDI® GOLD RUM is a smooth, amber-colored rum with a fuller body than BACARDI® LIGHT-DRY, and a pleasing woody flavor.

BACARDI® LIMÓN (pronounced "lee-MOAN") is a unique blend of BACARDI® rum and natural citrus flavors that delivers a blast of clean, crisp citrus taste unlike any other spirit. So distinctly smooth and flavorful, it is perfectly suited to be enjoyed straight, on the rocks, or mixed with juices or tonic.

BACARDI® SPICE RUM is a unique blend of rich golden rums, vanilla and cinnamon spices which combine for a smooth, flavorful taste experience. Terrific in cola, pineapple or cranberry juice.

BACARDI® SELECT RUM is the richest of all BACARDI® rums. It is a blend of selected aged rums with a rich flavor and full body that mixes great and makes the richest tasting drinks.

BACARDI® 151° RUM is a premium, high-proof golden rum, traditionally used for making delicious exotic island drinks. Enjoy it in Mai-Tais, Rum Runners, and punches.

For additional recipes, visit our website at
http://www.bacardi.com

ACAPULCO

1¼ oz. BACARDI®
LIGHT-DRY RUM

¼ oz. Hiram Walker
Triple Sec

½ oz. Major Peters'
Lime Juice

½ Egg White

½ tsp. Sugar

Mix in shaker or blender with ice and strain into a cocktail glass.

APPLE COOLER

1¼ oz. BACARDI®
LIGHT-DRY RUM

3 oz. Apple Juice

Pour into a highball glass and fill with ice.

APPLE PIE COCKTAIL

¾ oz. BACARDI® LIGHT-DRY RUM

¼ oz. Martini & Rossi
Rosso Vermouth

¼ oz. Apple Brandy

½ oz. Lemon Juice

dash Major Peters'
Grenadine

Stir in a mixing glass with ice and strain into a chilled cocktail glass. Garnish with twist of a lemon peel.

APPLE RUM RICKEY

¾ oz. BACARDI® LIGHT-DRY or GOLD RUM

½ oz. Apple Brandy

Soda

Pour rum in a highball glass filled with ice. Add apple brandy and fill with soda. Squeeze a wedge of lime and add.

APPLE RUM SWIZZLE

¾ oz. BACARDI® LIGHT-DRY or GOLD RUM

½ oz. Apple Brandy

1 oz. Major Peters'
Lime Juice

1 tsp. Sugar

Bitters

Place sugar in bottom of a highball glass and add several dashes of bitters. Add rum, lime juice and apple brandy and fill glass with shaved or crushed ice. Stir until frosty.

BACARDI® & COKE (CUBA LIBRE)

1½ oz. BACARDI® GOLD RUM

Coca Cola® Classic

Pour rum into glass filled with ice. Fill with Coca-Cola Classic. Garnish with a generous squeeze of lime.

BACARDI® BLOSSOM

1¼ oz. BACARDI® LIGHT-DRY RUM

1 oz. Orange Juice

½ oz. Lemon Juice

½ tsp. Sugar

Mix in a shaker or blender with ice and strain into a cocktail glass.

BACARDI® BUCK

1¼ oz. BACARDI® LIGHT-DRY or GOLD RUM

Ginger Ale

Pour rum in highball glass filled with ice. Add ginger ale and garnish with twist of a lemon peel.

BACARDI® COCKTAIL*

1¼ oz. BACARDI® LIGHT-DRY RUM

1 oz. Major Peters' Lime Juice

½ tsp. Sugar

½ oz. Major Peters' Grenadine

*Mix in shaker or blender with ice and strain into a chilled cocktail glass or serve on the rocks. *The NY Supreme Court ruled in 1936 that a Bacardi® Cocktail is not a Bacardi® Cocktail unless it's made with Bacardi® Rum.*

BACARDI® COLLINS

1¼ oz. BACARDI® LIGHT-DRY RUM

1¼ oz. Lemon or Major Peters' Lime Juice

1 tsp. Sugar

Club Soda

Mix rum, juice and sugar in shaker or blender with ice and pour into a tall glass. Fill with soda and garnish with a cherry and fruit slice.

BACARDI® DAIQUIRI*

1¼ oz. BACARDI® LIGHT-DRY RUM

½ oz. Lemon Juice

½ tsp. Sugar

*Mix in shaker or blender with ice and strain into a chilled cocktail glass or serve on the rocks. *The original Daiquiri was made with Bacardi® Rum in 1896.*

BACARDI® FIRESIDE

1¼ oz. BACARDI® LIGHT-DRY or GOLD RUM

1 tsp. Sugar

Hot Tea

In a mug place sugar and rum. Fill with very hot tea and one cinnamon stick. Stir well. Top with a slice of lemon.

BACARDI® FIZZ

1¼ oz. BACARDI®
LIGHT-DRY RUM

¼ oz. Lemon Juice

¼ oz. Major Peters'
Grenadine

Soda

Pour rum and lemon juice in a highball glass filled with ice. Add the grenadine and fill with soda.

BACARDI® GINGER-N-SPICE

1½ oz. BACARDI® SPICE
RUM

Ginger Ale

In a tall glass with ice, add rum and fill with ginger ale.

BACARDI® GIMLET

1¼ oz. BACARDI® LIGHT-
DRY RUM

½ oz. Major Peters'
Lime Juice

Stir in a mixing glass with ice and strain into a chilled cock-tail glass or serve on the rocks.

BACARDI® GRASSHOPPER

1 oz. BACARDI® LIGHT-
DRY RUM

¼ oz. Hiram Walker Green
Creme de Menthe

½ oz. Cream

Mix in shaker or blender with ice and strain into a cocktail glass.

BACARDI® MOJITO

1½ oz. BACARDI® LIGHT-
DRY RUM

12 Mint Leaves

½ Lime

2 dashes Angostura Bitters

4 tsp. Sugar

Club Soda

In a collins glass, place mint leaves and lime. Crush well with the back of a spoon. Add bitters and sugar. Fill glass with ice. Add rum and top with club soda. Stir well and garnish with sprig of mint or lime wheel.

BACARDI®
OLD-FASHIONED

1¼ oz. BACARDI® GOLD
RUM

2 dashes Bitters

splash Club Soda

1 tsp. Sugar

In old-fashioned glass dissolve sugar in bitters and club soda. Add 2 ice cubes and fill with rum. Garnish with fruit.

BACARDI®
PIÑA COLADA

1¼ oz. BACARDI® LIGHT-
DRY or GOLD RUM

2 oz. Unsweetened
Pineapple Juice

1 oz. Coco Lopez Cream
of Coconut

Mix in a shaker or blender with crushed ice, or stir and serve on the rocks. Garnish with a pineapple spear, if desired. For best results, blend.

BACARDI® RICKEY

1¼ oz. BACARDI®
LIGHT-DRY RUM

½ oz. Lemon or Lime
Club Soda

Squeeze lemon or lime into a tall glass filled with ice. Add rum and fill with club soda.

BACARDI® RUM PUNCH

1 oz. BACARDI® LIGHT-
DRY RUM

¼ oz. Hiram Walker White
Creme de Menthe

Milk or Cream

Pour rum and white Creme de Menthe into a tall glass half filled with ice. Fill with milk or cream.

BACARDI® SELECT
CALYPSO COFFEE

1½ oz. BACARDI®
SELECT RUM

¾ oz. Hiram Walker Dark
Creme de Cacao

In a coffee cup, mix ingredients and fill with hot black coffee. Top with whipped cream and cinnamon.

BACARDI® SELECT
DIRTY COLADA

1½ oz. BACARDI®
SELECT RUM

2 oz. Pineapple Juice

1 oz. Coco Lopez Cream
of Coconut

In a blender with ice, combine only 1 oz. rum, pineapple juice and cream of coconut. Blend until frothy and serve in a tall stemmed glass. Top with ½ oz. rum. Garnish with a pineapple wedge.

BACARDI® SELECT EGGNOG

1¼ oz. BACARDI® SELECT RUM

1 Egg

1 tsp. Sugar

Milk

Mix in a shaker and strain into a tall glass. Sprinkle with nutmeg.

BACARDI® SELECT HOT-BUTTERED RUM

1¼ oz. BACARDI® SELECT RUM

1 tsp. Sugar

½ tsp. Butter

4 Whole Cloves

In a mug, mix sugar, butter, rum and cloves. Fill with boiling water and stir.

BACARDI® SELECT HOT CHOCOLATE

1½ oz. BACARDI® SELECT RUM

1 cup Hot Chocolate

Mix ingredients and top with whipped cream.

BACARDI® SELECT IRISH COFFEE

1¼ oz. BACARDI® SELECT RUM

Hot Black Coffee

In a mug, pour rum and hot coffee. Top with whipped cream.

BACARDI® SELECT MANHATTAN

2 oz. BACARDI® SELECT RUM

¾ oz. Martini & Rossi Rosso Vermouth

In a shaker with cracked ice, add ingredients. Shake and strain into a martini glass. Garnish with a Maraschino cherry.

BACARDI® SELECT NIGHTCAP

1¼ oz. BACARDI® SELECT RUM

Pour into glass filled with cracked ice. Garnish with twist of lemon.

BACARDI® SOUR

1¼ oz. BACARDI® GOLD RUM

1 oz. Lemon Juice

½ tsp. Sugar

Mix in a shaker with ice and strain into a sour glass. Garnish with a red cherry and half an orange slice.

BACARDI® SOUTH BEACH ICED-TEA

½ oz.   BACARDI® SPICE RUM

½ oz.   BACARDI® LIMÓN

½ oz.   BACARDI® LIGHT-DRY RUM

3 oz.   Major Peters' Sweet & Sour Mix

In a tall glass, combine ingredients. Add a splash of cola.

BACARDI® SPARKLING COCKTAIL

1 oz.   BACARDI® LIGHT-DRY RUM

Martini & Rossi Asti

1 tsp.   Sugar

dash   Bitters

In tall glass, mix rum, sugar and bitters. Fill with Martini & Rossi Asti.

BACARDI® SPICE CUDA

1½ oz.   BACARDI® SPICE RUM

4 oz.   Pineapple Juice

splash   Major Peters' Grenadine

In a tall glass with ice, combine ingredients. Garnish with a lime wedge.

BACARDI® SPICE ON THE BEACH

1½ oz.   BACARDI® SPICE RUM

1 oz.   Peach Schnapps

half   Cranberry Juice

half   Orange Juice

Pour ingredients into a glass with ice. Garnish with mini umbrella.

BACARDI® SPICE WHACKER

1 oz.   BACARDI® SPICE RUM

2 oz.   Coco Lopez Cream of Coconut

1 oz.   Kahlua

Shake with ice and serve on the rocks.

BACARDI® SPICED COCOA

1¼ oz.   BACARDI® SPICE RUM

Add rum to a large mug. Fill with hot chocolate. Top with whipped cream.

BACARDI® SPICE
MAD COW

1 oz. BACARDI® SPICE
RUM

1 oz. Kahlua

Pour rum and Kahlua into a glass with ice. Fill with cream over ice.

BACARDI® SPI-DER
(Spiced Cider)

1½ oz. BACARDI® SPICE
RUM

Apple Juice

Add rum to glass with ice. Fill with apple juice and garnish with cinnamon stick. For a hot n' spicy drink, heat apple juice, add rum and serve in a coffee mug.

BACARDI® TOM
& JERRY

1 oz. BACARDI® LIGHT-
DRY or GOLD RUM

¼ oz. BACARDI® SELECT
RUM

1 Egg

1 tsp. Sugar

Separate yolk from white of egg and beat each separately. When white is fairly stiff, add sugar and beat to a stiff froth, combine white and yolk. Put rums in mug, add boiling water, 1 Tbsp. of egg mixture and sprinkle with nutmeg.

BACARDI® TOP GUN

1¼ oz. BACARDI® SPICE
RUM

¼ oz. BACARDI® 151° RUM

half Orange Juice

half Pineapple Juice

Pour Bacardi® Spice Rum into a glass filled with ice and add juices. Top with floater of Bacardi® 151° Rum.

BALI HAI

1¼ oz. BACARDI®
LIGHT-DRY RUM

Martini & Rossi Asti

2 oz. Lemon Juice or
Major Peters' Lime
Juice

½ oz. Major Peters'
Grenadine

¼ oz. Orgeat Syrup

Pour rum, lemon or lime juice and grenadine into a tall glass filled with crushed or shaved ice. Add the orgeat syrup and fill with champagne.

BANANA MAN

1 oz. BACARDI® LIGHT-DRY RUM

¼ oz. Hiram Walker Banana Liqueur

½ oz. Lemon or Major Peters' Lime Juice

Mix in a blender with ice and blend until smooth. Pour into a cocktail glass.

BAT BITE

1¼ oz. BACARDI® SELECT RUM

fill Cranberry Juice

In 10 oz. glass filled with ice, squeeze and drop in 1 lime or lemon wedge. Stir and serve.

BEACH PARTY

1¼ oz. BACARDI® LIGHT-DRY or GOLD RUM

1 oz. Pineapple Juice

1 oz. Orange Juice

1 oz. Major Peters' Grenadine

Mix in a shaker or blender with ice and pour into a tall glass.

BEACHCOMBER

1 oz. BACARDI® LIGHT-DRY or GOLD RUM

¼ oz. Hiram Walker Cherry Liqueur

1 oz. Lemon or Major Peters' Lime Juice

Mix in a shaker or blender with ice and strain into a cocktail glass.

BEACHCOMBER'S SPECIAL

1 oz. BACARDI® LIGHT-DRY RUM

¼ oz. Hiram Walker Orange Curacao

¾ oz. Lemon or Major Peters' Lime Juice

¼ tsp. Sugar (optional)

Mix in a shaker or blender with ice and strain into a cocktail glass or serve on the rocks.

BISHOP COCKTAIL

1 oz. BACARDI® LIGHT-DRY or GOLD RUM

¼ oz. Red Wine

¼ oz. Lemon or Major Peters' Lime Juice

¼ tsp. Sugar (optional)

Mix in a shaker or blender with ice and strain into a cocktail glass.

BOLERO COCKTAIL

¾ oz. BACARDI® LIGHT-DRY or GOLD RUM

¼ oz. Hiram Walker Apple-flavored Brandy

¼ oz. Martini & Rossi Rosso Vermouth

Stir in a mixing glass with ice and strain into a chilled cocktail glass. Garnish with a twist of lemon peel.

BONBINI

1 oz. BACARDI® LIGHT-DRY or GOLD RUM

¼ oz. Hiram Walker Orange Curacao

Bitters

Stir in a mixing glass with ice and strain into a chilled cocktail glass.

BONGO DRUM

1 oz. BACARDI® LIGHT-DRY RUM

¼ oz. Hiram Walker Blackberry-flavored Brandy

Pineapple Juice

Pour rum into a tall glass half filled with ice. Fill with pineapple juice and float the black-berry-flavored brandy on top.

BROADWAY COOLER

1 oz. BACARDI® LIGHT-DRY or GOLD RUM

¼ oz. Hiram Walker Green Creme de Menthe

½ oz. Lemon or Major Peters' Lime Juice

Soda

Pour rum, creme de menthe and juice into a tall glass filled with ice. Fill with soda and garnish with a sprig of mint.

BUCK-A-ROO

1¼ oz. BACARDI® LIGHT-DRY or GOLD RUM

Root Beer

Pour rum into a highball glass filled with ice. Fill with root beer and garnish with lemon or lime wedge.

CALIFORNIA COOL-AID

1¼ oz. BACARDI® LIGHT-DRY or GOLD RUM

Orange Juice

Milk

Pour rum into a tall glass half filled with ice. Add half orange juice and half milk. Stir.

CALIFORNIA LEMONADE

1¼ oz. BACARDI®
LIGHT-DRY RUM

3 oz. Lemon Juice

1½ tsp. Sugar

Bitters

Club Soda

Pour rum, lemon juice, sugar and bitters into a tall glass half filled with ice. Fill with club soda and stir.

CALM VOYAGE

1 oz. BACARDI® LIGHT-DRY or GOLD RUM

¼ oz. Hiram Walker Apple-flavored Brandy

1 oz. Orange Juice

dash Orange Bitters

Mix in a shaker or blender with ice and strain into a cocktail glass.

CALYPSO COOL-AID

1¼ oz. BACARDI® LIGHT-DRY RUM

1 oz. Pineapple Juice

½ oz. Lemon or Major Peters' Lime Juice

½ tsp. Sugar

Soda

Mix rum, juices and sugar in a shaker or blender with ice and pour into a tall glass. Fill with soda and garnish with pineapple spear and lime wheel.

CARIBBEAN COCKTAIL

1¼ oz. BACARDI® LIGHT-DRY RUM

1 oz. Orange Juice

1 oz. Lemon or Major Peters' Lime Juice

Soda

Pour rum and juice into a tall glass filled with crushed or shaved ice. Fill with soda and garnish with an orange slice and red cherry.

CARIBBEAN JOY

1¼ oz. BACARDI® LIGHT-DRY RUM

1 oz. Pineapple Juice

¾ oz. Lemon Juice

Mix in shaker or blender with ice and strain into a cocktail glass.

CASA BLANCA

¾ oz. BACARDI® LIGHT-DRY RUM

¼ oz. Hiram Walker Cherry Liqueur

¼ oz. Hiram Walker Orange Curacao

dash Bitters

Stir in a mixing glass with ice and strain into a chilled cocktail glass.

CHICAGO STYLE

¾ oz. BACARDI® LIGHT-DRY RUM

¼ oz. Hiram Walker Triple Sec

¼ oz. Romana Sambuca

½ oz. Lemon or Major Peters' Lime Juice

Mix in a shaker or blender with ice and strain into a cocktail glass.

CHOCOLATE CREAM

¾ oz. BACARDI® GOLD RUM

¼ oz. Hiram Walker Dark Creme de Cacao

¼ oz. Hiram Walker White Creme de Menthe

1 oz. Cream

Mix in a shaker or blender with ice and strain into a cocktail glass.

CLASSIC DAIQUIRI

1½ oz. BACARDI® LIGHT-DRY RUM

½ oz. Major Peters' Lime Juice or Sweet & Sour Mix

½ tsp. Sugar

In a shaker with ice, add rum, lime juice and sugar. Shake well and serve in a rocks glass.

Variations:

BANANA DAIQUIRI - *Add one banana.*

ORANGE DAIQUIRI - *Add 1 oz. orange juice.*

PEACH DAIQUIRI - *Add peeled fresh peach half.*

PINEAPPLE DAIQUIRI - *Add ½ slice canned pineapple.*

STRAWBERRY DAIQUIRI - *Add 1 cup of strawberries. Substitute your favorite fruit or two or more fruits for your own Special Daiquiri.*

COCONUT PUNCH

1¼ oz. BACARDI® LIGHT-DRY or GOLD RUM

2 oz. Coco Lopez Cream of Coconut

½ oz. Lemon Juice

3-4 Tbs. Vanilla Ice Cream

Mix all ingredients in a shaker or blender with crushed ice and pour into a tall glass.

COFFEE CREAM COOLER

1¼ oz. BACARDI® LIGHT-DRY or GOLD RUM

Cold Coffee

Cream

Pour rum into a tall glass half filled with ice. Fill with cold coffee and cream to desired proportions.

CONTINENTAL

1 oz. BACARDI® LIGHT-
DRY RUM

¼ oz. Hiram Walker Green
Creme de Menthe

¾ oz. Major Peters'
Lime Juice

¼ tsp. Sugar (optional)

Mix in a shaker or blender with ice and strain into a cocktail glass.

CORKSCREW

¾ oz. BACARDI® LIGHT-
DRY RUM

¼ oz. Brandy

¼ oz. Port Wine

½ oz. Lemon or Major
Peters' Lime Juice

Stir in a mixing glass with ice and strain into a cocktail glass.

COW PUNCHER

1 oz. BACARDI® LIGHT-
DRY or GOLD RUM

1 oz. Hiram Walker White
Creme de Cacao

Milk

Pour rum and creme de cacao into a tall glass half filled with ice. Fill with milk.

CRICKET

¾ oz. BACARDI® LIGHT-
DRY RUM

¼ oz. Hiram Walker White
Creme de Cacao

¼ oz. Hiram Walker Green
Creme de Menthe

1 oz. Cream

Mix in a shaker or blender with ice and strain into a cocktail glass.

DERBY DAIQUIRI

1¼ oz. BACARDI® LIGHT-
DRY RUM

½ oz. Lemon or Major
Peters' Lime Juice

½ oz. Orange Juice

dash Bitters

¼ tsp. Sugar (optional)

Mix in a shaker or blender with ice and strain into a cocktail glass.

DUNLOP COCKTAIL

1 oz. BACARDI® LIGHT-
DRY or GOLD RUM

1 oz. Sherry

dash Bitters

Stir in a mixing glass with ice and strain into a cocktail glass.

EYE OPENER

½ oz. BACARDI® LIGHT-
       DRY RUM

¼ oz. Romana Sambuca

¼ oz. Hiram Walker
       Orange Curacao

¼ oz. Hiram Walker White
       Creme de Cacao

1 Egg Yolk

Mix in a shaker or blender with ice and strain into a cocktail glass.

FLORIDA SUNRISE

1¼ oz. BACARDI® LIGHT-
        DRY RUM

½ oz. Major Peters'
       Grenadine

Orange Juice

Pour grenadine into the bottom of a tall glass. Fill with crushed ice. Pour in rum and fill with orange juice.

GARTER BELT

1¼ oz. BACARDI® GOLD
        RUM

Serve in a shot glass.

GRAPE PUNCH

1¼ oz. BACARDI® LIGHT-
        DRY RUM

Grape Juice

Lime or Lemon
Wedge

Pour rum into a tall glass filled with ice. Fill with grape juice and garnish with a squeeze of lime or lemon.

HARD HAT

1¼ oz. BACARDI® LIGHT-
        DRY RUM

1¼ oz. Fresh Lime Juice

1 tsp. Sugar

¼ oz. Major Peters'
       Grenadine

Club Soda

In a shaker with ice, all but club soda. Strain into 10 oz. glass. Fill with club soda. Garnish with red cherry.

HAVANA MARTINI

1½ oz. BACARDI® LIGHT-
        DRY RUM

½ oz. Major Peters' Lime
       Juice

½ tsp. Sugar

In a shaker with ice, combine ingredients. Shake and strain into a chilled martini glass. Garnish with a twist of lime.

HAWAIIAN NIGHT

1 oz. BACARDI® LIGHT-DRY RUM

¼ oz. Hiram Walker Cherry-flavored Brandy

Pineapple Juice

Pour rum into a tall glass half filled with ice. Fill with pineapple juice and float cherry-flavored brandy on top.

HEAT WAVE

1¼ oz. BACARDI® LIGHT-DRY or GOLD RUM

4 oz. Orange Juice

In a blender with ½ cup ice, blend until smooth. Pour into a 10 oz. glass. Serve immediately.

JACK-O-LANTERN JUICE

1 oz. BACARDI® 151° RUM

1½ oz. Orange Juice

1½ oz. Cranberry Juice

1½ oz. Pineapple Juice

½ oz. Hiram Walker Banana Liqueur

In a hurricane glass with ice, combine ingredients. Fill with Sprite®.

JAMAICAN-ME-SPICY

1½ oz. BACARDI® SPICE RUM

½ oz. Hiram Walker Blue Curacao

2 oz. Pineapple Juice

2 oz. Orange Juice

1 oz. Major Peters' Sweet & Sour Mix

In a tall glass with ice, combine rum, curacao and juices. Add sour mix to taste.

LIMÓN BLOODY MARY

1¼ oz. BACARDI® LIMÓN

4 oz. Tomato Juice

dash Worcestershire Sauce

Salt

Pepper

Pour Limón and tomato juice into a tall glass filled with ice. Add Worcestershire sauce, salt and pepper to taste. Garnish with squeeze of lemon or lime.

LIMÓN COSMOPOLITAN

2 oz. BACARDI® LIMÓN

1 oz. Hiram Walker Triple Sec

½ oz. Major Peters' Lime Juice

splash Cranberry Juice

In shaker with ice, add all ingredients. Shake and strain into a chilled martini glass. Garnish with lemon or orange twist.

LIMÓN DROP

1½ oz. BACARDI® LIMÓN chilled

Lemon Wedge

Sugar

Bite into a sugar-coated lemon wedge, but do not swallow. With the pulp still in your mouth, drink down the chilled Limón.

LIMÓN IN BEER

1½ oz. BACARDI® LIMÓN

Add to your favorite beer.

LIMÓN MARGARITA

½ oz. BACARDI® LIMÓN

½ oz. Hiram Walker Triple Sec

2 oz. Major Peters' Lime Juice

In a shaker with ice, add ingredients. Shake vigorously and pour into a margarita glass.

LIMÓN ON-THE-ROCKS

1¼ oz. BACARDI® LIMÓN

Pour Limón over ice or crushed ice and garnish with a twist of lemon peel.

LIMÓN & CRANBERRY

1½ oz. BACARDI® LIMÓN

Pour into a glass with ice and fill with cranberry juice. Add a squeeze of lime.

LIMÓN & TONIC

1¼ oz. BACARDI® LIMÓN

Tonic

Pour Limón into a tall glass filled with ice. Fill with tonic and garnish with a slice of lime or lemon.

LUCKY LADY

¾ oz. BACARDI® LIGHT-DRY RUM

¼ oz. Romana Sambuca

¼ oz. Hiram Walker White Creme de Cacao

¾ oz. Cream

Mix in a shaker or blender with ice and strain into a cocktail glass.

MAI-TAI

¾ oz. BACARDI® LIGHT-
       DRY RUM

¼ oz. BACARDI 151° RUM

½ oz. Hiram Walker
       Orange Curacao

½ oz. Major Peters'
       Lime Juice

½ oz. Orgeat Syrup

½ oz. Simple Syrup

*In an old-fashioned or stem
glass half filled with cracked
ice, put juice, syrups and
orange curacao (or use Mai-Tai
mix). Add rums and stir gently.
Garnish with mint sprigs,
pineapple spear and red cherry.*

MIAMI
SPECIAL

1 oz. BACARDI® LIGHT-
       DRY RUM

¼ oz. Hiram Walker White
       Creme de Menthe

¾ oz. Lemon or Major
       Peters' Lime Juice

*Mix in a shaker or blender with
ice and strain into a cocktail
glass.*

OLD SAN JUAN
COCKTAIL

1¼ oz. BACARDI® GOLD
        RUM

¼ oz.   Pineapple Juice

¼ oz.   Major Peters'
        Grenadine

½ oz.   Lemon Juice or
        Major Peters' Lime
        Juice

*Stir in a mixing glass with ice
and strain into a cocktail glass.*

OLD SAN JUAN
SIPPER

1 oz.   BACARDI® GOLD
        RUM

¼ oz.   *Hiram Walker White
        Creme de Menthe*

1 oz.   Lemon Juice or
        Major Peters' Lime
        Juice

¼ oz.   Major Peters'
        Grenadine

*Mix in a shaker or blender with
ice and strain into a cocktail
glass.*

PIÑA VERDE

1 oz. BACARDI® LIGHT-DRY RUM

¼ oz. Hiram Walker Green Creme de Menthe

Pineapple Juice

Pour rum into a tall glass half filled with ice. Fill with pineapple juice and float the green creme de menthe on top.

PINK PANTHER

1¼ oz. BACARDI® LIGHT-DRY RUM

¾ oz. Lemon Juice

¾ oz. Cream

½ oz. Major Peters' Grenadine

Mix in a shaker or blender with ice and strain into a cocktail glass.

PLANTER'S PUNCH

1¼ oz. BACARDI® LIGHT-DRY RUM

splash BACARDI® GOLD RUM

2 tsp. Sugar

2 oz. Orange Juice

dash Major Peters' Grenadine

Place sugar in shaker or blender and dissolve with fruit juice. Add rum, cracked ice and mix well or blend until frothy. Strain into an 8-ounce glass with cracked ice. Float dark rum on top. Garnish with orange and cherry.

RACER'S EDGE

1 oz. BACARDI® LIGHT-DRY RUM

¼ oz. Hiram Walker Green Creme de Menthe

Grapefruit Juice

Pour rum into a tall glass half filled with ice. Fill with grapefruit juice and float the green creme de menthe on top.

RED HOT MAMA

1¼ oz. BACARDI® LIGHT-DRY RUM

4 oz. Cranberry Juice

2 oz. Chilled Club Soda

In a 10 oz. glass. Garnish with lime wedge.

RUDOLPH'S NOSE

1¼ oz. BACARDI® LIGHT-DRY or GOLD RUM

Cranberry Juice

1½ oz. Lemon Juice

½ oz. Major Peters' Grenadine

Mix in a tall glass. Add ice and garnish with lemon wedge.

RUM RUNNER

1 oz. BACARDI® SELECT RUM

½ oz. BACARDI® 151° Rum

1 oz. Hiram Walker Blackberry-flavored Brandy

1 oz. Hiram Walker Banana Liqueur

½ oz. Major Peters' Grenadine

½ oz. Major Peters' Lime Juice

In a blender with ice, combine ingredients and blend until frothy. Serve in a tall stemmed glass.

RUM-TA-TUM

1½ oz. BACARDI® LIGHT-DRY RUM

2 cups Pineapple Juice

½ cup Fresh Lemon Juice

½ oz. Major Peters' Grenadine

1 liter Chilled Club Soda

In 2½ quart pitcher, add ice cubes. Pour into 8 oz. glasses with ice. Garnish with half orange slices. Serves 8.

SAN JUAN COCKTAIL

1 oz. BACARDI® LIGHT-DRY RUM

¼ oz. BACARDI® 151° RUM

1 oz. Grapefruit Juice

½ oz. Lemon or Major Peters' Lime Juice

¼ oz. Coco Lopez Cream of Coconut

Mix light rum, juices and cream of coconut in a shaker or blender with ice. Strain into a cocktail glass and float the Bacardi® 151° Rum on top.

SAN JUAN COLLINS

1 oz. BACARDI® LIGHT-DRY RUM

¼ oz. Hiram Walker White Creme de Menthe

Lemon Juice

Sugar

Pour rum into a tall glass half filled with ice. Fill with lemon juice and sugar to taste. Float White Creme de Menthe on top and garnish with lemon slice and a red cherry.

SAN JUAN SUNSET

1 oz. BACARDI® LIGHT-DRY RUM

¼ oz. Hiram Walker Cherry-flavored Brandy

Orange Juice

Pour rum into a tall glass half filled with ice. Fill with orange juice and float the cherry-flavored brandy on top. Serve with straws.

TAILGATE

1¼ oz. BACARDI® LIGHT-DRY RUM

1 tsp. Sugar

3 oz. Hot Water

In 8 oz. mug or tankard. Fill with hot water and stir well. Add 1 twist lemon or orange peel.

TAZMANIAN DEVIL SHOT

1½ oz. BACARDI® SPICE RUM

small dash Tabasco Sauce

few drops Major Peters' Lime Juice

Chill a shot glass. Add rum, tabasco sauce and a few drops of lime.

TEXAS SUNDOWNER

1 oz. BACARDI® LIGHT-DRY RUM

½ oz. Romana Sambuca

½ oz. Major Peters' Grenadine

Pour into an old-fashioned glass with ice.

THE LIMÓN CRANTINI

1½ oz. BACARDI® LIMÓN

¼ oz. Martini & Rossi Extra Dry Vermouth

splash Cranberry Juice

In a shaker with cracked ice, add Limón and vermouth. Add a splash of cranberry juice. Shake and strain into a martini glass. Garnish with a twist of lemon.

TROPICAL STORM

1 oz. BACARDI® LIGHT-DRY RUM

¼ oz. Hiram Walker Blackberry-flavored Brandy

Grapefruit Juice

Pour rum into a tall glass half filled with ice. Fill with grapefruit juice and float the blackberry-flavored brandy on top.

YELLOW BIRD

¾ oz. BACARDI® GOLD RUM

¼ oz. Liquore Galliano

¼ oz. Hiram Walker Creme de Banana

2 oz. Pineapple Juice

2 oz. Orange Juice

Shake well. Pour into a tall glass with ice cubes and decorate with a pineapple ring, cherry and orange slice.

ZOMBIE

¾ oz. BACARDI® LIGHT-DRY RUM

¼ oz. BACARDI® GOLD RUM

¼ oz. BACARDI® 151° RUM

1 oz. Pineapple Juice

1 oz. Orange Juice

1 oz. Lemon or Major Peters' Lime Juice

1 tsp. Powdered Sugar (optional)

Mix rums and juices with ice in a shaker or blender and pour into a tall glass. Garnish with a pineapple spear and red cherry. If desired, float ¼ tsp. Bacardi® 151° Rum on top with 1 tsp. powdered sugar.

Add your favorite Bacardi® recipes here.

For additional recipes, visit our website at
http://www.bacardi.com

© Foley Publishing Corp

BEEFEATER DRY GIN

PRODUCT KNOWLEDGE
History

Beefeater gin, the gin that defines gin, was established by James Burrough, a pharmacist, of London, England. Burrough experimented with an exotic array of recipes for all manner of spirit and cordials, but had a particular fascination for gin, believing that he could make a better product than anyone else. When he came to chose a name for his creation, he looked no further than a few miles along the River Thames to the Tower of London.

This Royal Palace, built by William the Conqueror in the 11th century, was guarded by Yeoman Warders, whose fearsome strength was attributed, by the Grand Duke of Tuscany in 1669, to the fact that "a very large ration of beef is given to them daily at court, and that they might be called *Beef-eaters.*"

Beefeater, today, continues to be closely linked to the city of London as the only gin distilled in the city of London using the same secret recipe for almost 170 years. Beefeater is the world's #1 premium gin, sold in over 140 countries.

Quality

The Beefeater difference is defined by the complex recipe using high quality, exotic botanicals from throughout the world, the skillful distilling process and the quality and con-sistency of production that determines Beefeater's unique, exceptional taste.

The quality begins with the production of the highest quality alcohol made from only the choicest maize and care-fully blended with selected strains of barley to produce a pure grain spirit.

Beefeater uses only the finest botanicals, gathered from around the world, to produce a distinctively dry and aromatic gin. Juniper berries, angelica root, corriander, lemon and orange peels are just a few of the ingredients used in the making of this most perfect gin.

The method of distillation, *steeping*, creates a far more complex and interesting gin, full of subtlety and nuance. It possesses a particularly fresh, clean and crisp gin with subtle citrus and fruit edge, making it the perfect base for mixed drinks and classic cocktails like the martini.

Terms

Gin comes from the Dutch word for Juniper: Genever. Gin was created in Holland in the late 16th century by Dr. Franciscus Sylvius.

Botanicals are ingredients that come from plants; botanicals are the flavoring agents for distilled gin.

Juniper is the primary botanical used in the making of all distilled gin.

London Dry Gin is a style of gin that differentiates London Dry gin from sweet gin and from Dutch gin.

London Distilled Dry Gin differentiates Beefeater as the only gin distilled in the city of London.

Steeping process is a very subtle and slow approach to making gin. The botanicals are allowed to infuse with the neutral grain spirit for 24 hours before the distillation process begins. This delivers a more complex and consistent flavor than other methods.

For additional recipes, visit our website at http://www.beefeaterginvodka.co.uk

THE BEEFEATER MARTINI

2 oz.   BEEFEATER DRY GIN

Dash   Martini & Rossi Extra Dry Vermouth

Stir in cocktail glass with ice. Strain and serve straight up or on the rocks with some ice in cocktail glass. Add lemon twist or olive. OR: Shake and strain and serve up or on the rocks with some ice.

Many customers and Bartenders agree that shaking will ruin a Martini because of the slight taste of the metal from the shaker. Use your own judgment!

Below are a few variations:

ALIZÉ:	Replace Martini & Rossi Vermouth with Alizé
ALIZÉ PASSIONATE:	Replace Martini & Rossi Vermouth with Alizé and dash of cranberry juice
CORNET:	Replace Martini & Rossi Vermouth with Port Wine
DEWEY:	Add dash orange bitters
DILLATINI:	Dilly Bean (try and find one)
ELEGANT:	Add dash Grand Marnier
FASCINATOR:	Add dash Pernod and sprig mint
GIBSON:	Add onion
GIMLET:	Replace Martini & Rossi Vermouth with Major Peters' Lime Juice. Garnish with lime.
GYPSY:	Add cherry
HOMESTEAD:	Add orange slice muddled
ITALIAN:	Replace Martini & Rossi Vermouth with Hiram Walker Amaretto
JACKSON:	Replace Martini & Rossi Vermouth with Dubonnet and dash of bitters
LADIES' CHOICE:	Add ¼ oz. Hiram Walker Kummel
LONE TREE:	Add dash lemon juice

MICKEY FINN:	Add splash of Hiram Walker White Creme de Menthe, garnish with mint
NAKED MARTINI:	Just Beefeater Dry Gin
NAVAL COCKTAIL:	Replace Martini & Rossi Extra Dry with Martini & Rossi Rosso Vermouth, add onion and twist
ORANGETINI:	Add splash of Hiram Walker Triple Sec and orange peel
PERFECTION:	Replace Martini & Rossi Extra Dry Vermouth with Martini & Rossi Rosso Vermouth
QUEEN ELIZABETH:	Add splash Benedictine
RED PASSION:	Replace Martini & Rossi Vermouth with Alizé Red Passion
RICHMOND:	Replace Martini & Rossi Vermouth with Lillet, add twist of lemon
ROSA:	Add Hiram Walker Cherry Flavored Brandy
ROSALIN RUSSELL:	Replace Martini & Rossi Vermouth with Aquavit
ROSELYN:	Add Major Peters' Lime Juice, Grenadine and lemon twist
ROUGE:	Add a dash of Chambord
SAKITINI:	Replace Martini & Rossi Vermouth with Sake
SILVER BULLET:	Float Cutty Sark on top
SOUR KISSES:	Add egg white, SHAKE
TRINITY aka TRIO PLAZA:	Replace Martini & Rossi Extra Dry Vermouth with half Martini & Rossi Rosso and half Extra Dry. Equal parts of Vermouth and Beefeater Dry Gin
VELOCITY:	Add orange slice and SHAKE
WALLICK:	Add dash of Hiram Walker Orange Curacao
WARDEN:	Add dash of Pernod

ABBEY
COCKTAIL

1½ oz. BEEFEATER
DRY GIN

1 oz. Orange Juice

dash Orange Bitters

Maraschino Cherry

Shake.

ALASKA
COCKTAIL

1¼ oz. BEEFEATER
DRY GIN

¼ oz. Yellow Chartreuse

2 dashes Orange Bitters

Stir.

ALEXANDER
COCKTAIL

1 oz. BEEFEATER
DRY GIN

1 oz. Hiram Walker White
Creme de Cacao

1 oz. Cream

Nutmeg

Shake.

ALFONSO
SPECIAL

½ oz. BEEFEATER
DRY GIN

1 oz. Hiram Walker
Triple Sec

½ oz. Martini & Rossi Dry
Vermouth

4 dashes Martini & Rossi
Sweet Vermouth

dash Angostura Bitters

Stir or shake.

ALLIES
COCKTAIL

1 oz. BEEFEATER
DRY GIN

1 oz. Martini & Rossi Dry
Vermouth

2 dashes Kummel

Stir.

ANGEL FACE

½ oz. BEEFEATER
DRY GIN

½ oz. Hiram Walker
Apricot Brandy

½ oz. Hiram Walker
Apple Brandy

Shake.

ARTILLERY

1½ oz. BEEFEATER DRY GIN

1½ tsp. Martini & Rossi Sweet Vermouth

2 dashes Bitters

Stir with ice and strain into cocktail glass.

BARBARY COAST COCKTAIL

½ oz. BEEFEATER DRY GIN

½ oz. Cutty Sark

½ oz. Hiram Walker Creme de Cacao

½ oz. Cream

Shake.

BEAUTY SPOT

1½ oz. BEEFEATER DRY GIN

2 tsp. Hiram Walker White Creme de Cacao

½ tsp. Major Peters' Grenadine

Shake and strain.

BEEFEATER ALOHA

1½ oz. BEEFEATER DRY GIN

¾ oz. Hiram Walker Triple Sec

1 Tbs. Pineapple Juice

Shake with ice and strain. Pour into a cocktail glass.

BEEFEATER BEACHBALL

1¼ oz. BEEFEATER DRY GIN

3 oz. Grapefruit Juice

3 oz. Orange Juice

Mix ingredient in ice-filled highball glass. Serve with a slice of orange.

BEEFEATER BLUE DEVIL

1 oz. BEEFEATER DRY GIN

¼ oz. Lemon Juice

dash Maraschino Liqueur

dash Hiram Walker Blue Curacao

a little Powdered Sugar

Mix well with ice in shaker and strain into tumbler.

BEEFEATER BUCK

2 oz. BEEFEATER DRY GIN

Juice of ½ Lemon

Ginger Ale chilled

Pour over ice.

BEEFEATER CASSIS

3 parts BEEFEATER DRY GIN

1 part Hiram Walker Creme de Cassis

Stir on the rocks.

BEEFEATER DAISY

2 oz. BEEFEATER DRY GIN

1 oz. Lemon Juice

½ tsp. Sugar

1 tsp. Raspberry Syrup (or grenadine)

Fresh Fruit

Shake and strain.

BEEFEATER DRIVER

1¼ oz. BEEFEATER DRY GIN

4 oz. Orange Juice

Tonic Water

In a tall glass filled with ice, add gin and orange juice. Fill with tonic water.

BEEFEATER FIZZ

2 oz. BEEFEATER DRY GIN

1 tsp. Sugar

1 oz. Lemon Juice

Club Soda chilled

Stir and strain.

BEEFEATER GIMLET

1¼ oz. BEEFEATER DRY GIN

¾ oz. Major Peters' Lime Juice

Pour over ice in a cocktail glass. Stir. Garnish with a slice of lime.

BEEFEATER GIN RUMMY

1 oz. BEEFEATER DRY GIN

½ oz. Martini & Rossi Dry Vermouth

dash Bitters

dash Lemon Juice

Shake well with ice. Strain into martini glass.

BEEFEATER HIGHBALL

2 oz. BEEFEATER DRY GIN

Ginger Ale or Club Soda

Pour into highball glass over ice cubes and fill with ginger ale or club soda. Add a twist of lemon peel, if desired, and stir.

BEEFEATER LEMONEATER

2 oz. BEEFEATER DRY GIN

Lemonade

Add gin to a glass filled with ice. Fill with lemonade.

BEEFEATER RED COAT

1½ oz. BEEFEATER DRY GIN

5 oz. Cranberry Juice

Serve in a tall glass over ice.

BEEFEATER RICKEY

2 oz. BEEFEATER DRY GIN

Juice of ½ Lime

Club Soda, chilled

Maraschino Cherry

Stir.

BEEFEATER STINGER

1 oz. BEEFEATER DRY GIN

¼ oz. Hiram Walker White Creme de Menthe

Stir well on the rocks.

BEEKMAN PLACE

½ oz. BEEFEATER DRY GIN

1 oz. Hiram Walker Sloe Gin

1 tsp. Lemon Juice

1 oz. Major Peters' Grenadine

Shake.

BEL AIR COCKTAIL

1 oz. BEEFEATER DRY GIN

½ oz. Hiram Walker Apricot Brandy

1 tsp. Major Peters' Grenadine

Shake.

BELMONT COCKTAIL

2 oz. BEEFEATER DRY GIN

1 tsp. Major Peters' Grenadine

¾ oz. Cream

Shake.

BENNETT COCKTAIL

1½ oz. BEEFEATER DRY GIN

½ oz. Major Peters' Lime Juice

½ tsp. Sugar

2 dashes Angostura Bitters

Shake.

BERMUDA HIGHBALL

½ oz. BEEFEATER DRY GIN

½ oz. Hiram Walker Brandy

½ oz. Martini & Rossi Dry Vermouth

Ginger Ale or Club Soda

Pour into highball glass over ice. Fill with ginger ale or club soda. Add a twist of lemon peel and stir.

BITCH ON WHEELS

1¼ oz. BEEFEATER DRY GIN

¼ oz. Martini & Rossi Extra Dry Vermouth

¼ oz. Pernod

¼ oz. Hiram Walker White Creme de Menthe

Shake ingredients with ice and strain into a chilled martini glass.

BLACK MARTINI

1½ oz. BEEFEATER DRY GIN

splash Chambord

Shake and strain.

BLONDE BOMBSHELL

1½ oz. BEEFEATER DRY GIN

½ oz. Hiram Walker Curacao

1 tsp. Hiram Walker White Creme de Menthe

2 tsp. Heavy Cream

Shake and strain.

BLUE CANARY

¾ oz. BEEFEATER DRY GIN

3 Tbs. Grapefruit Juice

1 Tbs. Hiram Walker Blue Curacao

Combine ingredients with ice in mixing glass and stir gently. Strain into chilled cocktail glass filled with crushed ice. Garnish with a mint sprig.

BLUE DEVIL

1 oz. BEEFEATER DRY GIN

¼ oz. Lemon Juice

dashes Maraschino Liqueur

dashes Hiram Walker Blue Curacao

a little Powdered Sugar

Mix well with ice in shaker and strain into tumbler.

BOOTLEGGER MARTINI

1½ oz. BEEFEATER DRY GIN

¼ oz. Southern Comfort

Lemon Twist

Shake and strain.

BRONX SILVER COCKTAIL

¾ oz. BEEFEATER DRY GIN

¼ oz. Martini & Rossi Dry Vermouth

¼ oz. Martini & Rossi Sweet Vermouth

Juice of ¼ Orange

Slice of Orange

Shake and strain.

BULLDOG

1½ oz. BEEFEATER DRY GIN

1½ oz. Orange Juice

Ginger Ale

Stemmed Cherry

Orange Slice

Stir juice and gin over ice in a collins glass, fill with ginger ale. Garnish with cherry or orange.

BUMPY SUNSET

Start with BEEFEATER DRY GIN over ice. Add orange juice to taste and a dash of Major Peters' Grenadine. Garnish with lime.

CLOVER CLUB COCKTAIL

1½ oz. BEEFEATER DRY GIN

Juice of ½ Lime or Lemon

2 tsp. Major Peters' Grenadine

Sprig of Fresh Mint

Shake and strain.

COPENHAGEN

¾ oz. BEEFEATER
DRY GIN

¾ oz. Absolut Vodka

¼ oz. Martini & Rossi Dry
Vermouth

Green Olive

Shake and strain.

COPPER ILLUSION
MARTINI

1 oz. BEEFEATER
DRY GIN

½ oz. Hiram Walker
Triple Sec

½ oz. Campari

Served with an orange slice.

COSMOPOLITAN

1½ oz. BEEFEATER
DRY GIN

¼ oz. Hiram Walker
Triple Sec

dashes Cranberry Juice

dashes Major Peters'
Lime Juice

Lemon Peel

*Shake vigorously over ice and
strain into a chilled martini
glass. Twist lemon peel over
drink and drop into glass.*

DEMPSEY COCKTAIL

1 oz. BEEFEATER
DRY GIN

1 oz. Hiram Walker
Apple Brandy

½ tsp. Pernod

2 dashes Major Peters'
Grenadine

Stir and strain.

DEPTH CHARGE

¾ oz. BEEFEATER
DRY GIN

¾ oz. Lillet

¼ oz. Pernod

Orange Peel

Shake and strain.

DUBONNET COCKTAIL

¾ oz. BEEFEATER
DRY GIN

¾ oz. Dubonnet

1 tsp. Lemon Juice

Shake and strain.

EARTHQUAKE

½ oz. BEEFEATER
DRY GIN

½ oz. Makers Mark

½ oz. Pernod

Shake and strain.

EMERALD ISLE COCKTAIL

2 oz. BEEFEATER DRY GIN

dash Hiram Walker Green Creme de Menthe

2 dashes Bitters

Stir with ice and strain into cocktail glass.

FALLEN ANGEL

¾ oz. BEEFEATER DRY GIN

¼ oz. Hiram Walker Apricot Brandy

¼ oz. Hiram Walker Brandy

Shake. Serve up.

FLAMINGO

1 oz. BEEFEATER DRY GIN

2 oz. Pineapple Juice

1 oz. Cream of Coconut

1 oz. Major Peters' Sweet & Sour Mix

Blend together with cracked ice until smooth. Strain and serve in chilled glass.

FLORIDA

½ oz. BEEFEATER DRY GIN

1½ tsp. Hiram Walker Kirschwasser

1½ tsp. Hiram Walker Triple Sec

1 oz. Orange Juice

1 tsp. Lemon Juice

Shake with ice and strain into cocktail glass.

FRENCH "75"

1½ oz. BEEFEATER DRY GIN

Juice of 1 Lemon

2 tsp. Sugar

Champagne chilled

Stir in collins glass. Then, add ice cubes, fill with Champagne. Decorate with lemon or orange and a cherry.

GIBSON

2 oz. BEEFEATER DRY GIN

Martini & Rossi Dry Vermouth, as desired

Two Pearl Onions

Mix with a generous amount of ice and strain into a chilled martini glass. Garnish with onions.

GIN & SIN

1½ oz. BEEFEATER
DRY GIN

¾ oz. Orange Juice

¾ oz. Lemon Juice

dashes Major Peters'
Grenadine

Stemmed Cherry

Shake vigorously over ice and strain into a chilled cocktail glass, or serve over ice in a highball glass.

GIN TART

1 oz. BEEFEATER
DRY GIN

½ oz. Major Peters' Lime
Juice

½ oz. Lemon Juice

Fill mixing glass with ice, add gin, lime and lemon juice, strain into cocktail glass, garnish with lime.

GIN & TONIC

2 oz. BEEFEATER
DRY GIN

Tonic Water

Lime Wedge

Pour gin over ice in a collins glass, add lime wedge.

GOLDEN DAWN

1 oz. BEEFEATER
DRY GIN

¼ oz. Hiram Walker
Apricot Brandy

1 oz. Orange Juice

Shake and strain.

GOLF COCKTAIL

1 oz. BEEFEATER
DRY GIN

½ oz. Martini & Rossi Dry
Vermouth

2 dashes Angostura Bitters

Stir and strain.

GOLLY DOLLY

¾ oz. BEEFEATER
DRY GIN

½ oz. Hiram Walker
Peach Brandy

1 tsp. Major Peters'
Grenadine

½ oz. Heavy Cream

Shake.

GREEN DEVIL

1½ oz. BEEFEATER
DRY GIN

2 tsp. Hiram Walker Green
Creme de Menthe

½ oz. Major Peters'
Lime Juice

Fresh Mint Leaves

Shake and strain.

GREYHOUND

1½ oz. BEEFEATER
DRY GIN

¾ oz. Grapefruit Juice

Shake and strain.

GYPSY LIFE

1 oz. BEEFEATER
DRY GIN

½ oz. Benedictine

1-2 dashes Angostura Bitters

Shake and strain.

HAWAIIAN COCKTAIL

1 oz. BEEFEATER
DRY GIN

¼ oz. Hiram Walker
Triple Sec

½ oz. Pineapple Juice

Shake and strain.

HULA HULA

½ oz. BEEFEATER
DRY GIN

¾ oz. Orange Juice

¼ tsp. Powdered Sugar

*Shake with ice. Strain into
cocktail glass. Decorate with
pineapple.*

LAST TANGO

¾ oz. BEEFEATER
DRY GIN

1 oz. Orange Juice

¼ oz. Hiram Walker
Triple Sec

Shake and strain.

LEAVE-IT-TO-ME
COCKTAIL

¾ oz. BEEFEATER
DRY GIN

¼ oz. Hiram Walker
Apricot Brandy

¼ oz. Martini & Rossi Dry
Vermouth

2 dashes Lemon Juice

1 dash Major Peters'
Grenadine

Shake and strain.

LITTLE DEVIL COCKTAIL

½ oz. BEEFEATER DRY GIN

½ oz. BACARDI® Light-Dry Rum

¼ oz. Hiram Walker Triple Sec

Juice of ¼ Lemon

Shake and strain.

LONDON CAPE

1¼ oz. BEEFEATER DRY GIN

2½ oz. Cranberry Juice

Stir and serve over ice.

LONDON JEWEL

1 part BEEFEATER DRY GIN

1 part Hiram Walker Peach Schnapps

Stir on the rocks.

LONDON SPIDER

1¼ oz. BEEFEATER DRY GIN

dash Bitters

Ginger Ale

In a tall glass filled with ice, add gin and bitters and fill with ginger ale.

LONDON TRIO

1 oz. BEEFEATER DRY GIN

½ oz. Hiram Walker Triple Sec

1 oz. Pineapple Juice

Fill shaker half way with ice, add gin, pineapple juice and lemon juice, shake well, pour into old-fashioned glass.

MAIDEN'S BLUSH COCKTAIL

1½ oz. BEEFEATER DRY GIN

1 tsp. Hiram Walker Triple Sec

1 tsp. Major Peters' Grenadine

2 dashes Lemon Juice

Shake and strain.

MAIDEN'S PRAYER

¾ oz. BEEFEATER DRY GIN

¾ oz. Hiram Walker Triple Sec

½ oz. Lemon Juice

Shake and strain.

MANHASSET MAULER

1 oz. BEEFEATER DRY GIN

½ oz. Hiram Walker Sloe Gin

Lemon Zest

Shake and strain.

MARTINI

2 oz. BEEFEATER DRY GIN

Martini & Rossi Vermouth, as desired

Olives

Lemon Peel

Mix with generous amount of ice and strain into a chilled martini glass. Garnish with olives or lemon twist.

MIDNIGHT MARTINI

Stir BEEFEATER DRY GIN and Martini & Rossi Dry Vermouth over ice and strain into chilled glass. Garnish with black olive.

MOONSHOT

1¼ oz. BEEFEATER DRY GIN

3 oz. Clam Juice

dash Red Pepper Sauce

Stir over ice cubes.

NAPOLEON

¾ oz. BEEFEATER DRY GIN

¼ oz. Dubonnet Rouge

¼ oz. Hiram Walker Triple Sec

In a mixing glass, combine all of the ingredients. Stir well. Strain into a cocktail glass.

NEGRONI

½ oz. BEEFEATER DRY GIN

½ oz. Martini & Rossi Rosso Vermouth

½ oz. Campari

Lemon Peel

Stir with ice in an aperitif glass, twist lemon peel over drink and drop into glass.

NINETEEN-TWENTY

½ oz. BEEFEATER DRY GIN

½ oz. Martini & Rossi Dry Vermouth

½ oz. Hiram Walker Kirschwasser

dash Pernod

Shake and strain.

NINETEENTH HOLE

¾ oz. BEEFEATER DRY GIN

¼ oz. Martini & Rossi Dry Vermouth

1 tsp. Martini & Rossi Sweet Vermouth

dash Angostura Bitters

Stir and strain. Serve with impaled green olive.

ORIENT EXPRESS

½ oz. BEEFEATER DRY GIN

½ oz. Makers Mark

½ oz. Hiram Walker Brandy

Stir and strain.

PARISIAN

½ oz. BEEFEATER DRY GIN

½ oz. Martini & Rossi Dry Vermouth

½ oz. Hiram Walker Creme de Cassis

Shake and strain.

PARK AVENUE

1 oz. BEEFEATER DRY GIN

½ oz. Martini & Rossi Sweet Vermouth

1 oz. Pineapple Juice

1-2 dashes Hiram Walker Curacao (optional)

Shake and strain.

PARK WEST

1½ oz. BEEFEATER DRY GIN

2 oz. Pineapple Juice

2 oz. Grapefruit Juice

Shake.

PICCADILLY COCKTAIL

¾ oz. BEEFEATER DRY GIN

¼ oz. Martini & Rossi Dry Vermouth

dash Pernod

dash Major Peters' Grenadine

Stir and strain.

PINK LADY

1¼ oz. BEEFEATER DRY GIN

2 tsp. Major Peters' Grenadine

3 oz. Half & Half

Shake with ice and strain into cocktail glass or serve on the rocks.

PINK PUSSYCAT

1½ oz. BEEFEATER DRY GIN

2 oz. Pineapple Juice

2 oz. Grapefruit Juice

dash Major Peters' Grenadine

Pour over rocks in tall glass and stir.

POLO

1¼ oz. BEEFEATER DRY GIN

Grapefruit Juice

Orange Juice

In a tall glass with ice, fill with half grapefruit juice and half orange juice.

PURPLE PASSION

1½ oz. BEEFEATER DRY GIN

3 oz. Grapefruit Juice

3 oz. Grape Juice

Pour over rocks in tall glass.

RED RUBY

1 oz. BEEFEATER DRY GIN

½ oz. Major Peters' Grenadine

½ oz. Martini & Rossi Dry Vermouth

In a mixing glass half filled with ice cubes, combine all ingredients. Stir well. Strain into cocktail glass.

SIDECAR IN LONDON

1 oz. BEEFEATER DRY GIN

¼ oz. Hiram Walker Triple Sec

¼ oz. Lemon Juice

Shake with ice and serve on the rocks or up in a sugar-rimmed glass.

SINGAPORE SLING

1 oz. BEEFEATER DRY GIN

½ oz. Lemon Juice

1 tsp. Major Peters' Grenadine

½ oz. Hiram Walker Cherry Brandy

Club Soda, chilled

Slice of Lemon or Lime

Maraschino Cherry

Mix all but club soda. Top with club soda.

SLIM GIN

¼ oz. BEEFEATER DRY GIN

In a tall glass filled with ice and your favorite diet soda.

SMOOTH MELODY

1 oz. BEEFEATER DRY GIN

1 oz. Orange Juice

Ginger Ale

Fill glass with ice, add juice and gin, fill rest with ginger ale stir, garnish with maraschino cherry.

TOM COLLINS

1 ½ oz. BEEFEATER DRY GIN

¾ oz. Lemon Juice

½ oz. Sugar Syrup

Soda

Stemmed Cherry

Lemon Slice

Stir the first three ingredients well with ice in a collins glass, fill with soda, garnish with cherry and lemon.

YELLOW FELLOW

1 oz. BEEFEATER DRY GIN

¼ oz. Yellow Chartreuse

Shake, strain into cocktail glass.

XANTHIA

1 oz. BEEFEATER DRY GIN

½ oz. Martini & Rossi Dry Vermouth

½ oz. Hiram Walker Triple Sec

Mix and serve on the rocks.

Add your favorite Beefeater recipes here.

© Foley Publishing Corp

CANADIAN CLUB

Looking back on Canadian Club's nearly 140 years of tradition, it becomes apparent that the seeds of its success were sown long, long ago.

In 1858, Hiram Walker (yes, there was a real Hiram Walker) created a company founded on a simple basic, solid premise: If you put uncompromising quality into everything you make and relentlessly search for innovation in everything you do, from distribution to packaging to advertising and beyond, then you can't help but have a successful product.

By any measure, Canadian Club truly is one of the most successful brands in the history of the spirits industry. In the United States, Canadian Club is a clear-cut leader among Canadian whiskies where it is the No. 1 on-premise call brand, has the largest consumer base and also has the largest on- and off-premise distribution base in its category. Worldwide, well over a billion bottles of Canadian Club have been sold. And Canadian Club is the No. 1 selling whisky in Canada, home of Canadian whiskies, as well as the top-selling Canadian whisky internationally.

The reasons for its success are many. By law, Canadian whisky has to be aged three years. By comparison, Canadian Club is aged a full six years to ensure its smooth, light flavor. Additionally, C.C. is barrel blended using a proprietary process. The C.C. family of whiskies are the only whiskies in the world blended in the barrel at the start of the maturation period, allowing the best possible "marriage" in white oak casks and resulting in exceptional richness and smoothness.

Discriminating consumers who appreciate its long, smooth, delicate and always consistent taste enjoy Canadian Club at home as well as in restaurants and taverns. In fact, "C.C." undoubtedly will go down in history as the most famous bar call ever.

Playing a major role in the success and popularity of Canadian Club are advertising and promotion. Previous campaigns, from the Adventure Series to the classic Hide-A-Case, sought to involve consumers, capture their imagination and create the right image for the brand. C.C.'s latest campaign, "Club Rules..." follows in that tradition of advertising excellence.

Additionally, Canadian Club's packaging has been given a distinctive, new look that is contemporary, but also captures the tradition and heritage of the brand. The new packaging features a "double label" that successfully communicates the premium whisky values of the brand, while retaining long-standing brand trademarks such as a script logo, amber bottle, black, white and gold color palette and the whisky's heritage dating back to 1858.

"C.C." appears on the neck to reinforce bar-call recognition, while the year the brand was established is now more visible to provide consumers a tangible tie to Canadian Club's extensive history and heritage. The main label calls attention to the barrel blended process, the logo is stacked in slightly bolder typeface to allow for quicker consumer recognition and "WHISKY" is bigger and bolder to better position C.C. against other premium whiskies. The 6-year-old age claim is predominantly displayed on the lower label, along with the word "Imported" to reinforce Canadian Club's new tag line—Aged And Barrel Blended, Because It Matters.

But, it's the same great whisky in the bottle that consumers have been asking for by name for some 140 years. Canadian Club continues to apply the same qualities that its founder, Hiram Walker, established decades ago by producing a high-quality, consistent product.

Few brands can boast of the stability Canadian Club

currently enjoys. And, Canadian Club drinkers are among the most loyal group of consumers in the world with their continuing patronage an endorsement of the quality and excellence that have become this brand's stock in trade.

So, when you open a bottle of Canadian Club, not only does the smooth, mellow, consistently good taste come pouring out, pride does, as well.

Canadian Whisky
Fascinating Facts

1. Canadian whisky originated in the grist mills of Upper Canada (Ontario). Millers, who received $\frac{1}{10}$ of each farmer's grain in return for grinding it, soon began turning the excess grain into whisky.

2. The first still license was issued in 1794 in Canada. For the next 50 years, distilled beverages were the number one source of revenues for the government, prompting one historian to speculate that Canada "drank herself to nationhood."

3. One bushel of grain yields 3 gallons of whisky.

4. Pioneer whisky was sold in bulk rather than by the bottle.

5. In 1879, Hiram Walker became the first Canadian distiller to give his whisky brand names, and to sell it in bottles.

6. Hiram Walker's "Club" whisky became "Canadian Club" after American distillers insisted on a law that whisky imported into the U.S. had to state its country of origin.

7. Whisky was not aged in oak barrels in Canada until the middle of the 19th century.

8. The first export of Canadian whisky to Europe was made in 1821. The distiller was John Molson, better known today for his brewing than his distilling.

9. Canada's early distilleries fattened cattle and hogs on spent whisky mash.

10. Americans drink 86% of Canada's whisky production.

CANADIAN CLUB
Born in Canada

Not long after 1858, when Hiram Walker created his uniquely smooth and mellow blend of whisky, he decided not to put it into barrels, which was the general practice of the times, for fear that it might be diluted, or worse yet, confused with inferior spirits. Instead, he bottled his whisky—ensuring that each individually-sealed bottle would retain its superior quality. He labeled his elegant blend "Club Whisky," because his whisky has been enjoyed at fine clubs everywhere. It became the favorite bar call at fine clubs everywhere, because by asking for "Canadian Club," its members could always be sure they were getting the best Canadian whisky—which was not often the case in those days. Today, 135 years later, Canadian Club remains the finest quality blend of Canadian whisky, thanks to the foresightedness of a man called Hiram Walker—and his incredibly high standards.

The Shot Enjoyed Round The World

To date, Canadian Club is distributed and enjoyed in over 150 countries, with more than one billion bottles having been sold worldwide, making it the favorite Canadian Whisky internationally. It's also one of the leading spirit brands in the United States. And it's the number one Canadian whisky in Canada—home of Canadian whisky. The reason is simple: Canadian Club is one of the smoothest, most mixable blends of Canadian whisky. That is undoubtedly why "C.C." has withstood the test of time, and will surely go down in history as the most famous Canadian ever called for.

CANADIAN CLUB DRINK CLASSICS: These are the basics to be included in everyone's repertoire of whisky drinks. These true classics will be enjoyed to the fullest by appreciative audiences everywhere, when made with Canadian Club.

THE CANADIAN DRY MANHATTAN

1½ oz. CANADIAN CLUB

½ oz. Martini & Rossi Dry Vermouth

Pour ingredients into ice filled mixing glass and stir. Strain into prechilled cocktail glass. Add olive and/or lemon twist as desired.

THE CANADIAN PERFECT MANHATTAN

1½ oz. CANADIAN CLUB

¼ oz. Martini & Rossi Sweet Vermouth

¼ oz. Dry Vermouth

Pour ingredients into ice filled mixing glass and stir. Strain into prechilled cocktail glass. Add cherry, olive, or lemon twist as desired.

THE CANADIAN SWEET MANHATTAN

1½ oz. CANADIAN CLUB

½ oz. Martini & Rossi Sweet Vermouth

Pour ingredients into ice filled mixing glass and stir. Strain into prechilled cocktail glass. Add maraschino cherry as garnish or lemon twist if desired.

THE TRADITIONAL CANADIAN MANHATTAN

1½ oz. CANADIAN CLUB

½ oz. Martini & Rossi Sweet Vermouth

2 dashes Angostura Bitters

Pour ingredients into ice filled mixing glass and stir. Strain into prechilled cocktail glass. Add maraschino cherry as garnish or lemon twist if desired.

CANADIAN CLUB COCKTAIL GLASS TIME: How did the "cocktail" get it's name? No one seems to agree, but the following story is one of the more intriguing. It seems that during the Revolutionary War, there was a tavern in New England run by a Miss Betsy Flanagan. The officers who regularly frequented her tavern, often complained to her about a prosperous Tory who lived in luxury while they barely had enough to eat. One night, so the story goes, Miss Betsy served the officers a drink mixed with fruit juice decorated with a feather from the Tory's favorite rooster. The officers cheered the drink—especially the garnish. One of the French officers was heard to shout—"Vive le coq's tail!" And thus, it is said, the word "cocktail" was born. From then til now, the cocktail has become the pre-eminent predinner libation with hundreds, perhaps thousands of variations. We present here the most noted of the whisky cocktails, employing the best whisky to make them with, Canadian Club. A votre sante.

ALLEGHENY

1 oz. CANADIAN CLUB

½ oz. Martini & Rossi Dry Vermouth

1½ tsp. Hiram Walker Blackberry-flavored Brandy

Pour ingredients into ice filled mixing glass and stir. Strain into a prechilled cocktail glass. Garnish with a twist of lemon.

BLACK HAWK

1½ oz. CANADIAN CLUB

½ oz. Hiram Walker Sloe Gin

Pour ingredients into ice filled mixing glass and stir. Pour into a prechilled cocktail glass. Garnish with a cherry.

BOUNTY

1½ oz. CANADIAN CLUB

¼ oz. Martini & Rossi Sweet Vermouth

¼ oz. Benedictine

Pour ingredients into ice filled mixing glass and stir vigorously. Strain into prechilled cocktail glass. Lemon or orange twist is an optional garnish.

CANADIAN ALEXANDER

1½ oz. CANADIAN CLUB

½ oz. Hiram Walker Dark Creme de Cacao

¾ oz. Heavy Cream

Shake all ingredients with cracked ice. Strain into a cocktail glass. Sprinkle with nutmeg.

CANADIAN ALGONQUIN

1½ oz. CANADIAN CLUB

¼ oz. Martini & Rossi Dry Vermouth

¼ oz. Pineapple Juice

Pour ingredients into ice filled mixing glass. Stir and pour into prechilled cocktail glass.

CANADIAN BEAUTY

1½ oz. CANADIAN CLUB

½ oz. Martini & Rossi Dry Vermouth

¼ tsp. Hiram Walker White Creme de Menthe

1 Tbs. Orange Juice

1 Tbs. Major Peters' Grenadine

1 dash Port

Shake first 5 ingredients with ice. Strain into a cocktail glass. Finish with a dash of Port.

CANADIAN BOOMERANG

1½ oz. CANADIAN CLUB

½ oz. Martini & Rossi Dry Vermouth

1 dash Angostura Bitters

1 dash Maraschino

Pour ingredients into ice filled mixing glass and stir. Strain into a prechilled cocktail glass and top with a twist of lemon.

CANADIAN BOSTON

¾ oz. CANADIAN CLUB

¾ oz. Hiram Walker Apricot-flavored Brandy

Juice of ¼ Lemon

1½ tsp. Major Peters' Grenadine

Pour ingredients into ice filled mixing glass and stir. Strain into a prechilled cocktail glass.

CANADIAN CLUB COCKTAIL

2 oz. CANADIAN CLUB

1 tsp. Sugar Syrup

1 dash Angostura Bitters

Pour ingredients into ice filled mixing glass. Strain into a prechilled cocktail glass. Top with a cherry.

DIXIE WHISKY

2 oz. CANADIAN CLUB

½ tsp. Hiram Walker White Creme de Menthe

¼ tsp. Hiram Walker Triple Sec

½ oz. Sugar Syrup

Pour ingredients into an ice filled mixing glass and stir vigorously. Strain into a cocktail glass.

FOX RIVER

2 oz. CANADIAN CLUB

1 Tbs. Hiram Walker Dark Creme de Cacao

4 dashes Angostura Bitters

Pour ingredients into ice filled mixing glass and stir. Strain into a cocktail glass.

FRISCO

1½ oz. CANADIAN CLUB

½ oz. Benedictine

Stir ingredients with cracked ice. Strain into a cocktail glass and top with a twist of lemon.

IRISH CANADIAN

1½ oz. CANADIAN CLUB

½ oz. Irish Mist

Stir ingredients with ice until well mixed. Strain into a cocktail glass.

LADIES NIGHT OUT*

2 oz. CANADIAN CLUB

½ tsp. Romana Sambuca

2 dashes Angostura Bitters

Stir all ingredients with ice. Strain into a cocktail glass. Top with a pineapple stick.
* Originally called "Ladies Day"

LAWHILL

1½ oz. CANADIAN CLUB

¾ oz. Martini & Rossi Dry Vermouth

¼ tsp. Romana Sambuca

¼ tsp. Maraschino

1 dash Angostura Bitters

Pour ingredients into ice filled mixing glass. Strain into a cocktail glass.

LINSTEAD

1½ oz. CANADIAN CLUB

¾ oz. Pineapple Juice

¼ tsp. Romana Sambuca

¼ tsp. Lemon Juice

½ tsp. Granulated Sugar

Shake all ingredients with ice (vigorously) and strain into a cocktail glass.

MAPLE LEAF

1 oz. CANADIAN CLUB

½ oz. Irish Mist

1 tsp. Hiram Walker Creme de Cacao

1 oz. Heavy Cream

Shake all ingredients with ice (vigorously) and strain into a cocktail glass.

METS MANHATTAN

1½ oz. CANADIAN CLUB

¼ oz. Martini & Rossi Dry Vermouth

¼ oz. Hiram Walker Strawberry Schnapps

Pour ingredients into ice filled mixing glass and stir vigorously. Strain into a prechilled cocktail glass. Optional strawberry garnish.

MONTE CARLO

1 oz. CANADIAN CLUB

1 oz. Dubonnet

1 dash Angostura Bitters

Pour ingredients into ice filled mixing glass and stir vigorously. Strain into a prechilled cocktail glass. Top with a twist of lemon.

MR. NEVINS

1½ oz. CANADIAN CLUB

1½ tsp. Hiram Walker Apricot-flavored Brandy

1 Tbs. Grapefruit Juice

1½ tsp. Lemon Juice

1 dash Angostura Bitters

Pour ingredients into ice filled mixing glass and stir vigorously. Strain into a prechilled cocktail glass. Top with a twist of lemon.

CANADIAN CLUB OLD-FASHIONED ENJOYMENTS: The classic Old-Fashioned is truly a magnificent cocktail and is but one drink served in what is called an "old-fashioned" glass. Herewith, we present a batch to be served in the aforementioned glassware, and to be enjoyed for their old-fashioned flavor, their old-fashioned elegance—their old-fashioned ambiance. Point being, there is nothing old-fashioned about an old-fashioned — especially if it's made with the premier Whisky — Canadian Club. Here's looking at you.

CANADIAN COCKTAIL

In an old-fashioned/rocks glass place:

2 dashes Angostura Bitters

¼ oz. Hiram Walker Triple Sec

½ tsp. Superfine Sugar

1 oz. Soda or Water

1¼ oz. CANADIAN CLUB

Stir first three ingredients until sugar dissolves, then add soda and Canadian Club. Stir and add cherry and lemon peel garnish.

CANADIAN OLD-FASHIONED

1 oz. Soda or Water

½ tsp. Superfine Sugar

2 dashes Angostura Bitters

1½ oz. CANADIAN CLUB

Place first three ingredients into an old-fashioned glass and stir. Then add ice cubes and the Canadian Club. Garnish with cherry, orange slice and lemon peel.

COMMODORE COCKTAIL

1¼ oz. CANADIAN CLUB

2 dashes Angostura Bitters

1 oz. Major Peters' Sweet & Sour Mix

dash Major Peters' Lime Juice (optional)

Pour ingredients into cocktail shaker with ice and shake. Strain into prechilled glass.

OLD OLD-FASHIONED*

2 dashes Angostura Bitters

½ tsp. Superfine Sugar

1 oz. Soda or Water

1¼ oz. CANADIAN CLUB

Muddle sugar, bitters, and a cherry, a lemon peel and an orange slice in the bottom of the glass for ten seconds. Add ice cubes, soda or water, and Canadian Club. Stir and serve.
* At the turn of the century, this was the traditional method for preparing an old-fashioned and it most certainly resulted in more complex flavors.

PALMER COCKTAIL

1¼ oz. CANADIAN CLUB

2 dashes Angostura Bitters

1 oz. Lemon Juice

Pour ingredients into mixing glass filled with ice cubes. Stir and strain into prechilled glass.

QUEBEC

2 oz. CANADIAN CLUB

¼ oz. Martini & Rossi Sweet Vermouth

¼ oz. Campari

¼ oz. Maraschino Cherry Juice

Pour ingredients into cocktail shaker with ice. Shake and pour over ice cubes in a double old-fashioned/rocks glass. Garnish with cherry.

SHORT CUT OLD-FASHIONED·

1¼ oz. CANADIAN CLUB

2 dashes Angostura Bitters

1 oz. 7-Up

Place the ingredients in an old-fashioned/rocks glass filled with ice cubes and stir. Garnish with cherry, orange slice, and lemon peel.

YUKON COCKTAIL

1½ oz. CANADIAN CLUB

2 dashes Angostura Bitters

¼ oz. Hiram Walker Triple Sec

1 tsp. Superfine Sugar

Pour ingredients into cocktail shaker with ice and shake. Strain into prechilled glass.

CANADIAN CLUB SOURS— HOW SWEET THEY ARE:

The sour (or Delmonico) glass is "footed" for the same reason a cocktail glass is—to keep the drink chilled while it is enjoyed. It gives the drinker a "foot" to hold so as not to warm the glass with the hands. When you want a sour that's truly sweet—make sure it's made with Canadian Club. Bottoms up.

CANADIAN CITRUS SOUR

1¼ oz. CANADIAN CLUB

¾ oz. Major Peters' Sweet & Sour Mix

¾ oz. Orange Juice

¾ oz. Major Peters' Lime Juice

Pour ingredients into cocktail shaker with ice. Shake and strain into sour glass. Garnish with lemon, orange and/or lime slices.

CANADIAN CLUB SOUR

1¼ oz. CANADIAN CLUB

2 oz. Major Peters' Sweet & Sour Mix, or

2 oz. Lemon Juice & 1 tsp. Superfine Sugar

Pour ingredients into cocktail shaker with ice. Shake and strain into sour glass. Garnish with cherry and orange slice.

CANADIAN RAINBOW SOUR

½ oz. CANADIAN CLUB

½ oz. Hiram Walker Apricot-flavored Brandy

½ oz. Hiram Walker Peach Schnapps

½ oz. Hiram Walker Triple Sec

2 oz. Major Peters' Sweet & Sour Mix

Pour ingredients into cocktail shaker with ice. Shake and strain into double old-fashioned/rocks glass with ice cubes. Garnish with cherry, orange slice, and lime squeeze.

CANADIAN STONE SOUR

1¼ oz. CANADIAN CLUB

1 oz. Major Peters' Sweet & Sour Mix

1 oz. Orange Juice

Pour ingredients into cocktail shaker with ice. Shake and strain into sour glass. Garnish with cherry and orange slice.

CANADIAN WARD EIGHT

1¼ oz. CANADIAN CLUB

2 oz. Major Peters' Sweet & Sour Mix

¼ oz. Major Peters' Grenadine

Pour ingredients into cocktail shaker with ice. Shake and strain into sour glass. Garnish with cherry and orange slice.

STILETTO SOUR

1 oz. CANADIAN CLUB

½ oz. Hiram Walker Amaretto

2 oz. Major Peters' Sweet & Sour Mix

Pour ingredients into cocktail shaker with ice. Shake and strain into sour glass. Garnish with cherry and orange slice.

TWIN HILLS SOUR

(Also known as Frisco Sour)

1¼ oz. CANADIAN CLUB

½ oz. Benedictine

1½ oz. Major Peters' Sweet & Sour Mix

½ oz. Major Peters' Lime Juice

Pour ingredients into cocktail shaker with ice. Shake and strain into sour glass. Garnish with lemon and lime slices.

THE CANADIAN CLUB
COLLINS COLLECTION:
Collins - definition - A sour
served in a tall glass with ice
cubes to which carbonated
water (club soda/seltzer) has
been added.

The Origin of the Collins:
Created by Tom Collins, one of
eight children who was born
in Ireland. He immigrated to
America at the turn of the
century and became a bar-
tender in New York. Tom
liked "a touch of the brush"
while working, and was
inclined to sip what appeared
to be tall lemonades. He told
his employers these lemon-
ades kept him cool during the
hot summer and therefore he
could work longer and be
more productive. Some cus-
tomers noted him drinking
this new type of long drink
and asked Tom to make them
one. Everyone seemed to like
them, so Tom offered them
wherever he was working.
Thus...

BLACK HAWK COLLINS

1 oz. CANADIAN CLUB

½ oz. Hiram Walker
Blackberry-flavored
Brandy

2 oz. Major Peters'
Sweet & Sour Mix

Pour ingredients into cocktail
shaker with ice. Shake and
strain into collins glass filled
with ice cubes. Fill with soda,
garnish with cherry and lime
squeeze.

CANADIAN COLLINS

1¼ oz. CANADIAN CLUB

2 oz. Major Peters'
Sweet & Sour Mix

Pour ingredients into cocktail
shaker with ice. Shake and
strain into collins glass filled
with ice cubes. Fill with soda,
add cherry and orange slice
garnish, insert long straws.

CANADIAN COOLER

1¼ oz. CANADIAN CLUB
½ oz. Major Peters'
     Sweet & Sour Mix
½ oz. Orange Juice
½ oz. Pineapple Juice
½ oz. Cranberry Juice

Stir vigorously, fill with soda, and add lime squeeze as garnish. A dash of grenadine on top is optional.

CANADIAN SLING

1 oz. CANADIAN CLUB
½ oz. Hiram Walker Cherry-
     flavored Brandy
2 oz. Major Peters'
     Sweet & Sour Mix
dash Benedictine

Pour ingredients into cocktail shaker with ice. Shake and strain into collins glass filled with ice cubes. Fill with soda, add cherry & orange slice garnish, and insert long straws.

CANADIAN STONE COLLINS

1¼ oz. CANADIAN CLUB
1 oz. Major Peters'
     Sweet & Sour Mix
1 oz. Orange Juice

Pour ingredients into cocktail shaker with ice. Shake and strain into collins glass filled with ice cubes. Fill with soda, add cherry and orange slice garnish, and insert long straws.

FRENCH CANADIAN COLLINS

1 oz. CANADIAN CLUB
¾ oz. Courvoisier Cognac
¼ oz. Benedictine
2 oz. Major Peters'
     Sweet & Sour Mix

Pour ingredients into cocktail shaker with ice. Shake and strain into collins glass filled with ice cubes. Fill with soda, add cherry and orange slice garnish, and insert long straws.

WARD EIGHT COLLINS

1¼ oz. CANADIAN CLUB
2 oz. Major Peters'
     Sweet & Sour Mix
¼ oz. Major Peters'
     Grenadine

Pour ingredients into cocktail shaker with ice. Shake and strain into collins glass filled with ice cubes. Fill with soda, add lime squeeze garnish, and insert long straws.

WINDSOR COLLINS

1 oz.   CANADIAN CLUB

½ oz.   Hiram Walker
        Triple Sec

½ oz.   Hiram Walker Peach
        Schnapps

2 oz.   Major Peters'
        Sweet & Sour Mix

Pour ingredients into cocktail shaker with ice. Shake and strain into a collins glass with ice cubes. Add lime squeeze garnish.

The Canadian Club Mug, Cup and Goblet Trio

This glassware...highball, collins, sour, old-fashioned or cocktail are the drink carriers which hold the promise of other delicious and spirited enjoyments. Made with the premier Canadian whisky—Canadian Club—these unusually-served drinks are sure to be added to your serving repertory. Salud.

CANADIAN HOT TODDY

1½ oz.   CANADIAN CLUB

2½ oz.   Hot Water

1 tsp.   Granulated Sugar

Over sugar, fill mug ⅔ full with hot water. Add Canadian Club. Stir. Top with a slice of lemon and a dusting of nutmeg.

HOT BRICK TODDY

2 oz.   CANADIAN CLUB

1½ oz.   Hot Water

1 tsp.   Granulated Sugar

1 tsp.   Butter

2-3 pinches Cinnamon

In mug, dissolve sugar, butter and cinnamon with hot water. Add Canadian Club, stir and serve.

HOTEY TOTEY

1 oz.   CANADIAN CLUB

½ oz.   Hiram Walker
        Cinnamon Schnapps

½ oz.   Hiram Walker Dark
        Creme de Cacao

Fill with hot chocolate. Top with a half dozen mini-marshmallows.

Additional Canadian Club Recipes:

AVRIL

1½ oz.   CANADIAN CLUB

½ oz.   Cranberry Liqueur

Stir well. Strain into a cocktail glass.

BABY'S BOTTOM

1½ oz. CANADIAN CLUB

½ oz. Hiram Walker White Creme de Menthe

½ oz. Hiram Walker White Creme de Cacao

Stir well. Strain into a cocktail glass.

BARNSTORMER

1½ oz. CANADIAN CLUB

½ oz. Hiram Walker Peppermint Schnapps

splash Hiram Walker Dark Creme de Cacao

splash Hiram Walker White Creme de Cacao

½ oz. Lemon Juice

Shake. Strain into an old-fashioned glass with ice.

BENT NAIL

1½ oz. CANADIAN CLUB

½ oz. Drambuie

3 oz. Crushed Ice

Shake. Strain into cocktail glass.

BLENDER

¼ oz. CANADIAN CLUB

¼ oz. Hiram Walker White Creme de Cacao

Blend with crushed ice.

BLINKER

1¼ oz. CANADIAN CLUB

2½ oz. Grapefruit Juice

½ oz. Major Peters' Grenadine

Shake well with ice. Strain into old-fashioned glass.

BOILERMAKER

1½ oz. CANADIAN CLUB

8 oz. Beer

Drink the whiskey. Sip the beer.

CANADIAN APPLE PIE

Into a highball glass filled with ice pour:

1½ oz. CANADIAN CLUB

½ oz. Hiram Walker Cinnamon Schnapps

Apple Cider or Apple Juice

Stir and serve. Add orange slice garnish.

CANADIAN CLUB ICED TEA

1 oz. CANADIAN CLUB

1 oz. Absolut Vodka

2 oz. Major Peters' Sweet & Sour Mix

Cola

Pack a 12 oz. glass with ice. Add liquors and sweet & sour. Fill with cola. Garnish with lemon wheel or twist.

CC CIDER

1 oz. CANADIAN CLUB

½ oz. Hiram Walker
Cinnamon Schnapps

3 oz. Apple Cider

¼ Unpeeled Red Apple

Blend. Pour unstrained.

EARTHSHAKE

1 oz. CANADIAN CLUB

½ oz. Beefeater Dry Gin

½ oz. Romana Sambuca

Shake well with ice. Strain into cocktail glass.

GREATHEAD

1½ oz. CANADIAN CLUB

½ oz. Applejack

Stir well. Strain into a cocktail glass.

IRISH CANADIAN

1½ oz. CANADIAN CLUB

½ oz. Irish Mist

Stir well. Strain into a cocktail glass.

MILLIONAIRE MANHATTAN

1¼ oz. CANADIAN CLUB

¼ oz. Harvey's Bristol Cream

Serve on the rocks or up.

NIAGARA FALLS

1½ oz. CANADIAN CLUB

½ oz. Irish Mist

½ oz. Heavy Cream

Shake all ingredients. Serve up.

PREAKNESS

1¼ oz. CANADIAN CLUB

¼ oz. Martini & Rossi
Sweet Vermouth

¼ oz. Benedictine

1 dash Angostura Bitters

Stir and strain into prechilled cocktail glass.

T.N.T. COCKTAIL

¾ oz. CANADIAN CLUB

¾ oz. Romana Sambuca

Shake with cracked ice. Strain into cocktail glass.

YES YES

1¼ oz. CANADIAN CLUB

¼ oz. Black Sambuca

Serve on the rocks.

Add your favorite CC recipes here.

© Foley Publishing Corp

CHAMBORD

Chambord is renowned throughout the world as the Liqueur Royale de France. In the glorious time of King Louis XIV the nobility of France journeyed to their great chateaux where they had feasts crowned by elegant liqueurs. Created in this ancient time, Chambord is a magnificent liqueur made with rich framboises noires (small black raspberries) and other fruits and herbs combined with delicious honey.

After dinner lace your favorite liqueur glass with Chambord, sit back and enjoy its rich aroma and taste.

Add your favorite Chambord recipes here.

1800 BITE THE BERRY

¼ oz. CHAMBORD

1¼ oz. Jose Cuervo
1800 Tequila

½ oz. Hiram Walker
Triple Sec

2½ oz. Major Peters' Sweet
& Sour Mix

2 oz. Cranberry Juice

*Combine in a rocks glass.
Garnish with an orange slice.*

BLACK FOREST

⅓ oz. CHAMBORD

⅓ oz. Absolut Vodka

⅓ oz. Kahlua

4 oz. Milk

BLACK MARTINI

splash CHAMBORD

1½ oz. Absolut Kurant

*Stir ingredients and serve
straight up or over ice.
Invented at the Continental
Cafe in Philadelphia,
Pennsylvania.*

CADIZ

¾ oz. CHAMBORD

¾ oz. Amontillado Sherry

½ oz. Hiram Walker
Triple Sec

½ oz. Heavy Cream

1 scoop Crushed Ice

*Mix all the ingredients in a
shaker. Pour the mixture into a
chilled old-fashioned glass.*

CANDY ASS

1 oz. CHAMBORD

1 oz. Mozart

*Shake with ice and strain into a
shot glass.*

CHAMBORD &
CHANTAINE BRUT

Chantaine

dash CHAMBORD

*Pop goes the Chantaine, in
goes a dash of Chambord.*

CHAMBORD &
COGNAC & HEAT

½ oz. CHAMBORD

½ oz. Cognac

*Place in snifter glass and heat
in a microwave for 25 seconds
(or in a saucepan on high).*

CHAMBORD & CREAM

1¼ oz. CHAMBORD

dash Cream

Serve Chambord in cordial glass with dash of cream on top. (Pour over back of spoon.)

CHAMBORD ADRENALIN

Equal parts:

CHAMBORD

Absolut Vodka

Chilled.

CHAMBORD COLADA

1½ oz. CHAMBORD

1½ oz. Bacardi Rum

2 oz. Pineapple Juice

½ oz. Coco Lopez Cream of Coconut

¾ oz. Ice

Place all ingredients in a blender; process on high until smooth.

CHAMBORD DAIQUIRI

¾ oz. CHAMBORD

¾ oz. Bacardi Light Rum

juice of ½ Lime

1 tsp. Powdered Sugar

3-4 Black Raspberries (optional)

Add 1 cup crushed ice and mix in a blender for 30 seconds; strain into a champagne glass.

CHAMBORD FROST

1½ oz. CHAMBORD

juice of ¼ Lemon

1 cup Crushed Ice

Mix in a blender or shaker for 20 seconds. Pour into a cocktail glass with the ice.

CHAMBORD ICEBERG

½ oz. CHAMBORD

½ oz. Absolut Vodka

Pour one-half ounce of vodka into a tall champagne glass. Top with one-half ounce Chambord. Fill to the brim with ice cubes.

CHAMBORD KAMIKAZI

½ oz. CHAMBORD

1 oz. Absolut Vodka

¼ oz. Hiram Walker Triple Sec

¼ oz. Major Peters' Lime Juice

Shake with ice and strain into a shot glass.

CHAMBORD MARGARITA

¼ oz. CHAMBORD

¾ oz. Jose Cuervo Tequila

½ oz. Hiram Walker
        Triple Sec

juice of ½ Lime

Blend with ice.

CHAMBORD ROYALE SPRITZER

1½ oz. CHAMBORD

        Champagne, chilled

        Club Soda

Serve in champagne glass.

CHAMBORD SOUR

1½ oz. CHAMBORD

½ oz. Lemon Juice

¾ Tbs. Sugar

Shake well with ice; strain into a sour glass. Garnish with a slice of orange.

CHAMBORD SPIRIT

½ oz. CHAMBORD

½ oz. Wild Spirit

Pour over lots of ice.

CHAMBORLADA

1 oz. CHAMBORD

½ oz. Bacardi Light Rum

½ oz. Bacardi Dark Rum

3 oz. Pineapple Juice

2 oz. Coco Lopez Cream
      of Coconut

Combine all ingredients, except Chambord, with cracked ice in a blender. Blend. Pour the Chambord into the bottom of a wine glass. Pour the pina colada mixture on top. Top off with a little more Chambord.

CHAMU

½ oz. CHAMBORD

1 oz. Malibu

½ oz. Absolut Vodka

3 oz. Pineapple Juice

Combine ingredients in a tall glass with ice. Fill with pineapple juice.

DUCK PIN

1 oz. CHAMBORD

1 oz. Southern Comfort

½ oz. Pineapple Juice

Shake. Strain into a shot glass.

FRENCH DREAM

½ oz. CHAMBORD

1½ oz. Carolans Irish Cream

2 oz. Half & Half

4 oz. Ice Cubes

Blend.

FRENCH SUMMER

¾ oz. CHAMBORD

3 oz. Sparkling Water

slice Lemon

Pour the Chambord into a wine glass filled to the brim with ice. Add the sparkling water and the juice of a slice of lemon. Garnish with fruit. Stir.

FRENCH SUMMER #2

1 oz. CHAMBORD

Fill with sparkling water. Add a slice of orange.

GRAPE CRUSH

½ shot CHAMBORD

½ shot Absolut Vodka

dash Major Peters' Sweet & Sour Mix

Shake. Serve on the rocks or in a shot glass.

GRAPE CRUSH #2

1 oz. CHAMBORD

1 oz. Absolut Vodka

2 oz. Major Peters' Sweet & Sour Mix

1 oz. 7-Up

Shake all but 7-Up. Top with 7-Up.

HARBOR LIGHTS

1 part CHAMBORD

1 part Bacardi Rum

1 part Orange Juice

Shake with ice and strain into a shot glass.

HOLLYWOOD

1 part CHAMBORD

1 part Absolut Vodka

1 part Pineapple Juice

Shake with ice and strain into a shot glass.

INTERNATIONAL COFFEE

½ oz. CHAMBORD

½ oz. Carolans Irish Cream

5 oz. Coffee

Pour Carolans and Chambord into a cup of hot coffee.

IRISH HORSEMAN #2

¼ oz. CHAMBORD

¾ oz. Tullamore Dew Irish Whiskey

¼ oz. Hiram Walker Triple Sec

3 oz. Major Peters' Sweet & Sour Mix

8 oz. Crushed Ice

Combine whiskey, Triple Sec, and sweet & sour mix with crushed ice. Shake well. Pour into a highball glass. Top with Chambord.

IRISH RASPBERRY

½ oz. CHAMBORD

½ oz. Carolans Irish Cream

In a shaker with ½ cup ice. Shake and pour with the ice into a champagne glass. Top with whipped cream and serve with a straw.

IRISH RASPBERRY #2

½ oz. CHAMBORD

1 oz. Carolans Irish Cream

1 cup Ice

Blend with ice and serve.

KILLER KOOL-AID

1 part CHAMBORD

1 part Absolut Vodka

1 part Beefeater Dry Gin

1 part Bacardi Rum

2 oz. Cranberry Juice

1 oz. Major Peters' Sour Mix

Combine in a tall glass over ice.

KIR ROYALE

dash CHAMBORD

Wine

LA JOLLARITA

½ oz. CHAMBORD

1½ oz. Jose Cuervo Traditional Tequila

½ oz. Hiram Walker Triple Sec

Shake, strain, and serve.

LOBOTOMY

⅓ shot CHAMBORD

⅓ shot Hiram Walker Amaretto

⅓ shot Pineapple Juice

Shake. Serve in a shot glass.

MEXICAN BERRY

1½ oz. CHAMBORD

1 oz. Jose Cuervo Tequila

Shake with ice and strain into a shot glass.

MIDNIGHT MARTINI

½ oz. CHAMBORD

1½ oz. Absolut Vodka

Lemon twist garnish

Stir with ice and strain. Garnish with a lemon twist. From the Gallery Lounge Sheraton in Seattle, Washington.

MIDNIGHT ORCHID

¼ oz. CHAMBORD

1 oz. Absolut Vodka, chilled

2 oz. Pineapple Juice

½ oz. Cranberry Juice

½ oz. Half & Half

Shake. Serve over crushed ice or blend with ice.

MISTICO DESERT BERRY

dash CHAMBORD

1½ oz. Jose Cuervo Mistico

Stir and strain into a shot glass.

MISTRAL

1 oz. CHAMBORD

2 oz. Dry White Wine

1 Tbs. Frozen Strawberries or Raspberries

Mix in a blender with 3 tablespoons ice; pour with ice into a champagne glass.

MONT BLANC

1 oz. CHAMBORD

1 oz. Absolut Vodka

1 oz. Cream or Half & Half

1 scoop Vanilla Ice Cream

Mix in a blender for 20 seconds; pour into a wine glass.

MONTMARTRE

1 oz. CHAMBORD

1 oz. Hiram Walker Coffee Liqueur

1 oz. Cream or Half & Half

Mix in a blender with ½ cup crushed ice for 20 seconds; pour into a cocktail glass with ice.

NERVOUS BREAKDOWN

CHAMBORD

Absolut Vodka

Fill with sparkling water, splash cranberry juice and lime.

NUTS & BERRIES

½ oz. CHAMBORD

½ oz. Absolut Vodka

½ oz. Hiram Walker
Hazelnut Liqueur

4 oz. Cream

PURPLE HAZE

1 part CHAMBORD

1 part Absolut Vodka

1 part Cranberry Juice or
Major Peters' Sweet
& Sour Mix

Combine in a shot glass.

PURPLE HOOTER

¾ oz. CHAMBORD

¾ oz. Absolut Vodka

1½ oz. Major Peters' Sweet
& Sour Mix

Shaken over ice.

RASPBERRY BROWNIE

¾ oz. CHAMBORD

¾ oz. Kahlua

Float cream or milk.

RASPBERRY LIME RICKEY

1 oz. CHAMBORD

splash Major Peters' Lime
Juice

Fill with sparkling water.

RASPBERRY MARTINI

splash CHAMBORD

1 part Mozart Chocolate
Liqueur

1 part Absolut Vodka

*Combine with ice and shake
well. Serve in a glass whose
rim has been dipped in powdered sugar.*

RASPBERRY SMASH

¼ shot CHAMBORD

¾ shot Absolut Vodka

splash Raspberry Syrup

Shake. Serve in a shot glass.

RAZZ-MA-TAZZ

½ oz. CHAMBORD

1½ oz. Absolut Vodka

1½ oz. Club Soda

*Serve over ice in a tall glass,
chilled.*

SEX ON THE BEACH

¾ oz. CHAMBORD

¾ oz. Midori Melon
Liqueur

3 oz. Pineapple Juice

*Pour over ice; fill the glass with
cranberry juice.*

SEX ON THE BEACH #1

¾ oz. CHAMBORD

¾ oz. Midori Melon
Liqueur

2 oz. Pineapple Juice

splash Cranberry Juice

*Combine in a mixing glass.
Shake or stir. Pour in a shot
glass. Can also be served over
ice in a rocks glass.*

SIMPLY BONKERS

1 part CHAMBORD

1 part Bacardi Rum

1 part Cream

Combine in a shot glass.

ST. MORITZ

*CHAMBORD in a cordial glass
with dash of cream on top.
(Pour over back of spoon.) The
fresh taste of the cream with
the luscious framboise (black
raspberry) taste of Chambord
is superb. A very special treat.*

SWEET TART

¼ oz. CHAMBORD

1 oz. Absolut Vodka

¼ oz. Major Peters' Lime
Juice

¼ oz. Pineapple Juice

*Shake with ice and strain into a
shot glass.*

THE HOLLYWOOD

½ oz. CHAMBORD

½ oz. Absolut Vodka

4 oz. Pineapple Juice

VAMPIRE

⅓ shot CHAMBORD

⅓ shot Absolut Vodka

⅓ shot Cranberry Juice

Shake. Serve in a shot glass.

ZIPPERHEAD

CHAMBORD

Absolut Vodka

*Pour Chambord, then Absolut
over ice. Splash with sparkling
water, sip through a large straw.*

Add your favorite Chambord recipes here.

© Foley Publishing Corp

JOSE CUERVO

THE FIRST FAMILY OF TEQUILA

Time and Tradition

For over 200 years, the Jose Cuervo family has produced the finest tequila in the world. This untamed spirit, steeped in legend and mystique, can trace its origins back as far as the 1770s. It is here that the story of tequila begins.

History tells of Mexico's highly advanced Aztec civilization producing a sour, milky drink fermented from the agave plant. This beverage, called "pulque," was discovered by the Spanish conquistadors upon their arrival in the 16th century. However, longing for their more potent and palatable brandies, the Spaniards introduced their knowledge of distilling to the Aztecs "pulque," using sugars from the local agave plant to produce a new spirit named mezcal.

However, it wasn't until 1758, that the Jose Cuervo story truly began. It was then that King Charles IV of Spain granted a large section of land to Don Jose Antonio de Cuervo. This was done in appreciation for the protection he offered the local parish. The extremely fertile soil on this land, located in the volcanic highlands of what is now Jalisco, had a natural abundance of the blue agave plant. Don Jose, establishing a distillery, used the blue agave found there to make a type of wine called "vine de mescal." This wine would eventually assume the name tequila after the town of Tequila, Mexico. The word tequila in Mexican Indian literally means "lava hill," making Tequila home to some of the best blue agaves in all of Mexico.

From 1784-1795, Mexico placed a national ban on the distillation of alcohol, and tequila production was stopped. Fortunately for the Cuervo family, after the eleven year ban was lifted, Don Jose Maria Guadalupe de Cuervo was granted the first royal permit to produce tequila. It was then that he established the La Rojena distillery in Tequila, Mexico. Although today there are nearly 50 tequila producers, only agaves from the state of Jalisco and three other small regions can be used, according to Mexican law, to produce tequila.

The Heart of Tequila:

At the heart of tequila production is the blue agave plant. This plant, not a cactus, is actually a member of the lily family, and is known botanically as "agave tequilana Weber, variedad azul." The average blue agave takes from 8 to 10 years to mature and can grow from 6 to 8 feet tall. In the final stage of growth, a rapid growing stalk called a "quiote" begins to grow from the center of the plant. If permitted to grow, it will flower and kill the plant. Therefore, the ideal time to harvest the blue agave is just before the appearance of the quiote.

The plants are harvested using razor sharp, paddled shaped metal spades called "coas" by harvesters called "jimadores." The coas are used to remove the spikes of the blue agave, leaving only the heart or "pina." These pinas, weighing upwards of 200 lbs., are brought to the distillery and steamed in giant antique stone ovens for many days.

Conversion:

The time spent steaming the pinas converts their starches into sugars. In order to extract the sugars, the pinas are crushed, releasing the juices called "aguamiel" or honey water. Yeast is then added to the solution, and the mixture is double distilled (eliminating the "heads and tales" or impurities). The resulting product is a 150 proof clear white tequila.

Depending upon the type of tequila being created, the final phase differs. In order to make white tequila (known as silver or blanco), the liquid must be married with demineralized water for 30 days. Other kinds of tequilas include reposado and añejo. These are all made from tequila that has been aged in oak barrels for varying amounts of time. The amount of time spent aging determines the color, taste, identification and name. Reposado is Spanish for "rested," and tequilas that carry this label have been aged for a minimum of 2 months. Añejo, meaning "aged," is used to describe tequila that has been aged for at least one year. These tequilas are gold in color.

BRAND	CREDENTIALS	USAGE
Cuervo White	White tequila; clean, crisp, smooth tequila taste	Substitute for other traditional white spirit drinks—Bloody Maria, Tequila Sunrise or with fruit juices or tonic; also great for margaritas
Cuervo Gold	World's most popular and largest-selling tequila	Ideal for margaritas or shots
Jose Cuervo Margarita Mix	The #1 margarita mix—out-selling all other margarita mixes combined	Triple sec and sweet and sour flavorings, specially blended to compliment Jose Cuervo tequilas for the perfect margarita, 3 parts mix to 1 part tequila
1800 Reposado	A blend of reposado and añejo tequilas	Perfect for the ultimate margarita or shots
Jose Cuervo Tradicional	Clean, 100% blue Agave reposado tequila	Ideal chilled straight or with a splash of lime or orange liqueur
1800 Añejo	A 100% blue Agave añejo tequila	Perfect for straight consumption
Jose Cuervo Reserva de la Familia	The most sought after tequila in the world. Multi-year old, 100% blue Agave aged in new oak barrels	Ideal for sipping or with your favorite cigar

For additional recipes, visit our website at http://www.cuervo.com

18 CARAT GOLD

½ oz. 1800 REPOSADO

½ oz. Goldschlager

Combine ingredients in a shot glass.

1800 BITE THE BERRY

1¼ oz. 1800 REPOSADO

½ oz. Hiram Walker Triple Sec

¼ oz. Chambord

2 oz. Cranberry Juice

Combine over ice in rocks glass. Garnish with orange slice.

1800 BLOODY MARIA

1½ oz. 1800 REPOSADO

6 oz. Major Peters' Bloody Mary

Chilled Lime Wedge

Place ice cubes in a large wine glass and add tequila. Fill glass with Bloody Mary. Stir and garnish with lime wedge.

1800 CELEBRATION

½ oz. 1800 REPOSADO

Fill glass with champagne.

1800 LEMON DROP

1¼ oz. 1800 REPOSADO

½ oz. Hiram Walker Triple Sec

1 oz. Major Peters' Sweet & Sour Mix

1 oz. Lemon Lime Soda

squeeze of Fresh Lemon Float

Pour ingredients over ice in rocks glass. Mix. Add fresh lemon juice float. Garnish with fresh lemon.

1800 ULTIMATE MARGARITA

1½ oz. 1800 REPOSADO

2 oz. Major Peters' Sweet & Sour Mix

splash Cointreau

Frozen or on the rocks. The ultimate taste.

1800 SUNSET

1 oz. 1800 REPOSADO

glass Champagne

splash Major Peters' Grenadine

ALMOND PEACH MARGARITA

1¼ oz. 1800 REPOSADO

2½ oz. Major Peters' Sweet & Sour Mix

½ oz. Hiram Walker Peach Schnapps

½ oz. Fresh Lime Juice

In shaker combine all ingredients with ice. Pour into stemmed glass. Garnish with a lime wedge.

ARIBA

1½ oz. CUERVO GOLD

3 oz. Orange Juice

¼ oz. Grand Marnier

Mix orange juice and Cuervo Gold in a tall glass with ice. Float Grand Marnier on top.

AZTEC RUIN

1 part JOSE CUERVO TRADICIONAL

1 part Major Peters' Lime Juice

Either as a chilled shot or in a martini glass.

AZTEC STINGER

2 oz. CUERVO GOLD

¼ oz. Hiram Walker White Creme de Menthe

Shake. Serve up or on the rocks.

BLUE AGAVE

1 oz. JOSE CUERVO TRADICIONAL

1 oz. Hiram Walker Blue Curacao

Shake, strain and serve.

BLUE MOON-A-RITA

1½ oz. CUERVO WHITE

½ oz. Hiram Walker Blue Curacao

½ oz. Hiram Walker Triple Sec

1½ oz. Major Peters' Lime Juice

Serve on the rocks.

CHERRY BOMB

1½ oz. JOSE CUERVO TRADICIONAL

2 oz. Cherry Juice

½ oz. Hiram Walker Cherry Liqueur

Strain and serve.

CUERVO ACAPULCO FIZZ

1½ oz. CUERVO GOLD

1½ oz. Cream

2 oz. Orange Juice

3 Ice Cubes

2 tsp. Granulated Sugar

2 dashes Orange Bitters

1 whole Egg

Blend all ingredients together. Pour into a highball glass. Garnish with orange slice.

CUERVO AGUA FRESCA

1 cup Water

2 Tbs. Superfine Sugar

⅓ cup Cubed Fresh Pineapple

⅓ cup Fresh or frozen Whole Strawberries

⅓ cup Fresh or frozen cubed or Ripe Mango

2 sprigs Fresh Mint

½ cup Ice (3 oz.)

1 Tbs. Fresh Lime Juice

In blender combine all drink ingredients. Blend until smooth. Strain into pitcher. Chill. Makes about 8 drinks. For each serving: in 13 oz. hurricane glass, place about ½ cup ice. Add 1½ oz. Cuervo Gold. Fill glass with Agua Fresca mixture, about 5 oz. Garnish with strawberry and straw.

CUERVO BAJA GOLD

2 oz. CUERVO GOLD

1½ oz. Simple Syrup

¾ oz. Fresh Lime Juice

¾ cup Ice

4 oz. Chilled Beer

Blend in blender until smooth. Pour into chilled mug. Top with beer. Lime garnish.

CUERVO BRAVE BULL

1½ oz. CUERVO WHITE

1½ oz. Hiram Walker Coffee Liqueur

Combine ingredients in rocks glass with ice. Garnish with a lemon twist.

CUERVO CACTUS COOLER

1½ oz. CUERVO GOLD

½ oz. Hiram Walker Peppermint Schnapps

Club Soda

Pour Cuervo Gold and club soda over rocks in a tall glass. Top with Peppermint Schnapps and lime wheel garnish.

CUERVO CARAMBA!

1½ oz. CUERVO WHITE

3 oz. Grapefruit Juice

1 Tbs. Sugar

Club Soda

Shake all ingredients, except club soda, with well-cracked ice. Add club soda, serve in highball glass.

CUERVO CHILI COCKTAIL

2 oz. CUERVO GOLD

3 dashes Tabasco

Serve in a shot glass.

CUERVO CRANDADDY

1 oz. CUERVO GOLD

1 oz. Hiram Walker
Triple Sec

5 oz. Cranberry Juice

Fill large glass with ice. Stir.

CUERVO GOLD MARGARITA

1½ oz. CUERVO GOLD

1 oz. Hiram Walker
Triple Sec

2 oz. Major Peters'
Lime Juice

2 oz. Major Peters'
Sweet & Sour Mix

Blend ingredients with ice and pour into a margarita glass over ice or frozen.

CUERVO GOLDEN BREEZE

1½ oz. CUERVO GOLD

4 oz. Grapefruit Juice

2 oz. Cranberry Juice

squeeze Fresh Lime

Pour Cuervo over 12-13 oz. glass. Add juices, stir and drop lime in glass.

CUERVO LOLITA

1½ oz. CUERVO GOLD

1 tsp. Honey

Juice of One Lime

dash Bitters

Combine all ingredients in cocktail shaker with ice. Pour into cocktail glass.

CUERVO MACARENA

Start with a shaker and add the following:

1 oz. CUERVO GOLD

½ oz. Coconut Rum

3 oz. Jose Cuervo
Margarita Mix

Equal parts: Pineapple &
Orange Juice

Top with splash of Cranberry Juice. Shake and pour over ice into a 16 oz. tumbler. Garnish with pineapple, orange and a cherry.

CUERVO MARGARITA COOLER

1 oz. CUERVO GOLD
½ oz. Hiram Walker Triple Sec
4 oz. Club Soda
1 oz. Pineapple Juice
1 oz. Major Peters' Lime Juice
1 oz. Jose Cuervo Margarita Mix

Combine in tall glass over ice. Drop lime wedge in glass.

CUERVO MEXICAN COFFEE

1 oz. 1800 REPOSADO
¾ oz. Kahlua Coffee Liqueur
fill Fresh Hot Coffee

Add Cuervo 1800 and Kahlua Coffee Liqueur to mug of fresh, hot coffee. Top with whipped cream.

CUERVO MOCHA MELT

1 oz. CUERVO GOLD
5 oz. Fresh, strong hot coffee
1 envelope (single serving) Hot Cocoa Mix
½ oz. Coffee Brandy

In a mug, combine coffee and hot cocoa mix. Mix in Cuervo Gold and Coffee Brandy. Top with whipped cream.

CUERVO PINATA

1½ oz. CUERVO GOLD
5 oz. Pineapple Juice

Fill tall glass with ice. Pour Cuervo and juice. Garnish with fresh pineapple.

CUERVO RASPBERRY MARGARITA

1½ oz. CUERVO GOLD
1 oz. Hiram Walker Triple Sec
1 oz. Major Peters' Lime Juice
½ cup Raspberries (frozen)
Garnish Raspberries (fresh)

In blender combine ½ cup ice with ingredients. Blend until frothy.

CUERVO SANTA FE MAGGIE

1¼ oz. CUERVO GOLD
½ oz. Hiram Walker Triple Sec
2 oz. Major Peters' Sweet & Sour Mix
2 oz. Cranberry Juice

Blend ingredients briefly with ice and pour into unsalted margarita glass. Squeeze in lime wedge and drop into glass.

CUERVO SIDE OUT

1½ oz. CUERVO GOLD

1 oz. Hiram Walker
Triple Sec

2 oz. Cranberry Juice

1½ oz. Major Peters'
Lime Juice

Blend all ingredients with crushed ice and strain into large margarita glass. Lime wheel for garnish.

CUERVO SLAMMER

½ oz. CUERVO GOLD

1 oz. Sprite

Serve as a shot.

CUERVO SPIKE

1½ oz. CUERVO GOLD

fill Grapefruit juice

Ice Cubes

Pour "The Gold" over ice in a tall glass, add grapefruit juice, stir and serve.

CUERVO SUNBURN

1½ oz. CUERVO GOLD

1½ oz. Cranberry Juice

1½ oz. Pineapple Juice

1½ oz. Freshly Squeezed
Orange Juice

Shake drink ingredients with ½ cup ice. In 13 oz. balloon glass place ½ cup ice. Strain drink over ice. Garnish with orange wedge and maraschino cherry.

CUERVO SUNRISE

1¼ oz. CUERVO GOLD

1½ oz. Orange Juice

2 dashes Major Peters'
Lime Juice

Serve on the rocks.

CUERVO-RITA

1¼ oz. 1800 REPOSADO

½ oz. Hiram Walker
Triple Sec

3 oz. Pineapple Juice

2 oz. Cream of Coconut

1 oz. Jose Cuervo
Margarita Mix

Serve blended and garnished with fresh pineapple.

DOUBLE GOLD MEDALS

½ oz. CUERVO GOLD

½ oz. Goldwasser

Combine ingredients in a shot glass.

DURANGO DROP

1½ oz. CUERVO GOLD

½ oz. Lemon Juice

Serve in a sugar-coated rimmed shot glass.

FUZZY RITA

1½ oz. CUERVO GOLD

½ oz. Hiram Walker Peach Liqueur

½ oz. Hiram Walker Triple Sec

2 dashes Major Peters' Lime Juice

Serve on the rocks.

GOLDEN EYE

1½ oz. CUERVO GOLD

½ oz. Hiram Walker Peppermint Schnapps

Serve on the rocks or straight up.

GOLDEN IGUANA

1½ oz. CUERVO GOLD

1½ oz. Pineapple Juice

1½ oz. Orange Juice

Pour ingredients over ice and stir.

GOLDDIGGER

1½ oz. CUERVO GOLD

½ oz. Hiram Walker Triple Sec

dash Major Peters' Grenadine

½ oz. Major Peters' Lime Juice

Shake with ice and serve on the rocks or as a shot.

GREEN IGUANA MARGARITA

½ oz. 1800 REPOSADO

1 oz. Midori Melon Liqueur

2 oz. Major Peters' Sweet & Sour Mix

Blend all ingredients with cracked ice and serve in a chilled margarita glass with a salted rim.

IN CUERVOGUE

2 oz. CUERVO GOLD

1 Maraschino Cherry

Serve in a brandy snifter with a cherry.

INOCULATION SHOT

1 oz. CUERVO GOLD

1 oz. Hiram Walker Blue Curacao

Serve in a shot glass.

JOSE & PEPE

½ part CUERVO GOLD

½ part Chambord

Serve in a shot glass.

JUNGLE JUICE

1½ oz. CUERVO GOLD

1½ oz. Pineapple Juice

1½ oz. Cranberry Juice

1½ oz. Freshly Squeezed
        Orange Juice

splash Lemon-Lime Soda

*Blend with ice. Pour in tall
glass with ice.*

LA BOMBA

1¼ oz. CUERVO 1800
        REPOSADO

¾ oz. Hiram Walker
        Triple Sec

1½ oz. Pineapple Juice

1½ oz. Orange Juice

2 dashes Major Peters' Grenadine

*Coat glass rim with sugar.
Shake until slushy and frothy.
Serve in salt-rimmed glass.
Garnish with a lime wheel.*

LA JOLLARITA

1½ oz. JOSE CUERVO
        TRADICIONAL

½ oz. Hiram Walker
        Triple Sec

½ oz. Chambord

Shake, strained, served.

LA SENORITA

1½ oz. CUERVO WHITE

½ oz. Hiram Walker
        Strawberry Liqueur

½ oz. Hiram Walker
        Triple Sec

1½ oz. Major Peters'
        Lime Juice

Strawberry for garnish.

LIZARD JUICE

½ oz. CUERVO GOLD

½ oz. Pineapple Juice

½ oz. Freshly Squeezed
        Orange Juice

float Hiram Walker
        Blue Curacao

*Combine all ingredients in
rocks glass with ice, except
Blue Curacao. Add Blue
Curacao float. Garnish with
orange slice.*

LOW RIDER

1½ oz. CUERVO GOLD

½ oz. Hiram Walker
        Triple Sec

splash Cranberry Juice

Shake and serve in a shot glass.

217

MACARENA PUNCH

1 oz. CUERVO GOLD
1 oz. Malibu Rum
       Cranberry Juice
       Pineapple Juice
       Major Peters'
       Sweet & Sour Mix

Serve in tall glass over ice.

MERRY WIDOW

1 oz. CUERVO GOLD
3 oz. Champagne
splash Orange Juice

Serve in a champagne glass with an orange wheel garnish.

MEXICAN MARTINI

fill JOSE CUERVO
      TRADICIONAL
splash Cointreau

Serve iced in a martini glass.

PINK CAD

1½ oz. 1800 REPOSADO
½ oz. Hiram Walker
       Triple Sec
4 oz. Jose Cuervo
       Margarita Mix
½ oz. Grand Marnier
1 oz. Fresh Lime Juice

Pour Cuervo 1800 over ice. Add Triple Sec, margarita mix, Grand Marnier and fresh juice. Stir gently and serve.

RED PEPPER

1½ oz. CUERVO GOLD
½ oz. Orange Juice
½ oz. Cranberry Juice

Shake with ice. Serve in a shot glass.

SOUTHERN TRADITION MARGARITA

1½ oz. JOSE CUERVO
        TRADICIONAL
⅝ oz. Southern Comfort
5 oz. Major Peters' Sweet
       & Sour Mix
½ oz. Fresh Orange Juice

Shake with ice and serve.

SUNSTROKE

1¾ oz. CUERVO WHITE
¼ oz. Hiram Walker
       Triple Sec
½ oz. Major Peters'
       Lime Juice
2 oz. Pineapple Juice

Serve on the rocks.

THE ULTIMATE SHOT

½ oz. 1800 REPOSADO
½ oz. Grand Marnier

Serve in a shot glass.

TEQUIL O'NEIL

1¼ oz. CUERVO GOLD

¼ oz. Orange Juice

⅛ oz. Club Soda

Serve in shot glass covered with basketball-type coaster and slam.

TIJUANA TEA

1½ oz. 1800 REPOSADO

¾ oz. Hiram Walker Triple Sec

1 oz. Jose Cuervo Margarita Mix

3 oz. Cola

TNT (CUERVO GOLD Tequila 'N Tonic)

1½ oz. CUERVO GOLD

4 oz. Tonic Water

splash Major Peters' Lime Juice

In 10 oz. footed highball glass, add ½ cup (3 oz.) ice. Pour in Cuervo Gold and tonic. Mix in lime juice. Garnish with lime.

UNTAMED MARGARITA

1 oz. CUERVO GOLD

½ oz. Hiram Walker Triple Sec

½ oz. Fresh Lime Juice

2½ oz. Major Peters' Sweet & Sour Mix

float Hiram Walker Blue Curacao

Combine all ingredients, except Curacao, in shaker with ice. Add Blue Curacao float. Garnish with lime slice and maraschino cherry.

YELLOW DEVIL MARGARITA

1½ oz. CUERVO WHITE

¾ oz. Hiram Walker Triple Sec

3 oz. Major Peters' Sweet & Sour Mix

¼ oz. Galliano

Serve on the rocks.

Add your favorite Cuervo recipes here.

© Foley Publishing Corp

CUTTY SARK

SCOTS WHISKY

On the 23rd of March 1923, at a luncheon in the pine-paneled parlour of their early 18th century premises at 3 St. James's Street, London, the partners of Wine and Spirit Merchants Berry Bros. were discussing the launch of a new Scots Whisky. A family-run business and Royal Warrant holders, Berry's had been established at No. 3 since the 1690s. Francis Berry, the senior partner, had a strong preference for whiskies which were naturally light in colour. He insisted that only the very finest of Scotland's classic malt whiskies should be selected for the new blend and that the whisky should be naturally light in colour. The partners' lunch guest that day was James McBey, a well-known Scottish artist. All the new Scots whisky lacked was a name and a symbol. At the time the famous clipper ship "Cutty Sark" was much in the news as she had just returned to England after many years' sailing under the Portuguese flag. McBey, who was a keen sailor, suggested that this would be an admirable name for the new whisky.

The name "Cutty Sark" was an inspired choice for a Scots Whisky. It was the name of the most famous and fastest of all the Scottish-built clipper ships. Appropriate too, for nothing could seem more Scottish, the name being taken from Robbie Burns' poem "Tam O'Shanter." (Cutty Sark means short shirt in the old Scots language.) McBey also volunteered to design the label which remains today almost exactly as he originally drew it, even to the hand-drawn lettering and the use of the correct descriptive word "Scots" rather than the more common "Scotch." Only the colour of the label is different. McBey had suggested a creamy shade to imply age. The printers, by accident, used a bright yellow so striking in its effect that the partners decided to keep it.

The Story Behind the Name "Cutty Sark"

The origins of the name "Cutty Sark" lie deep in Scottish folklore. The epic poem "Tam O'Shanter" by Robert Burns, Scotland's famous eighteenth century poet tells the story in verse.

A farmer named Tam (or Thomas) was riding his grey mare home late one stormy night after a hard evening's drinking with friends. As he was nearing Alloway churchyard he heard the wailing of bagpipes so reined his horse for a closer look.

To his astonishment he saw a group of ugly, old witches dancing frenziedly. He was just about to move on when a young beautiful witch emerged from the shadows of the tombs, scantily dressed in a "Cutty Sark" or short shirt. As her dancing became wilder and more abandoned, he involuntarily cried out "Weel done, Cutty-sark!"

There was a flash of lightning followed by pitch darkness. Terrified, Tam spurred his stubborn mare and fled for his life, hotly pursued by the beautiful young witch. Miraculously he remembered that witches cannot cross running water, so made straight for the nearby bridge. Just as he reached it the young witch reached out and grabbed the tail of the mare, which came clean off in her hand.

That is why years later in 1869 when the sleek clipper ship was launched in Scotland, her owners named her "Cutty Sark" after Burns' fleet-footed witch and placed a figurehead of the witch with outstretched arm on the clipper's bow. In her racing days, after a fast passage, the apprentices would sometimes make a mare's tail from old rope, teased out and rubbed with grey paint to put in the figurehead's hand.

The Clipper Ship "Cutty Sark"

Of the hundreds of majestic clipper ships which used to

cross the oceans of the world during the golden age of sail in the nineteenth century, only the "Cutty Sark" remains.

"Cutty Sark," built in Dumbarton, Scotland in 1869 was named after the fleet-footed young witch in the poem "Tam O'Shanter" by Scotland's famous eighteenth century poet Robert Burns.

Built for speed, "Cutty Sark" began her career in the China Tea trade when the first clipper reaching London with each season's new crop received the highest prices for her cargo. She also raced against her great rivals to bring the season's first wool home from Australia, braving the mountainous seas of the "roaring forties." The fastest clipper ship of her time, "Cutty Sark" was to make many memorable voyages and to this day she still holds the record for the run from Australia to England of 69 days in 1887. During her career she also made several voyages to the U.S.A. bringing wool from Australia to New York in 1880, and jute from the Philippines in 1881.

In 1922, at the end of an illustrious career, she was purchased by a retired English sea captain who devoted much time and money to re-rigging and lovingly restoring her. During the late 1930s and 1940s she became a Merchant Navy training vessel. Later funds were raised and a trust established for "Cutty Sark" to be preserved in dry dock in Greenwich, London. In 1957, she was opened to the public by Her Majesty The Queen and has now become one of London's major tourist attractions visited by half a million people each year.

Definition of a Blended Scotch Whisky

A blended Scotch whisky is a mixture of grain and malt Scotch whisky. The grain and malt whiskies must be distilled, matured in cask for a minimum of 3 years and blended in Scotland.

There are hundreds of blended Scotch whiskies. Each different blend is made from its own secret recipe. Grain whisky will form the base of a blend and will be mixed with malts from some or all of the malt whisky distilling regions: Lowland, Highland, Speyside, and Islay.

The Cutty Sark Blend

A great deal of time and care is given to the meticulous selection of malt and grain whiskies for the Cutty Sark blend. Cutty Sark is a whisky blend created by fine wine merchants, established in 17th century, who pride themselves in the superlative quality of all the products they offer.

Since the Cutty Sark blend was created in the early 1920s the partners and directors have insisted that only whiskies from Scotland's best distilleries are tasted and selected for Cutty Sark as we have always proudly stated on the label.

Unlike most of our competitors Cutty Sark is independently owned so is free to choose only those whiskies considered to be of exceptional quality. The basis of the Cutty Sark blend is a high proportion of the finest, old, Speyside Malts from famous distilleries such as Glenrothes. All the malt whiskies chosen for the Cutty Sark blend are carefully selected for their fragrant *individual/special qualities.*

All the malt whiskies destined for the Cutty Sark blend are gently matured in the pure air and cool damp cellars that only The Highlands and Islands of Scotland can offer. These malts are aged for up to 12 years, sometimes even longer depending upon the time needed for each individual cask to reach the peak of maturity.

This quiet, slow maturation in American oak casks and Spanish Sherry casks, greatly contributes to the delicate, elegant character of Cutty Sark. Each cask chosen for maturing Cutty Sark whiskies is individually selected too.

Fino sherry casks give a fine and more delicate colour and character to the whisky and American oak a subtle hint of wood after many years.

"Marrying"

When the individual whiskies selected for the Cutty Sark blend have reached maturity they are blended together in a large vat (vatted) and returned to oak casks for a second period of maturation known as "marrying." The Cutty Sark blend is returned to oak casks and "married" for up to 9 months. Marrying allows the malt and grain whiskies within the blend to harmonize and develop a smoother more balanced taste. Only outstanding blends enjoy this final period of togetherness to achieve perfection.

After marrying Cutty Sark has a pale natural colour drawn from the casks in which it has matured. No coloring is added except for the minimum which is sometimes needed to maintain consistency from bottle to bottle.

Many other brands are a much deeper colour as they may have caramel added to their blends.

Every cask destined for the Cutty Sark blend is checked for quality before blending. The blender will reject any casks which do not reach the high standard required or which have been exhausted by maturation. By the time Cutty Sark is bottled each whisky in the blend will have been nosed by an expert at least 6 times. Only the finest whiskies are accepted.

Cutty Sark has a unique character which differentiates it from all other Scotch whiskies. Cutty Sark is naturally light in colour, with a delicate fragrant nose, smooth, long satisfying flavor and crisp taste.

For additional recipes, visit our website at
http://www.cutty-sark.co.uk

ABERDEEN SOUR

1½ oz. CUTTY SARK
1 oz. Orange Juice
1 oz. Lemon Juice
½ oz. Hiram Walker
     Triple Sec
1 scoop Crushed Ice

Shake or blend. Pour into an old-fashioned glass.

AFFINITY

1 oz. CUTTY SARK
½ oz. Martini & Rossi
     Sweet Vermouth
½ oz. Martini & Rossi
     Dry Vermouth
2 dashes Orange Bitters

Stir well. Strain into a cocktail glass.

BANNOCK-BURN

1 measure CUTTY
     SARK (Scottish Spirit)
     Tomato Juice
     (English Blood)
dash Worcestershire Sauce
slice Lemon
     Ice

Shake and let them fight it out to the finish.

BARBARY COAST

½ oz. CUTTY SARK
½ oz. Beefeater Dry Gin
½ oz. Hiram Walker
     White Creme de
     Cacao
½ oz. Heavy Cream

Blend. Pour into cocktail glass.

BLACK JACK

1 oz. CUTTY SARK
½ oz. Kahlua
½ oz. Hiram Walker
     Triple Sec
½ oz. Lemon Juice

In a shaker half-filled with ice, combine all ingredients. Shake well. Strain into a cocktail glass.

BLIMEY

1½ oz. CUTTY SARK
½ oz. Major Peters' Lime
     Juice
1½ tsp. Superfine Sugar

In a shaker half filled with ice, combine all ingredients. Shake well. Strain into a cocktail glass.

BLINDER

1½ oz. CUTTY SARK

4 oz. Grapefruit Juice

dash Major Peters' Grenadine

Pour the Cutty Sark and grapefruit juice into a highball glass filled with ice. Drop the grenadine into the drink.

BOBBY BURNS

1 oz. CUTTY SARK

¼ oz. Martini & Rossi Sweet Vermouth

3 dashes Benedictine

Stir and serve.

CELTIC MIX COCKTAIL

1 oz. CUTTY SARK

½ oz. Tullamore Dew

½ oz. Lemon Juice

1 dash Bitters

Shake. Strain into a cocktail glass.

CUTTY CARIBBEAN

1 oz. CUTTY SARK

½ oz. CocoRhum

½ oz. Hiram Walker Blue Curacao

Shake well. Pour into cocktail glass; garnish with lemon slice and two straws.

CUTTY CLIPPER

1 oz. CUTTY SARK

1 oz. Hiram Walker Creme de Cacao

1 oz. Cream

Add to ice in shaker and shake well. Pour into cocktail glass, add a dash of Major Peters' Grenadine; garnish with orange and add two straws.

CUTTY COLLINS

2 oz. CUTTY SARK

5-6 dashes Lemon Juice

2-3 lumps Ice

Pour into a large glass with ice and fill with soda.

CUTTY COOLER

Equal parts:

CUTTY SARK

Hiram Walker Creme de Noyaux

Over ice. Fill with half pineapple, half orange juice and splash of Major Peters' Sweet & Sour Mix.

CUTTY CROWS NEST

1 oz. CUTTY SARK

1 oz. Stones Ginger
Wine

1 oz. Tia Maria

Add to ice in shaker. Shake
well, pour into cocktail glass.
Float layer of cream on top
and sprinkle with grated
chocolate.

CUTTY LIFESAVER

1 oz. CUTTY SARK

1 oz. Galliano

squeeze Lime

dash Fresh Cream

Add to ice in shaker. Shake
thoroughly, pour into long
glass and top with orange juice
and mint leave garnish.

CUTTY MIZZEN

1 oz. CUTTY SARK

½ oz. Martini & Rossi
Dry Vermouth

½ oz. Midori Melon
Liqueur

dash Hiram Walker
Blue Curacao

Stir with ice in tall glass. Pour
into cocktail glass.

CUTTY OCEAN

Add 1 oz. Galliano,
1 oz. CUTTY SARK to ice and
stir in tall glass; pour into cocktail glass and using a straw like
a pipette, drop a dash of Blue
Curacao through the center of
the drink to rest at the bottom
of the glass. Ice, Creme de
Almond, Pineapple Juice,
Orange Juice, Major Peters'
Sweet & Sour Mix.

CUTTY SARK SOUR

1½ oz. CUTTY SARK

3 oz. Major Peters'
Sweet & Sour Mix

Shake with sour mix over ice.
Top with club soda.

CUTTY SIDECAR

1 oz. CUTTY SARK

¼ oz. Hiram Walker
Triple Sec

¾ oz. Sweetened Lemon
Juice

Shake and serve in cocktail
glass with sugar rim.

CUTTY SQUARE RIGGER

1 oz. CUTTY SARK

½ oz. Martini & Rossi Dry Vermouth

dash Major Peters' Lime Juice

Add to ice in shaker. Stir and pour into glass. Top with ginger ale.

CUTTY SURFER

1 oz. CUTTY SARK

½ oz. Hiram Walker Orange Curacao

½ oz. Hiram Walker Blue Curacao

Add to ice in shaker. After shaking, top with soda water, orange slice and green cherry garnish.

DERBY FIZZ

1 oz. CUTTY SARK

5 dashes Lemon Juice

1 tsp. Powdered Sugar

1 Egg

3 dashes Hiram Walker Curacao

Club Soda

Stir. Pour into a tall glass over ice.

DUDE

1 oz. CUTTY SARK

dash Major Peters' Grenadine

½ oz. Harvey's Bristol Cream

Build in rocks glass with ice. Float Harvey's.

EARTHQUAKE

⅓ CUTTY SARK

⅓ Beefeater Dry Gin

⅓ Romana Sambuca

Shake, serve in a rocks glass over ice.

FLYING SCOTSMAN

3 measures CUTTY SARK

2½ measures Martini & Rossi Dry Vermouth

1 Tbs. Angostura Bitters

1 Tbs. Sugar Syrup

Shake, serve in a rocks glass over ice.

GALE WARNING

1 oz. CUTTY SARK

3 oz. Pineapple Juice

2 oz. Cranberry Juice

Serve over ice in tall glass.

GODFATHER

2 parts CUTTY SARK

2 parts Hiram Walker
Amaretto

Stir on the rocks.

GRAND MASTER

2 oz. CUTTY SARK

½ oz. Hiram Walker
Peppermint
Schnapps

3 oz. Club Soda

1 Lemon Twist

*Stir well. Garnish with the
lemon twist.*

GREEN MIST

1 oz. CUTTY SARK

1 oz. Hiram Walker Green
Creme de Menthe

½ oz. Lemon Juice

*Shake the ingredients, strain
into cocktail glass. Garnish with
slice of kiwi and sprig of mint.*

HEATHCLIFF

1 oz. CUTTY SARK

1 oz. Calvados

½ oz. Beefeater Dry Gin

1 tsp. Heather Honey or
Sugar Syrup

1 scoop Crushed Ice

*Shake. Strain into cocktail
glass.*

HEATHER COFFEE

1 oz. CUTTY SARK

¼ oz. Drambuie

Coffee

*Fill mug with coffee; top with
whipped cream.*

HIGHLAND FLING

2 oz. CUTTY SARK

½ oz. Martini & Rossi
Sweet Vermouth

2 dashes Orange Bitters

1 Maraschino Cherry

*Stir. Strain into cocktail glass.
Garnish with cherry.*

INTERNATIONAL STINGER

1 oz. CUTTY SARK

¼ oz. Hiram Walker
Peppermint
Schnapps

*Serve chilled in a Manhattan
glass.*

LASER DISK

½ oz. CUTTY SARK

½ oz. Drambuie

½ oz. Lemonade

Shake. Serve in shot glass.

MAMIE TAYLOR

1¼ oz. CUTTY SARK

¼ oz. Fresh Lime Juice

Ginger Ale

Build in tall glass with ice. Top with ginger ale.

OLD ROB

¾ oz. CUTTY SARK

¾ oz. Martini & Rossi
Sweet Vermouth

¼ tsp. sugar

dash Angostura Bitters

Stir. Serve over rocks.

PERFECT ROB ROY

1¼ oz. CUTTY SARK

¼ oz. Martini & Rossi
Sweet Vermouth

¼ oz. Martini & Rossi
Dry Vermouth

Serve in rocks glass with ice. Garnish with lemon twist.

PIRATE'S DELIGHT

1¼ oz. CUTTY SARK

3 oz. Orange Juice

¼ oz. Kahlua

Mix Cutty Sark and orange juice. Float Kahlua.

PURPLE HEATHER

1 measure CUTTY SARK

1 tsp. Hiram Walker
Creme de Cassis

Ice

Pour into a tall glass and top up with club soda.

REAL MCCOY

2 oz. CUTTY SARK

3 oz. Water or Club Soda

Serve in a tall glass.

ROB ROY

Equal measure:

2 oz. CUTTY SARK

½ oz. Martini & Rossi
Sweet Vermouth

dash Angostura Bitters

RUSTY NAIL

1½ oz. CUTTY SARK

½ oz. Drambuie

Serve on the rocks.

SCARLET SCHOONER

2 oz. CUTTY SARK

1 oz. Hiram Walker
Peach Schnapps

2 oz. Cranberry Juice

Stir in tall glass with ice.

SCOTCH COLLINS

2 oz. CUTTY SARK

1½ oz. Major Peters'
Sweet & Sour Mix

7-Up

Serve in tall glass with ice.
Garnish with red cherry.

SCOTCH HORSE'S NECK

1 oz. CUTTY SARK

5-6 dashes Lemon Juice

1 dash Angostura Bitters

Pour into a large glass and top
with ginger ale.

SCOTCH RICKEY

2 oz. CUTTY SARK

1 lump Ice

juice Half lime

juice Quarter lemon

Club Soda

Stir. Pour into a tall glass with
ice.

SCOTCH OLD-FASHIONED

2 oz. CUTTY SARK

½ tsp. Sugar

2 dashes Angostura Bitters

splash Soda

Put sugar, bitters, red cherry,
lemon twist, orange slice and
muddle. Add ice and top with
club soda.

SCOTCH TODDY

1½ oz. CUTTY SARK

Hot Water

Sugar

Heap teaspoon sugar in warm
glass; add little boiling water
to dissolve sugar. Add 1 oz.
Cutty Sark and stir. Pour in
more boiling water and top
with ½ oz. more Cutty Sark.

SCOTTY DOG

1¼ oz. CUTTY SARK

1½ oz. Major Peters'
Lime Juice

Shake. Garnish with a slice of lime.

STAIRCASE

1 oz. CUTTY SARK

¼ oz. Martini & Rossi
Dry Vermouth

¼ oz. Martini & Rossi
Sweet Vermouth

¼ oz. Drambuie

Serve in rocks glass with ice.

STARBOARD

1½ oz. CUTTY SARK

1 oz. Grapefruit Juice

½ oz. Martini & Rossi
Dry Vermouth

1 scoop Crushed Ice

Shake. Serve in a chilled old-
fashioned glass.

TARTANTULA

1½ oz. CUTTY SARK

½ oz. Martini & Rossi
Sweet Vermouth

½ oz. Benedictine

1 Lemon Twist

Stir. Strain into a cocktail glass.

TASTE OF HONEY

2 oz. CUTTY SARK

½ oz. Honey

1 oz. Heavy Cream

Blend with ice. Serve in cocktail glass.

ULTIMATE SOUR

2 oz. CUTTY SARK

4 oz. Major Peters'
Sweet & Sour Mix

splash Orange Juice

Shake. Serve in an old-fashioned glass with ice.

WHISPER

Equal measures:

CUTTY SARK

Martini & Rossi
Dry Vermouth

Martini & Rossi
Sweet Vermouth

Over cracked ice.

WOOD-WARD

1½ oz. CUTTY SARK

½ oz. Martini & Rossi Extra
Dry Vermouth

1 oz. Grapefruit Juice

Combine with ice; shake well. Strain into an old-fashioned glass with ice.

Add your favorite Cutty Sark recipes here.

© Foley Publishing Corp

DRAMBUIE

History

The Drambuie that we enjoy today dates back some 250 years to the personal life and times of Prince Charles Edward Stuart. Cultured, proud and charismatic, Bonnie Prince Charlie, as he is more commonly known, was a man inspired by a vision. And his dream?

To restore the Stuart name to the British throne, following his grandfather's deposal around sixty years previously.

Embarking upon a bold campaign, the Prince's initial encounters encouraged a march southwards on the British throne. His place in Scottish folklore, and Drambuie's are immortalised in the tale of his most gallant escapade.

Progressing to within 127 miles of London, news of counter government forces amassing and outnumbering them six to one reached the Scottish encampment. Retreat was imperative.

Only aspirations died in the Midlands that day. But soon the killings started, ending in the slaughter of the Prince's remaining forces in the far North of Scotland, months later.

However, loyal troops and individuals shielded the Prince from his enemies, foiling all attempts at capture, before making good his eventual escape.

Of the faithful, none was as steadfast as Captain John MacKinnon, to whom the Prince gave the recipe for his personal liqueur as a mark of deep respect and genuine affection.

Legend has it that the MacKinnons kept the Prince's recipe in the family for over 150 years, keeping the liqueur solely for their own use. And not until 1906, was widespread appreciation of Drambuie made possible, after Malcolm

MacKinnon had moved from Skye to Edinburgh and forged a career in wines and spirits. He believed in Drambuie's finer qualities, and his quest to produce commercial volumes of the liqueur involved the judicious use of the age old, secret herbal essence, the recipe for which was always kept under lock and key by the family. And the painstaking and meticulous hand production process he employed provided further evidence of the unstinting devotion to quality for which the MacKinnons were already renowned.

Demand for Drambuie increased slowly, but nonetheless surely, in those early days. From Malcolm MacKinnon's initial production of 12 bottles in a fortnight, the company progressed to exporting cases to military regiments and then to expatriate Scots the world over.

Such was the spread of its popularity, that it became the first liqueur to be accepted into the cellars of the Houses of Parliament as well as into the Royal Household at Buckingham Palace. Yet whilst new production facilities were acquired in this period, neither the recipe, ingredients, nor quality of Drambuie were ever compromised. The MacKinnons saw to that.

Creating Drambuie

To this day, the original recipe is known only to the MacKinnons, who remain personally involved in the making of Drambuie. They confirm that there's a base of the finest aged malt whiskies tempered by lighter grain varieties plus their own 'home made' syrup and pure natural honey from a neighboring farm.

They insist that the specialist knowledge of skilled individuals is a crucial ingredient in the liqueur's production, be it in distilling the barley, blending in the cellar or drawing off the actual essence. Speaking of which: what are its secret constituents?

"They are of the very highest quality," is the ever evasive reply.

Now based rurally, eight miles west of Edinburgh in a purpose built liqueur manufacturing plant, Drambuie's production facility combines the best of both worlds. There, the craft of blending and bottling is augmented and enhanced by state of the art equipment, but only in those areas where improvements in overall quality can be attained.

For some things simply cannot be bettered. Like the human ability to 'nose-judge' the quality of Drambuie-suited malts, or the time-honored practice of rinsing out bottles with whisky prior to bottling. And the taste of this, the finest of liqueurs.

Drambuie Worldwide

Savoured today by millions the world over, Drambuie remains the only British liqueur exported to all global markets, which is an apt testament to the brand's quality and a comprehensive endorsement of its truly international appeal.

You'll find it not only in over 100 countries worldwide, but also on the aeroplanes, ships and trains that take you there and in Duty Free outlets prior to the departure.

All this, together with availability on Concorde, QE2 and the Orient Express, provides conclusive proof that Drambuie is undoubtedly a first class traveler.

Whatever the location, no matter the language, Drambuie is acclaimed as the quintessential Scottish liqueur epitomizing quality, refinement and taste.

Enjoying Drambuie

So having witnessed the kind of celebrated company that Drambuie keeps and the varied strata within which it circulates, one might deduce that it mixes well. And you would be right.

Something special in the Drambuie character makes it the perfect partner in classic and contemporary cocktails.

That sophisticated strength and subtlety is singularly superb over cubed or crushed ice and doubly delightful in a 'Rusty Nail'—equal parts Drambuie and your favorite scotch over ice.

Drambuie took its name from the Gaelic phrase "AN DRAM BUIDHEACH", meaning the drink that satisfies.

And it still does today. Throughout the world. No matter how you choose to drink it.

ALARM CLOCK

1 oz. DRAMBUIE
½ oz. Bacardi Dark Rum
½ oz. Canadian Club

Shake with ice and strain.

BACKDRAFT

1 oz. DRAMBUIE
1 oz. Hiram Walker Triple Sec

Serve as a shot.

BANILLA BOAT

1 oz. DRAMBUIE
½ oz. Hiram Walker Creme de Banana
4 oz. Vanilla Ice Cream

Blend until smooth. Serve in a champagne glass. Pour Chambord over top. Garnish with a banana slice and a filbert.

BENT NAIL

½ oz. DRAMBUIE
1½ oz. Canadian Club
1 tsp. Hiram Walker Kirschwasser

Fill mixing glass with ice. Add Canadian Club, Drambuie and Kirsch. Shake. Strain into a cocktail glass.

BLACK TARTAN

¼ oz. DRAMBUIE
1 oz. Cutty Sark
¼ oz. Tullamore Dew
¼ oz. Kahlua

Shake. Serve over rocks.

BONNIE PRINCE

¼ oz. DRAMBUIE
1½ oz. Beefeater Dry Gin
¼ oz. White Wine
Orange Peel

Combine all ingredients, except orange peel, in a cocktail shaker and shake well. Strain into chilled cocktail glass and garnish with orange peel.

BUTTERSCOTCH COLLINS

½ oz. DRAMBUIE
1 tsp. Sugar
Water
1½ oz. Cutty Sark
2 oz. Lemon Juice
1 oz. Soda

Dissolve sugar in water. Pour over ice in collins glass. Add Scotch, Drambuie and lemon juice. Stir, top with soda. Garnish with a cherry and orange slice.

DRAMBUIE AFTER

After dining pour Drambuie into cordial glass and serve neat.

DRAMBUIE COFFEE

Freshly brewed coffee lightly sweetened with the delicious flavor of Drambuie. Serve in a warm glass and top with fresh cream. Equally pleasing when served with hot tea instead of coffee. Satisfying and distinctly different.

DRAMBUIE MIST

Pour Drambuie over shaved ice and add a lemon twist.

DRAMBUIE ON ICE

A generous measure of Drambuie poured over crushed ice. An after dinner delight. Ice actually enhances the flavor!

DRAMBUIE RUSTY NAIL®

Half fill rocks glass with ice, add 1 oz. Drambuie and 1 oz. Cutty Sark Scotch or your own favorite. Stir.

DUNDEE

2 tsp. DRAMBUIE
1½ oz. Beefeater Dry Gin
2 Tbsp. Cutty Sark
1 tsp. Lemon Juice

Fill mixing glass with ice, add Gin, Scotch, Drambuie and lemon juice. Shake, strain into a rocks glass and add ice. Garnish with a cherry and a lemon twist.

ELECTRIC TICKLER

¼ oz. DRAMBUIE
1½ oz. Beefeater Dry Gin
¼ oz. Martini & Rossi Sweet Vermouth
Orange Juice
Club Soda

In a collins glass, shake with ice, strain over ice, fill with soda. Lemon garnish.

GASSER

1 oz. DRAMBUIE
1½ oz. Cutty Sark
1 Tbs. Martini & Rossi Sweet Vermouth
2 dashes Orange Bitters

In an old-fashioned glass, shake with ice, strain over ice. Add orange twist.

GLOWLIGHT

½ oz. DRAMBUIE

1½ oz. Beefeater Dry Gin

½ oz. Jose Cuervo Tequila

1 tsp. Major Peters' Grenadine

½ tsp. Bacardi Rum
Club Soda

2 Cherries

In a collins glass, pour over ice, fill with soda. Add grenadine and cherries. Float rum.

GUNRUNNER

½ oz. DRAMBUIE

½ oz. Cutty Sark

1½ oz. Hiram Walker Amaretto

1 Tbs. Bacardi Gold Rum

In a highball glass, shake with ice, strain over ice.

IGLOO MELTER

½ oz. DRAMBUIE

¾ oz. Canadian Club

¾ oz. Cutty Sark

1 tsp. Lemon Juice

2 drops Major Peters' Lime Juice

In an old-fashioned glass, shake with ice, strain over ice. Add lime juice.

JACK FROST

½ oz. DRAMBUIE

1 oz. Jack Daniel's

2 oz. Orange Juice

2 oz. Major Peters' Sweet & Sour Mix

splash Major Peters' Grenadine

Shake with ice and serve in tall glass.

JOLLY ROGER

½ oz. DRAMBUIE

1½ oz. Bacardi Light Rum

1 oz. Fresh Lime Juice

¼ tsp. Cutty Sark
Sparkling Water

Combine all ingredients, except sparkling water, with cracked ice in a cocktail shaker. Shake well and pour into chilled highball glass. Fill with sparkling water and stir gently.

KILTED BLACK LEPRECHAUN

½ oz. DRAMBUIE

1 oz. Carolans Irish Cream

½ oz. Bacardi Rum

Shake with ice. Strain. Serve as a shot.

KILTLIFTER

1 oz. DRAMBUIE

1 oz. Cutty Sark

splash Major Peters'
Lime Juice

Shake with ice. Serve over rocks.

KNUCKLE-BUSTER (also called Knuckle-Duster)

½ oz. DRAMBUIE

1½ oz. Cutty Sark

1 tsp. Bacardi 151° Rum

In an old-fashioned glass, pour over ice, stir.

LOCH LOMOND

½ oz. DRAMBUIE

1 oz. Cutty Sark

½ oz. Martini & Rossi Dry
Vermouth

1 Lemon Twist

In a mixing glass half filled with ice, combine the Scotch, Drambuie and Vermouth. Stir well. Strain into a cocktail glass. Garnish with the lemon twist.

OLD NICK

½ oz. DRAMBUIE

1½ oz. Canadian Club

½ oz. Orange Juice

½ oz. Lemon Juice

3 dashes Orange Bitters

1 Lemon Twist

1 Maraschino Cherry

In a shaker half filled with ice, combine Canadian Club, Drambuie, orange juice, lemon juice, and bitters. Shake well. Strain into an old-fashioned glass almost filled with ice cubes. Garnish with lemon twist and cherry.

PRINCE EDWARD

½ oz. DRAMBUIE

1 oz. Cutty Sark

½ oz. Lillet Blanc
Orange Slice

Combine all ingredients, except orange slice, with cracked ice in a cocktail shaker. Shake well and pour into chilled old-fashioned glass. Garnish with orange slice.

RASPBERRY DELIGHT

¾ oz. DRAMBUIE
¾ oz. Chambord
½ oz. Kahlua
      Fresh Raspberries
1 scoop Ice Cream
Blend with crushed ice.

SCREAMIN' HUDSON

½ oz. DRAMBUIE
1½ oz. Canadian Club
½ oz. Lemon Juice

In a shaker half filled with ice cubes, combine all of the ingredients. Shake well. Strain into a cocktail glass.

SCARLETT KISS

Mix Drambuie with cranberry juice and serve over ice in a tall glass.

SCOTTISH ICED TEA

One part Drambuie in a tall glass of freshly brewed unsweetened iced tea, garnished with lemon or a sprig of mint. Iced cold, a fantastic idea.

WHISKEY ZIPPER

1 Tbs. DRAMBUIE
2 oz. Canadian Club
½ oz. Maraschino Liqueur
1 tsp. Lemon Juice

In an old-fashioned glass, pour over ice, stir gently. Use Tullamore Dew for Irish Whiskey Zipper.

WIDOWMAKER

½ oz. DRAMBUIE
1 oz. Maker's Mark
½ oz. Cutty Sark
1 oz. Lemon Juice
1 oz. Orange Juice

In an old-fashioned glass, shake with ice, strain over ice.

Add your favorite Drambuie recipes here.

© Foley Publishing Corp

GOLDWASSER

"Der Lachs" the original Danziger Goldwasser is a mysterious blend of 25 herbs, spices and real 22 karat gold flakes. Since 1598, the unparalleled liqueur of choice...A dazzling experience for palate and eye. The original Danziger Goldwasser has been exclusively produced by the house of "Der Lachs" since 1598. Acquire a taste for gold—try Der Lachs Goldwasser straight up, on the rocks or in one of these intriguing mixed drinks.

For additional recipes, visit our website at
http://www.ourniche.com

BERRY GOLDWATER

(Very conservative and mellow)

1 part DER LACHS
GOLDWASSER

1½ parts Echte Kroatzbeere
Blackberry Liqueur

Pour over rocks.

COLD GOLD

1½ oz. DER LACHS
GOLDWASSER
(chilled)

Your favorite beer on the side.

DER LACHS ON
THE ROCKS

1½ oz. DER LACHS
GOLDWASSER

Shake bottle, pour over rocks and enjoy the dazzling experience for palate and eye.

GO FOR THE GOLD

1½ oz. DER LACHS
GOLDWASSER

Serve chilled; 25 herbs, spices and 22 karat gold flakes, the most exquisite liqueur in the world!

GOLD FREEZE

Keep bottle of DER LACHS GOLDWASSER in freezer; enjoy icy shots straight up.

GOLDEN BEE

½ DER LACHS
GOLDWASSER,
chilled

½ Honey Liqueur,
chilled

In a tooter glass, layered. Get Stung!

GOLDEN GIMLET

4 parts DER LACHS
GOLDWASSER

5 parts Major Peters'
Lime Juice

1 part Fresh Lime Juice

Shake ingredients together and pour over ice in a chilled cocktail glass.

GOLDEN KIR

½ part DER LACHS
GOLDWASSER

1 dash Hiram Walker Creme
de Cassis

Dry Champagne

Pour into fluted champagne glass.

GOLDEN SUNSET

1½ oz. DER LACHS
GOLDWASSER

Shake bottle, pour over ice and add a slice of orange. Refreshing!

GOLDFINGER

1½ oz. DER LACHS
GOLDWASSER,
chilled

Chilled and served in a shot glass. Chase down with your favorite beer.

GOLDMINERS DREAM

1 oz. DER LACHS
GOLDWASSER

Shake bottle before using. Pour over a generous helping of chocolate ice cream. Serve with a shovel!

OIL SLICK

¾ oz. DER LACHS
GOLDWASSER

splash Jagermeister

Serve in chilled shot glass. Save the environment and suck up an Oilslick!

Add your favorite Goldwasser recipes here.

© Foley Publishing Corp

HIRAM WALKER
LIQUEURS

Simply stated, a *liqueur* is a very flavorful distilled spirit containing at least 2½% sugar by weight. Two and one half percent by weight is a mild form of sweetening material (about one and a quarter tablespoons in a 750 ml package). Most liqueurs are heavier in sugar content.

There are three elements that make a liqueur great:

First, an outstanding flavor;

Second, long shelf life; and

Finally, stability after the bottle is opened.

Hiram Walker Liqueurs possess these three qualities in such measure that Hiram Walker can proudly claim that they are the finest liqueurs in the world.

The main basic liqueur flavors come from various fruits and/or botanicals. They are gathered from the four corners of the earth and are purchased at such times as they are considered of vintage quality, just as grapes grown in a particular year produce vintage wine.

Hiram Walker has no monopoly on these fruits and botanicals. Therefore, it is through scientific research and constant and exacting quality control that Hiram Walker is able to produce the finest cordials in the world—exquisite flavor, and with stability that maintains the flavor long after the bottle is opened.

In addition to this, Hiram Walker is one of the leading distillers in the field of analytical flavor research. Hiram Walker's purpose in this regard has been to attain liqueur flavors that are identical with the fruits and botanicals at the most succulent periods in their growing cycles and also to keep these flavors intact and free from deterioration once the bottle is opened.

The three major methods used to produce or obtain the flavor for liqueurs are: 1. Infusion; 2. Percolation; 3. Distillation.

DRAWING

The *Infusion* method, very much like making tea, is used primarily for making fruit liqueurs. By this method, the fruit is placed directly into a quantity of spirits and allowed to steep until almost all the flavor, aroma and color has been extracted.

Percolation is a method that compares exactly with the percolating of coffee and is used for making plant liqueurs.

The percolator is a large tank. Spirits are put into the bottom of the tank and the flavoring source, in the form of leaves or herbs, is placed in a basket-like container at the top of the tank. The spirits in the bottom of the tank are then pumped to the top, sprayed over the leaves or herbs, and drip back to the bottom. This percolation process is repeated until all the flavor and aroma has been extracted.

Whereas the brewing of tea or coffee percolating depend on boiling water—infusion and percolation methods of producing flavorings use room temperature spirits. Heat resulting from hot infusion or hot percolation would be harmful to the delicate flavor source.

For most liqueurs, infusion or percolation is only the beginning. After the flavors have been extracted by these methods, the heavily flavored spirits are distilled, resulting in the delicacy of flavor desired by the maker.

The *distillation* method in some instances is used alone. The flavoring source is placed in a still, covered with spirits, and distilled. The distillate carries off the flavor of the various ingredients.

Although there are three major methods of extracting flavor from fruits and botanicals, there is no best way. Research over the years has taught Hiram Walker that the most satisfactory results are obtained only by a careful blend of flavors extracted by one or more of the methods previously mentioned.

Most liqueurs have neutral, tasteless, odorless, high-proof alcohol as their base. The flavor of the finished product comes wholly from the flavoring agents, not from the spirit base. Some liqueurs, however, use brandy, Scotch or Irish Whiskies, bourbon, or even Canadian whisky as a base. In this case, the base will contribute significantly to the taste of the bottled liqueur. Hiram Walker Peppermint Schnapps, for example, has a special "gin-like" base spirit. It has all the delicate background flavors of gin without the dominant juniper berry or orange flavor.

Sweetening syrups are used widely in liqueur making and in many brands they have proved to be an unstable element because they crystallize when the bottle is opened. Hiram Walker's research has improved the methods of making syrups to a point where a water-clear liqueur such as Peppermint Schnapps stays water-clear. No haze or cloudiness will develop in the bottle.

Vastly important to Hiram Walker's flavor-blending of liqueurs are the special tanks and special measuring devices which are employed to measure syrup, water, flavors, spirits, etc. There cannot be any margin of error with these mechanical aids which make certain that only the right proportions of ingredients are used.

Also of extreme importance is the "marrying" or rest period, since some liqueurs require a longer aging time than others. Some producers do not take the necessary time.

Hiram Walker Liqueurs never leave the processing tanks until they have been rested, cured, matured, and found stable as to clarity, bouquet, and taste.

Hiram Walker Liqueurs offer a wide spectrum of flavors. They are served as cocktails and after-dinner drinks, and used in preparing main and side-dishes and desserts. There is something to suit every modern taste, mood and occasion. It is little wonder, therefore, that Hiram Walker is at the forefront of the liqueur business.

PROPER CORDIALS

These Cordial flavors are the essential ingredients for drinks that have remained popular through the years. They are the foundation of "Margaritas," "Grasshoppers," "Brandy Alexanders," and many more. Hiram Walker has built its reputation for quality and great taste with these Cordials. Try them and discover why they have endured the test of time.

Triple Sec

This product is made principally from imported orange peel—the wild Curacao orange and the sweet, aromatic Spanish Valencia.

Triple sec means "triple dry"...three distillations. The orange peel is softened in water, the spirit added, and they are distilled together. There are other complementary flavors in this product, but the exact types and amounts are closely guarded secrets. The extensive curing time, unique production techniques and exclusive flavor blending process, create the intriguing mystery of Triple Sec.

Anisette

Hiram Walker uses only the finest imported anise. Hiram Walker Anisette mixes beautifully with Hiram Walker Blackberry Flavored Brandy to make a "Jelly Bean."

Sloe Gin

Sloe Gin tends to mislead consumers with its name. Although it is made from sloeberries, it is not made from gin. The sloeberry is actually a wild plum and belongs to the same family as the plum and cherry. It is small, cherry size, with a large seed, thin fruit, and very sour. It is primarily used as a flavoring agent. Hiram Walker uses other fruits and supporting flavors to enhance the sloeberry flavor.

Creme de Menthe

Hiram Walker is the standard for true mint flavor. The color is rich, classic mint-green; the flavor balance is pleasant, satisfying, fresh; it is not super-sugary, or excessively sweet.

Mint is one of the most delicate flavors in Cordials. Since the flavor starts evaporating as soon as the mint is picked, the harvesting is quite interesting. A still is moved right into the mint field. The mint is picked and loaded immediately into the still. The oil of mint is collected just like a regular still run. To the oil and other complementary flavors, spearmint is added to give our product a softer, more subtle and delicate flavor.

There is no flavor/aroma difference in the Green and White Menthes.

Creme de Cacao

We have used a special blend of cacao nibs—Brazilian, Venezuelan, African, and Guatemalan. Each is roasted to a different color/flavor level to lend its distinctive quality to our cacao. True Madagascan vanilla adds an appetizing difference—a rich, heady aroma, a smooth velvet taste.

Supporting flavors are married to the vanilla/cacao combination. The final blend is aged to bring out all the distinctive characteristics.

Creme de Banana

Real banana flavor and aroma, with the natural sweetness and color of the fruit. Hiram Walker Creme de Banana makes the best tasting "Banana Daiquiri" you'll ever have.

Creme de Strawberry

Vine-ripened strawberries provide the magnificent taste and aroma. The fresh flavor will stand up in all your favorite mixed drinks.

Creme de Cassis

Imported black currants from France and other selected fruits and berries create this rare pleasure. Add Creme de Cassis to champagne to make a "Royal Kir."

Creme de Noyaux

A distinctive flavor and aroma from the combination of sweet and bitter almonds. Try the recipe for a "Pink Squirrel."

Orange Curacao

The flavor of wild Curacao oranges tamed by the sweet taste of Valencia oranges—the secret ingredient in many Polynesian drinks.

Blue Curacao

Blue Curacao has the same delightful orange flavor as Orange Curacao, with an interesting blue shade to make fun and colorful drinks. Combine Blue Curacao with vodka and pineapple juice for a "Blue Lagoon."

Rock & Rye

An old-time American favorite made with a special blend of aged rye whiskies and fresh fruit juices. A "Rock & Rye Sour" is a flavorful alternative to the common "Whiskey Sour."

Kirschwasser

A unique cherry liqueur made from Oregon and Washington cherries, and crushed cherry pits to add a hint of nut flavor. Tremendous poured over fresh fruit.

Amaretto

All natural flavors make this Amaretto rich in body and outstanding in quality. The combination of sweet and bitter almonds is blended with extracts of selected fruits and aromatic herbs, and enhanced with natural vanilla.

Amaretto & Cognac

Only Hiram Walker has the expertise to combine their Amaretto with fine French cognac to create a perfectly balanced liqueur that brings out the best of both—the sweetness of Amaretto smoothed and sophisticated with the robust character of Cognac.

Chocolate

These Liqueurs are the ultimate in indulgence. Exclusively from Hiram Walker, the taste says it all.

Chocolate Cherry

The combination of imported cacao and vintage crop cherries makes a wonderful after-dinner treat.

Chocolate Mint

This product is made from imported cacao and field-fresh mint. Experience the perfect after-dinner mint.

Hazelnut Liqueur

A distinctive blend of rich, aromatic imported hazelnuts, complemented by the robust character of wild hazelnuts. Other imported natural flavors are skillfully blended to develop this unique flavor.

SCHNAPPS

Schnapps are light, refreshing and full flavored fun! Hiram Walker's exclusive use of a "gin-like" base allows the fullest flavors and freshest taste of any Schnapps you'll ever know.

Schnapps can be enjoyed anytime, anywhere, in any way—as a shot, on the rocks, or in a mixed drink.

Peppermint Schnapps

One secret is the clean oil of peppermint. Hiram Walker uses three distillation processes—heat, vacuum, freeze-dry—to develop our unique flavor.

The spirit base is gin-like...a special distillation of low flavor gin.

Peach Schnapps

This represents a technical breakthrough in flavor development by Hiram Walker craftsmen.

Peach is skillfully blended from twenty-five different peach nectars—some for flavor, some for aroma, some for an incredibly delicate balance of flavor and aroma that has never before been achieved in the industry.

The peach aroma and flavor of this outstanding product are truly memorable—and a Hiram Walker exclusive.

Root Beer Schnapps

This is the Schnapps that is closest to one of America's favorite sodas, with the authentic flavor of old-time root beer. Try the recipe for a "Root Beer Float" found on the bottle for a nostalgic treat.

Cinnamon Schnapps

Here is a unique and crisp Schnapps flavor. Cinnamon Schnapps is great as a spicy addition to any hot or cold drink.

Spearmint Schnapps

An outstanding example of a true, clean, uncluttered Spearmint flavor. There is a richness unrivaled by any other producer.

Apricot Schnapps

Several varieties of tree-ripened apricots contribute to the delicious taste and aroma. These flavors are rounded and complemented by apricot and peach pits.

The lower spirits level and reduced fruit sugar ensure a true, natural apricot flavor unrivaled in the market.

FLAVORED BRANDIES

Our Flavored Brandies reflect the tradition of quality and expertise that has made Hiram Walker the finest Cordial producer over the last fifty years.

Flavored Brandies are usually enjoyed straight, as an after-dinner drink. However, their full body and flavor provide a richer taste in many mixed drinks.

Blackberry Flavored Brandy

Here is one of the finest examples of our Cordial makers' art. Why? Blackberries have a very low flavor and aroma level. To create a rich, distinctive taste requires complementary and supporting ingredients.

Cherries, strawberries, red raspberries and twelve additional flavors support and complement our Blackberry flavor. But, appreciate the balance...you taste only blackberry...the aroma is blackberry.

Apricot Flavored Brandy

Hiram Walker Apricot Flavored Brandy has a unique flavor, unequaled by any other Apricot product on the market. Developing this celebrated flavor is a Hiram Walker exclusive. We use several varieties of tree-ripened apricots. Each variety is used for its special characteristic...robust flavor, body, aroma, sweetness.

Peach Flavored Brandy

A variety of peaches are used for body, aroma and sweetness.

Coffee Flavored Brandy

The aroma and flavor is FRESH ROASTED. Hiram Walker Coffee Brandy is made from a unique blend of international coffees and other imported flavors.

Cherry Flavored Brandy

Only the finest "one-crop-a-year" cherries are used as they provide the richest of cherry flavors.

Ginger Flavored Brandy

The exclusive use of imported ginger from Jamaica and other natural ingredients bring out the wonderful taste of pure ginger.

AFTER DINNER MINT

1½ oz. HIRAM WALKER DARK CREME DE CACAO

½ oz. Carolans Irish Cream

2 drops HIRAM WALKER GREEN CREME DE MENTHE

Layer liquors in the order they are given. Serve in a shooter glass.

AFTER EIGHT

½ oz. HIRAM WALKER GREEN CREME DE MENTHE

½ oz. Kahlua

½ oz. Cream

Layer ingredients in the following order (Kahlua, Green Creme de Menthe, Cream). Serve in a shooter glass.

ALABAMA SLAMMER

1 part HIRAM WALKER AMARETTO

1 part HIRAM WALKER SLOE GIN

1 part Southern Comfort

splash Major Peters' Sweet & Sour Mix

Shake with ice and strain into shooter glass.

ALEXANDER SWISS

1 oz. HIRAM WALKER SWISS CHOCOLATE ALMOND

¾ oz. Courvoisier

1 oz. Cream

Blend with ice cubes. Serve in on-the-rocks glass.

ALMOND JOY SHOOTER

1 oz. HIRAM WALKER AMARETTO

½ oz. HIRAM WALKER DARK CREME DE CACAO

½ oz. Absolut Vodka

½ oz. Cream

Shake with ice. Strain and serve straight up. Serve in cocktail glass.

AMERICAN DREAM

½ oz. HIRAM WALKER AMARETTO

½ oz. HIRAM WALKER DARK CREME DE CACAO

½ oz. HIRAM WALKER HAZELNUT

½ oz. Kahlua

Shake with ice. Strain and serve straight up. Serve in cocktail glass.

APRICOT ALEXANDER

1 oz. HIRAM WALKER APRICOT FLAVORED BRANDY

1 oz. HIRAM WALKER WHITE CREME DE CACAO

4 oz. Vanilla Ice Cream

Mix in blender until smooth. Pour into on-the-rocks glass.

APRICOT SOURBALL

1½ oz. HIRAM WALKER APRICOT FLAVORED BRANDY

Juice of ½ Lemon

Juice of ½ Orange

In an on-the-rocks glass with ice, top with lemon and orange juices.

ATOMIC GREEN

¼ oz. HIRAM WALKER CREME DE BANANA

½ oz. MIDORI

½ oz. HIRAM WALKER PEACH SCHNAPPS

½ oz. Absolut Vodka

1 oz. Cream

Shake with ice. Strain and serve straight up in rocks glass.

BANANARAMA

½ oz. Kahlua

¾ oz. HIRAM WALKER AMARETTO

¾ oz. HIRAM WALKER CREME DE BANANA

½ oz. Cream

Layer liquors in the order given. Float cream on top. Serve in sherry glass.

BANANA SPLIT

1½ oz. HIRAM WALKER SWISS CHOCOLATE ALMOND

½ oz. HIRAM WALKER CREME DE BANANA

3 oz. Cream

Blend with cracked ice and pour into on-the-rocks glass.

BANSHEE

¾ oz. HIRAM WALKER CREME DE BANANA

¾ oz. HIRAM WALKER LIGHT CREME DE CACAO

3 oz. Cream

Blend with crushed ice. Serve in tulip glass.

BARBERRY COAST

1¼ oz. HIRAM WALKER RASPBERRY

1½ oz. Cranberry Juice

½ oz. Grapefruit Juice

Serve over ice in tall glass.

BEACH BUM

1 oz. MIDORI

1 oz. Absolut Vodka

1 oz. Cranberry Juice

Shake with ice. Strain and serve straight up. Serve in cocktail glass.

BEANBERRY

1¼ oz. HIRAM WALKER RASPBERRY

Hot Coffee

In a mug filled with hot coffee. Top with whipped cream.

BELLINI

1 oz. HIRAM WALKER PEACH SCHNAPPS

½ oz. Peach Puree

3 oz. Champagne

Serve in champagne glass.

BERRY BERRY

1¼ oz. HIRAM WALKER RASPBERRY

5 oz. Cranberry Juice

Serve over ice in a tall glass.

BERRY GOOD

1¼ oz. HIRAM WALKER RASPBERRY

4 oz. Club Soda

Serve in a tall glass with ice.

BLACK ANGEL

1½ oz. HIRAM WALKER BLACKBERRY FLAVORED BRANDY

Juice of 1 Lime

Soda

In an on-the-rocks glass packed with ice, add a splash of soda. Garnish with lime wedge.

BLACK PEARL

¼ oz. HIRAM WALKER BLACKBERRY FLAVORED BRANDY

1 oz. HIRAM WALKER PEACH SCHNAPPS

Serve on the rocks.

BLACK TIE

½ oz. HIRAM WALKER AMARETTO

½ oz. Drambuie

½ oz. Cutty Sark Scotch

Layer liquors in the order given. Serve in shooter glass.

BLACKBERRY BRANDY

¾ oz. HIRAM WALKER BLACKBERRY FLA-VORED BRANDY

¾ oz. HIRAM WALKER LIGHT CREME DE CACAO

3 oz. Cream

Frappe with shaved ice and strain into chilled saucer-type champagne glass. Sprinkle with nutmeg.

BLUE LEMONADE

¼ oz. HIRAM WALKER BLUE CURACAO

1¼ oz. Absolut Vodka

1 oz. Major Peters' Sweet & Sour Mix

Shake with ice. Strain and serve straight up. Serve in sherry glass.

BLUEMOON

1¼ oz. HIRAM WALKER BLUE CURACAO

¾ oz. Absolut Vodka

¾ oz. Cream

Layer ingredients in the following order (Blue Curacao, Vodka) float cream. Serve in shooter glass.

BOCCI BALL

¾ oz. HIRAM WALKER AMARETTO

1¼ oz. Absolut Vodka

1 oz. Orange Juice

Shake with ice. Strain and serve straight up. Serve in rocks glass.

BUBBLEGUM

½ oz. HIRAM WALKER CREME DE BANANA

½ oz. MIDORI

½ oz. Absolut Vodka

¼ oz. Major Peters' Grenadine

½ oz. Orange Juice

½ oz. Major Peters' Sweet & Sour Mix

Shake with ice. Strain and serve straight up. Serve in sherry glass.

BURRBERRY

1¼ oz. HIRAM WALKER
RASPBERRY

Hot Chocolate

In a mug filled with hot chocolate.

BUSTED CHERRY

¾ oz. HIRAM WALKER
CHERRY BRANDY

¾ oz. Kahlua

¾ oz. Cream

Layer ingredients in the following order (Kahlua, Cream, Cherry Brandy). Serve in shooter glass.

BUTTERY NIPPLE

¾ oz. HIRAM WALKER
BUTTERSCOTCH

¾ oz. Carolans Irish Cream

Shake with ice. Strain and serve straight up. Serve in rocks glass.

CAFE ITALIA

1½ oz. HIRAM WALKER
AMARETTO &
COGNAC

Fill with coffee. Top with whipped cream.

CHERRY LIFESAVER

¾ oz. HIRAM WALKER
AMARETTO

¾ oz. Absolut Vodka

1 oz. Cranberry Juice

Shake with ice; strain into cocktail glass.

CHOCOLATE BANANA CREAM PIE

¾ oz. HIRAM WALKER
CREME DE BANANA

¾ oz. HIRAM WALKER
CREME DE CACAO

1 oz. Cream

Shake with ice; strain into cocktail glass.

CHOCOLATE MINT CREAM

1½ oz. HIRAM WALKER
CHOCOLATE MINT

2 oz. Milk

Soda

Combine in tall glass filled with ice cubes. Top with soda. Garnish with mint sprig.

CHOCOLATE MINT FREEZE

1¼ oz. HIRAM WALKER CHOCOLATE MINT

4 oz. Vanilla Ice Cream

Combine in blender until smooth. Serve in champagne saucer and garnish with chocolate swirls.

CINNAMON COLA

1½ oz. HIRAM WALKER CINNAMON SCHNAPPS

Cola

In an on-the-rocks glass packed with ice, top with cola. Garnish with lime wedge.

CINNAMON STICK

1 oz. HIRAM WALKER CINNAMON SCHNAPPS

1 oz. HIRAM WALKER AMARETTO

3 oz. Vanilla Ice Cream

Combine in blender with cracked ice. Pour into on-the-rocks glass.

CONTINENTAL STINGER

1 oz. HIRAM WALKER AMARETTO & COGNAC

¾ oz. HIRAM WALKER PEPPERMINT SCHNAPPS

Combine in blender with cracked ice. Pour unstrained into on-the-rocks glass. Add mint leaf.

COOL ON THE ROCKS

2 oz. HIRAM WALKER PEPPERMINT SCHNAPPS

Pour over ice and stir.

CRAN MINT

1¼ oz. HIRAM WALKER PEPPERMINT SCHNAPPS

Cranberry Juice

In a tall glass with ice, fill with cranberry juice, stir well.

CREAMSICKLE

¾ oz. HIRAM WALKER AMARETTO

¾ oz. HIRAM WALKER TRIPLE SEC

1½ oz. Orange Juice

1½ oz. Cream

Blend with ice. Serve in wine glass.

DR. PEPPER

1½ oz. HIRAM WALKER
ROOTBEER
SCHNAPPS

8 oz. Beer

Pour Rootbeer Schnapps into shot glass. Fill 12 oz. beer glass ¾ full. Drop shot glass into beer.

FUZZ-BUSTER

½ oz. HIRAM WALKER
PEACH SCHNAPPS

½ oz. Chambord

½ oz. Absolut Vodka

5 oz. Orange Juice

Add ice and orange juice. Blend until frothy. Serve in a grande glass (16 oz.). Garnish with orange slice.

FUZZY NAVEL

1¼ oz. HIRAM WALKER
PEACH SCHNAPPS

5 oz. Orange Juice

Build over ice in a tall glass.

GIRL SCOUT COOKIE

¾ oz. HIRAM WALKER
PEPPERMINT
SCHNAPPS

½ oz. Kahlua

3 oz. Half & Half

Blend with ice.

GOLDEN PEACH

¾ oz. HIRAM WALKER
PEACH SCHNAPPS

1 oz. Beefeater Dry Gin

5 oz. Orange Juice

In a tall glass with ice, fill with orange juice, stir well.

GRASSHOPPER

¾ oz. HIRAM WALKER
GREEN CREME DE
MENTHE

¾ oz. HIRAM WALKER
LIGHT CREME DE
CACAO

3 oz. Cream

Blend with ice until smooth. Serve in a wine glass.

GRETEL

1½ oz. HIRAM WALKER
SWISS CHOCOLATE
ALMOND

½ oz. HIRAM WALKER
SLOE GIN

3 oz. Vanilla Ice Cream

Combine in blender until smooth. Serve in cocktail glass. Dust with shaved chocolate.

HEAD

¾ oz. HIRAM WALKER ROOT BEER SCHNAPPS

¾ oz. Half & Half or Heavy Cream

Shake with ice, serve on the rocks or in a shot glass.

HOT CHOCOLATE ALMOND

1 oz. HIRAM WALKER BUTTERSCOTCH SCHNAPPS

½ oz. HIRAM WALKER AMARETTO

5 oz. Hot Chocolate

Top with whipped cream.

HOT IRISH NUT

¾ oz. HIRAM WALKER HAZELNUT LIQUEUR

1 oz. Carolans Irish Cream

Fill with coffee. Top with whipped cream.

ITALIAN SPEAR

1 part HIRAM WALKER PEPPERMINT SCHNAPPS

1 part HIRAM WALKER AMARETTO

Build over ice in a rocks glass.

JELLY BEAN

1 part HIRAM WALKER BLACKBERRY FLAVORED BRANDY

1 part Romana Sambuca

Serve in rocks glass over ice.

MAI BERRY

1 oz. HIRAM WALKER RASPBERRY

¼ oz. HIRAM WALKER TRIPLE SEC

2 Tbs. Major Peters' Lime Juice

In a shaker, combine with ice and shake vigorously. Strain into a highball glass. Garnish with a pineapple spear and mint sprig.

MIDORI GREEN IGUANA MARGARITA

1 oz. MIDORI MELON LIQUEUR

1½ oz. Cuervo Tequila

3 oz. Major Peters' Sweet & Sour Mix

Blend and pour (salted glass optional).

MIDORI FROZEN DAIQUIRI

1 oz. MIDORI MELON LIQUEUR

½ oz. Bacardi White Rum

1 oz. Major Peters' Sweet & Sour Mix

Blend with crushed ice until frozen.

MIDORI FROZEN MARGARITA

1 oz. MIDORI MELON LIQUEUR

1 oz. Cuervo Tequila

1 oz. Major Peters' Sweet & Sour Mix

Blend with crushed ice.

MIDORI LUCKY CHARM

1 oz. MIDORI MELON LIQUEUR

1 oz. Carolans Irish Cream

Serve as a shooter.

MIDORI MELON BALL

2 oz. MIDORI MELON LIQUEUR

1 oz. Absolut Vodka

4 oz. Orange, Pineapple, or Grapefruit Juice

Pour in tall glass over ice.

MIDORI SOUR

1 oz. MIDORI MELON LIQUEUR

2 oz. Major Peters' Sweet & Sour Mix

Shake with ice. Serve in rocks glass.

MIDORI SUN OF A BEACH

1 oz. MIDORI MELON LIQUEUR

1 oz. Beefeater Dry Gin (optional)

6 oz. Orange Juice

Build over cubed ice in a tall glass.

MIDORI TEA

1½ oz. MIDORI MELON LIQUEUR

5 oz. Hot Tea

½ oz. HIRAM WALKER TRIPLE SEC

Slice of Lemon

Add Midori and Hiram Walker Triple Sec to hot tea. Add lemon to taste.

MINT DREAM

1½ oz. HIRAM WALKER SWISS CHOCOLATE MINT

Fill with coffee. Top with whipped cream.

PEACH COBBLER

1¼ oz. HIRAM WALKER
PEACH SCHNAPPS

5 oz. Hot Apple Cider

Serve in mug. Top with cream.

PEACH BLOSSOM

1 oz. HIRAM WALKER
PEACH SCHNAPPS

½ oz. HIRAM WALKER
AMARETTO

1 scp Vanilla Ice Cream

Mix in a blender until smooth.

PEACH CREAMY

¾ oz. HIRAM WALKER
PEACH SCHNAPPS

½ oz. HIRAM WALKER
WHITE CREME DE
CACAO

2 oz. Cream

Shake well with ice and strain into cocktail glass.

PEACH ON THE BEACH

¾ oz. HIRAM WALKER
PEACH SCHNAPPS

½ oz. Absolut Vodka

2 oz. Orange Juice

2 oz. Cranberry Juice

Build over cubed ice in a tall glass.

PEACH PIRATE

¾ oz. HIRAM WALKER
PEACH SCHNAPPS

½ oz. Bacardi Rum

Shake with ice and strain.

PEACH ROYAL

¾ oz. HIRAM WALKER
PEACH SCHNAPPS

3 oz. Champagne

Add schnapps to champagne glass. Fill to top with champagne.

PEACHY

1½ oz. HIRAM WALKER
PEACH FLAVORED
BRANDY

3 oz. Major Peters'
Sweet & Sour Mix

Blend with cracked ice and serve in a wine glass.

PEACH SOUR

1¼ oz. HIRAM WALKER
PEACH SCHNAPPS

3 oz. Sweetened
Lemon Mix

Shake with ice. Serve straight up or on the rocks. Garnish with peach slice.

PEPPERMINT PATTI

¾ oz. HIRAM WALKER
PEPPERMINT
SCHNAPPS

¾ oz. Kahlua

Serve over ice in a rocks glass.

PEPPERMINTINI

½ oz. HIRAM WALKER
PEPPERMINT
SCHNAPPS

1¼ oz. Absolut Vodka

*Shake with ice. Strain into a
cocktail glass. Stir on the rocks.*

PINK SQUIRREL

¾ oz. HIRAM WALKER
LIGHT CREME DE
CACAO

¾ oz. HIRAM WALKER
CREME DE NOYAUX

3 oz. Strawberry Ice Cream

*Combine in blender until
smooth.*

PINK VELVET

1 oz. HIRAM WALKER
CHOCOLATE CHERRY

1 oz. HIRAM WALKER
CREME DE CASSIS

3 oz. Vanilla Ice Cream

*Combine in blender until
smooth. Garnish with cherry.*

PURPLE ORCHID

¾ oz. HIRAM WALKER
BLACKBERRY
FLAVORED BRANDY

¾ oz. HIRAM WALKER
CREME DE CACAO

3 oz. Cream

Blend with ice.

RASPBERRY BROWNIE

¾ oz. HIRAM WALKER
RASPBERRY

½ oz. Kahlua

3 oz. Cream or Ice Cream

*Blend until frozen. Top with
whipped cream.*

RASPBERRY CREAM PIE

1¼ oz. HIRAM WALKER
RASPBERRY

5 oz. Hot Apple Cider

*In a mug filled with cider.
Garnish with a cinnamon stick.*

RASPBERRY KIR

1 oz. HIRAM WALKER
RASPBERRY

¼ oz. Champagne

*In a chilled fluted champagne
glass, garnish with Raspberry.*

RED HOT

1¼ oz. HIRAM WALKER
RED HOT
SCHNAPPS

Tabasco Sauce to
taste

Combine in shooter glass.

ROOT BEER RUSSIAN

1 part HIRAM WALKER
ROOT BEER
SCHNAPPS

1 part Kahlua

1 part Absolut Vodka

Shake, serve on the rocks.

ROOT BEER SUNRISE

1¼ oz. HIRAM WALKER
ROOT BEER
SCHNAPPS

3 oz. Orange Juice

Major Peters'
Grenadine

*Shake, top with a dash of
grenadine.*

ROOTY-TOOTY

1¼ oz. HIRAM WALKER
ROOT BEER
SCHNAPPS

3 oz. Orange Juice

*Mix with ice in a blender, serve
over ice in an on-the-rocks
glass.*

ROYAL KIR

splash HIRAM WALKER
CREME DE CASSIS

Champagne

*In a champagne glass; add
splash of cassis, fill with champagne.*

RUM RUNNER

½ oz. HIRAM WALKER
CREME DE BANANA

½ oz. HIRAM WALKER
BLACKBERRY
BRANDY

½ oz. Bacardi Light Rum

½ oz. Bacardi Dark Rum

1 oz. Major Peters'
Sweet & Sour Mix

4 oz. Pineapple Juice

½ oz. Major Peters'
Grenadine

Build over ice. Collins glass.

SEX ON THE BEACH, FL

½ oz. HIRAM WALKER
PEACH SCHNAPPS

½ oz. MIDORI

½ oz. Absolut Vodka

2 oz. Pineapple Juice

*Combine with ice and shake
well. Strain and serve straight
up. Serve in cocktail glass.*

SINGAPORE SLING

1¼ oz. Beefeater Dry Gin

¾ oz. HIRAM WALKER
CHERRY BRANDY

1½ oz. Major Peters'
Sweet & Sour Mix

Club Soda

Build over ice. Fill with soda. Float Cherry Brandy. Lime squeeze, red cherry garnish.

SLOE GIN FIZZ

1 oz. HIRAM WALKER
SLOE GIN

1½ oz. Major Peters'
Sweet & Sour Mix

Club soda

Blend Sloe Gin and sweet and sour. Pour with ice into 12 oz. fizz glass and fill with soda. Red cherry garnish.

SLOE SCREW

1 oz. HIRAM WALKER
SLOE GIN

2½ oz. Orange Juice

Build over cubed ice and stir. Serve in highball glass.

SNOWSHOE

1 part HIRAM WALKER
PEPPERMINT
SCHNAPPS

2 parts Maker's Mark
Bourbon

Serve as a shooter.

SNOWFLAKE

1 part HIRAM WALKER
PEPPERMINT
SCHNAPPS

1 part Beefeater Dry Gin

Stir in wine glass filled with crushed ice.

SNUGGLER

1¼ oz. HIRAM WALKER
PEPPERMINT
SCHNAPPS

5 oz. Hot Chocolate

Serve in a mug. Garnish with a sprig of mint. Top with whipped cream.

SON OF A PEACH

1½ oz. HIRAM WALKER
PEACH SCHNAPPS

2 oz. Pineapple Juice

3 oz. Orange Juice

1 oz. Major Peters'
Sweet & Sour Mix

Build over ice in a tall glass.

SPARK PLUG

1½ oz. HIRAM WALKER
AMARETTO &
COGNAC

Cola

In an on-the-rocks glass with ice, fill with cola and add lime wedge.

ST. MORITZ

1 oz. HIRAM WALKER
SWISS CHOCOLATE
ALMOND

½ oz. HIRAM WALKER
CHERRY FLAVORED
BRANDY

3 oz. Cream

Combine in blender with cracked ice until smooth. Serve in a wine glass.

STINGER

1 oz. Brandy

¾ oz. HIRAM WALKER
LIGHT CREME DE
MENTHE

Shake with ice and strain into chilled cocktail glass.

SWEET SUNSHINE

1 oz. HIRAM WALKER
COFFEE FLAVORED
BRANDY

1 oz. HIRAM WALKER
TRIPLE SEC

3 oz. Orange Juice

Combine in blender with cracked ice. Serve in a wine glass.

SWISS CHOCOLATE TROPICANA

1½ oz. HIRAM WALKER
SWISS CHOCOLATE
ALMOND

½ oz. HIRAM WALKER
CREME DE BANANA

3 oz. Cream

Combine in blender with cracked ice. Serve in a wine glass.

SWISS PEACH

1½ oz. HIRAM WALKER
SWISS CHOCOLATE
ALMOND

½ oz. HIRAM WALKER
PEACH FLAVORED
BRANDY

3 oz. Vanilla Ice Cream

Combine in blender with cracked ice. Serve in an on-the-rocks glass.

THE BOTCH-A-ME

1 oz. HIRAM WALKER
AMARETTO

2 oz. Orange Juice

dash Soda

Build over ice in an on-the-rocks glass. Garnish with a twist of lime.

TRAVELING WILDBURY'S

¼ oz. HIRAM WALKER TRIPLE SEC

¼ oz. Chambord

¼ oz. Absolut Vodka

¼ oz. Bacardi Rum

¼ oz. Beefeater Dry Gin

1 oz. Major Peters' Sweet & Sour Mix

Cola

Shake; pour into a tall glass, top with cola.

TRIPLE ORANGE

1½ oz. HIRAM WALKER TRIPLE SEC

5 oz. Orange Juice

In a tall glass with ice, fill with orange juice. Garnish with orange slice and cherry.

TUACA LEMON DROP

1 oz. TUACA

1½ oz. Major Peters' Sweet & Sour Mix

Shake with ice and strain into cocktail glass.

TUACA ITALIANO

1½ oz. TUACA

5 oz. Orange Juice

Build over cubed ice in a tall glass.

TUACA SODA

1½ oz. TUACA

Soda

Build over cubed ice in a tall glass.

TUACA KEY LIME PIE

Shake 1½ oz. TUACA and ¼ oz. lime juice with ice. Strain into shot glass. Top with fresh whipped cream.

TUACA HOT APPLE PIE

1½ oz. TUACA

6 oz. Apple Cider

Pour Tuaca into hot apple cider. Top with whipped cream and sprinkle with cinnamon.

TUACACCINO

1 oz. TUACA

2 tsp. Instant Cocoa

Pour in hot coffee. Serve in mug.

VELVET HAMMER

¾ oz. HIRAM WALKER CREME DE CACAO

¾ oz. HIRAM WALKER TRIPLE SEC

3 oz. Cream

Blend with ice. Serve in wine glass.

WHIPPER SCHNAPPER

1¼ oz. HIRAM WALKER
RASPBERRY

2 oz. Half & Half or Heavy
Cream

*Blend with crushed ice. Serve
in cordial glass topped with a
cherry.*

WILD IRISH BERRY

¾ oz. HIRAM WALKER
RASPBERRY

¾ oz. Carolans Irish Cream

*Shake, serve up or on the
rocks.*

WOO-WOO

¾ oz. HIRAM WALKER
PEACH SCHNAPPS

¾ oz. Absolut Vodka

1 oz. Cranberry Juice

*Shake with ice. Strain and
serve in a cocktail glass.*

Add your favorite Hiram Walker Liqueur recipes here.

IRISH PRODUCTS: CAROLANS

What is Carolans?

- Carolans is a superior tasting, genuine Irish Cream Liqueur—made in Ireland from Irish ingredients including fresh cream, fine Irish spirits and Irish whiskey.

- Carolans has excellent product quality: it has a more distinctive spirit note than its major competitor and a very subtle honey-like flavor.

- Alcohol content is 17% by volume.

- Attractive, elegant packaging gives the brand classical, premium values.

- Product quality is guaranteed: the company achieved ISO 9002 standards in 1991.

Positioning Statement

Brand Promise:

- Succumb to the luscious, sensual taste of Carolans Irish Cream.

Benefits:

- Drinking Carolans offers the sensual indulgence you expect from a perfect Irish Cream Liqueur.

- The pleasure provided by Carolans is enhanced by sharing it with close friends in a warm, intimate environment.

- Carolans has a rich, luscious creamy taste which closely reflects its self-indulgent image. No Irish Cream is more delicious—yet Carolans is also a very good value for the money.

BACKGROUND
The Product

Carolans Irish Cream is a unique tasting, high quality Irish cream liqueur. The fact that cream liqueurs originated in Ireland is no coincidence—since Ireland has a great tradition in producing fine quality dairy products and distilling spirits. (The oldest whiskey distillery in the world was founded in Ireland in 1608.)

It is the marrying of these two traditions with Irish expertise that lies behind the success story of Carolans. Carolans combines Irish spirits and whiskey with rich double cream and derives its superior taste from the subtle blending of flavors, principally honey.

This ingredient is particularly appropriate for a drink produced in Clonmel—the word, "Clonmel" is derived from the Gaelic "Cluain Meala" which means Vale of Honey.

Clonmel, in County Tipperary, is also set in Ireland's famed "Golden Vale," probably the best natural dairyland in the world. Only the best suppliers are considered, since the cream is such a vital component (making up nearly 40% of the product). It is this uncompromising quality and use of the finest cream that gives Carolans such a smooth consistency.

Production

Carolans production is a four stage process combining traditional expertise with modern, highly sophisticated technology.

1st Stage: Irish whiskey and neutral spirit are carefully blended together in a vat to prepare the alcohol base for Carolans. When the right blend is achieved, it is mixed with the cream at a nearby dairy.

2nd Stage: Cream, water and stabilizers are mixed together at high temperatures in large stainless steel tanks.

Stabilizers are essential to ensure that the product does not curdle. Achieving the right mixture is a delicate process and is tightly controlled using modern, sophisticated equipment.

3rd Stage: After an appropriate period, the cream mixture is fed through stainless steel piping to a homogenizer. During this process the spirits, honey and flavors are fed into the mixture. The homogenization process ensures that the cream does not separate and binds all the ingredients together.

The technology which binds the cream and spirit in Carolans is unique and highly specialized, ensuring long life and a full, fresh taste.

4th Stage: Following homogenization, the mixture is cooled and bottled at the plant. Prior to bottling, samples are taken from every batch of Carolans for analysis and quality control. This close attention to quality ensures that the highest standards are maintained and only the best is bottled.

Why does Carolans not Separate?

The secret behind the product's stability lies in the homogenization process. This breaks up the fat content into molecules which remain suspended in the liquid and bound to the other ingredients; thus the cream will not separate from the liquid.

How long will Carolans Last?

A technological advantage in the manufacturing process gives Carolans the best stability and longest shelf life of all Irish cream liqueurs. On average, Carolans will last two years unopened, although it is best drunk within 6 months of being opened. Whilst not essential, it is recommended that the bottle is refrigerated once opened, to keep it at its best.

BEAM ME UP SCOTTY

Equal parts:

> CAROLANS IRISH CREAM
>
> Kahlua
>
> Hiram Walker Creme de Banana

Combine ingredients and mix.

BRAIN

¾ shot CAROLANS IRISH CREAM

¼ shot Hiram Walker Peach Schnapps

Serve in a shot glass.

BRAIN HEMORRHAGE

¾ shot CAROLANS IRISH CREAM

¼ shot Hiram Walker Peach Schnapps

dash Major Peters' Grenadine

Serve in a shot glass.

BUTTER FINGER

¼ shot CAROLANS IRISH CREAM

¼ shot Absolut Vodka

¼ shot Hiram Walker Butterscotch Schnapps

¼ shot Kahlua

Serve as a shot.

BUTTERY NIPPLE

⅓ shot CAROLANS IRISH CREAM

⅓ shot Absolut Vodka

⅓ shot Hiram Walker Butterscotch Schnapps

Serve as a shot.

CAROLANS AFTER EIGHT

⅔ CAROLANS IRISH CREAM

⅓ Hiram Walker White Creme de Menthe

Shake and decorate with grated chocolate.

CAROLANS AVALANCHE

1 glass Cold Milk

> CAROLANS IRISH CREAM

1 Tbs. Vanilla Ice Cream

Pour a little Carolans Irish Cream into a glass, top up with milk and add a scoop of ice cream.

CAROLANS B 52

Simply follow the order here, pouring equal measures of each ingredient slowly and carefully over a teaspoon:

> Kahlua
>
> CAROLANS IRISH CREAM
>
> Hiram Walker Triple Sec

CAROLANS FRENCH CREAM

Equal parts:

> CAROLANS IRISH CREAM
>
> Courvoisier

Mix and serve over ice.

CAROLANS MUDSLIDE

Equal Parts:

> CAROLANS IRISH CREAM
>
> Kahlua
>
> Absolut Vodka

Mix and serve in a tall glass over ice.

CAROLANS NUTTY IRISHMAN

Equal parts:

> CAROLANS IRISH CREAM
>
> Hiram Walker Hazelnut Liqueur

Combine ingredients and mix.

CAROLANS STEAMY AFFAIR

> Hot Black Coffee

2 tsp. Sugar

measure CAROLANS IRISH CREAM

measure Kahlua

Stir sugar, Carolans and Kahlua into a goblet containing hot coffee. Float cream on top.

CAROLANS WILD ROVER

Equal parts:

> CAROLANS IRISH CREAM
>
> Irish Mist

Mix and serve over ice.

CAROLANS 747

Equal parts:

> CAROLANS IRISH CREAM
>
> Hiram Walker Hazelnut Liqueur
>
> Kahlua

Serve in a tall glass over ice.

Add your favorite Carolans Irish Cream drink recipes here.

CAROLARETTO

1 part CAROLANS IRISH CREAM

1 part Hiram Walker Amaretto

Shake or stir on the rocks.

CREAM WHISKEY

1 part CAROLANS IRISH CREAM

2 parts Canadian Club

Stir well on the rocks.

CREAMED SHERRY

2 parts CAROLANS IRISH CREAM

1 part Duff Gordan Cream Sherry

Stir well on the rocks.

DIRTY GIRL SCOUT COOKIE

⅔ shot CAROLANS IRISH CREAM

⅓ shot Hiram Walker Green Creme de Menthe

Serve as a shot.

DIRTY NELLY

Equal parts:

CAROLANS IRISH CREAM

Tullamore Dew Irish Whiskey

Mix and serve over ice.

ERIE TOUR

⅓ shot CAROLANS IRISH CREAM

⅓ shot Irish Mist

⅓ shot Tullamore Dew

Serve over ice.

ERIN GO BURRR

3 oz. CAROLANS IRISH CREAM, well chilled

Serve chilled Carolans straight up in a chilled cocktail glass.

EXTRA NUTTY IRISHMAN

Equal parts:

CAROLANS IRISH CREAM

Irish Mist

Frangelico

Shake. Top with whipped cream. Serve in a goblet glass.

FRUITY IRISHMAN

2 parts CAROLANS IRISH CREAM

1 part Midori Melon Liqueur

Stir well on the rocks.

GINOLANS

2 parts CAROLANS IRISH CREAM

1 part Beefeater Dry Gin

Stir well and serve on the rocks.

INTERNATIONAL COFFEE

½ oz. CAROLANS IRISH CREAM

½ oz. Chambord

Hot Coffee

Serve in a mug.

IRISH CHARLIE

½ shot CAROLANS IRISH CREAM

½ shot Hiram Walker Dark Creme de Cacao

Shake with ice. Serve in a shot glass.

IRISH CREAM STINGER

3 parts CAROLANS IRISH CREAM

1 part Hiram Walker White Creme de Menthe

Stir well on the rocks.

IRISH DREAM

½ oz. CAROLANS IRISH CREAM

½ oz. Hiram Walker Hazelnut Liqueur

½ oz. Hiram Walker Dark Creme de Cacao

1 scoop Vanilla Ice Cream

Combine ingredients in a blender with ice. Blend thoroughly. Pour into a collins or parfait glass. Serve with a straw.

IRISH HEADLOCK

¼ oz. CAROLANS IRISH CREAM

¼ oz. Tullamore Dew

¼ oz. Hiram Walker Amaretto

¼ oz. Brandy

Layer in above order.

IRISH PENANCE

1 part CAROLANS IRISH
CREAM

1 part Hiram Walker
Triple Sec

Shake slowly and serve on the rocks.

JELLYFISH

¼ shot CAROLANS IRISH
CREAM

¼ shot Hiram Walker White
Creme de Cacao

¼ shot Hiram Walker
Amaretto

¼ shot Major Peters'
Grenadine

Pour first three ingredients directly into glass. Pour grenadine in center of glass.

LIMP MOOSE

½ shot CAROLANS IRISH
CREAM

½ shot Canadian Club

Chill.

MILK & HONEY

Equal Parts:

CAROLANS IRISH
CREAM

Irish Mist

Serve in a rocks glass.

NUTTY IRISHMAN

½ shot CAROLANS IRISH
CREAM

½ shot Hiram Walker
Hazelnut Liqueur

Serve as a shot or on the rocks.

ORIENTAL RUG

¼ shot CAROLANS IRISH
CREAM

¼ shot Hiram Walker
Hazelnut Liqueur

¼ shot Jagermeister

¼ shot Kahlua

dash Cola

Serve as a shot.

VULCAN MIND PROBE

⅓ shot CAROLANS IRISH
CREAM

⅓ shot Hiram Walker
Peppermint
Schnapps

⅓ shot Bacardi 151° Rum

Layer. Suck drink down through straw in one gulp.

Add your favorite Irish drink recipes here.

© Foley Publishing Corp

IRISH MIST

The History of Irish Mist

Irish Mist was the first liqueur to be produced in Ireland when commercial production began in 1947 at Tullamore, County Offaly. Tullamore is the hometown of the Williams family who were the original owners of Irish Mist. The company history goes back to 1829 when the Tullamore Distillery was founded to produce Irish Whiskey. In the mid-1940s the demand for Irish Whiskey fell and Desmond E. Williams began the search for an alternative, yet unrelated, product. The search ended with the discovery of Irish Mist, a product whose origin is over 1,000 years old and based on the ancient recipe for heather wine.

Heather wine, a spirit combined or married with honey, herbs and spices, had been drunk by the chieftains and nobles of Ireland's ancient clans throughout the centuries. However, the secret of this legendary drink disappeared with the last great exodus of the Irish Earls in 1691, an event which has passed into Irish History as "The Flight of the Wild Geese."

The recipe was thought to have been lost forever until a traveler from Europe arrived, quite fortuitously, with an old manuscript he had found. Desmond Williams recognized it as the ancient recipe for heather wine and transformed it into Irish Mist, setting up the Irish Mist Liqueur Company.

The first major breakthrough for Irish Mist was an order from Shannon Duty Free Shop. In 1950, Irish Mist was first exported to the U.S.A. This was soon followed by Canada in 1953 and Australia and the UK in 1954. By 1980, the brand was enjoyed in over 100 countries worldwide. In 1985, the Cantrell & Cochrane Group purchased the Irish Mist Liqueur Company from the Williams family and throughout 1986 and 1987, an extensive evaluation of the brand took place.

As a result, in September 1987, Irish Mist was relaunched in an exciting, new, distinctive bottle. The product was felt to be just right and the recipe of Irish Mist remained the same, maintaining all the care and time-honored maturation that goes into making the product. Blending still takes place in Tullamore, County Offaly, the birthplace of Irish Mist.

The Product

Irish Mist is an Irish Whiskey based liqueur that is truly unique, there being no other product with its combination of Irish Whiskey, honey and herbs.

The rich smoothness of the flavor and attractive amber color of the liquid are both attributes of the blending process that goes into Irish Mist. This process is outlined below.

Stage 1 - Maturation

Premium quality whiskies are matured in wood for a minimum of five years and stored in bonded warehouses in Tullamore, County Offaly.

During the maturation process the harsher constituents in the whiskey are removed, the whiskey becomes smoother, gains flavor and draws color from the oak sherry casks in which it is stored.

Stage 2 - Blending

A number of quality malt and grain whiskies are used in the base blend for Irish Mist. The blending or "marrying" process entails the mixing of two different whiskies of a special type which are allowed to rest for two weeks when other whiskies are added and the total blend is allowed to rest and marry for a further four weeks.

Stage 3 - Storage

After the six week blending and marrying process, the base blend is transferred into storage tanks of which there are six each with a capacity of 45,000 liters, and then they are sealed by the revenue authorities.

Stage 4 - Addition of Other Ingredients to the Base Blend

The base blend is transferred from storage tanks to mixing tanks where herbs, honey, sugar and distilled water are added. Laboratory samples are drawn for test, and water and caramel are added until the blend has reached the correct levels of alcohol/volume percentage, BRIX (sugar level) and color.

The whole mixture spends one week in the mixing tank for initial marrying before it is transferred to resting tanks for a minimum of four weeks.

Stage 5 - Filtration and Bottling

After resting, the blend is then filtered in a 40 chamber filtering press to remove the natural fall-out and to achieve the brilliant color and clarity of Irish Mist.

The liquid has now become Irish Mist which is sent in bulk to the bottling facility in Clonmel, County Tipperary.

Brand Positioning

Irish Mist is a high quality, contemporary Irish Whiskey liqueur whose ease of drinking and unique taste experience encourages and enhances warmth and intimacy between friends in every day social situations.

● Irish Mist's taste is very accessible and easy to drink.

● Irish Mist's whiskey base means that it delivers strength—the pleasure of having a drink.

● Irish Mist also delivers on the pleasure of drinking because it is smooth, rich, full of flavor and provides a warming after-glow.

- The honey content helps to make it smooth and flavorsome.

- The combination of strength and sweetness makes Irish Mist the ideal base for many cocktails.

Benefit

Irish Mist makes drinking a real pleasure. It is easy to drink, smooth and subtle, perfect for every drinking occasion. Enjoying Irish Mist makes informal occasions something to treasure.

Brand Image

Irish Mist is a unique, accessible drink which helps to foster warmth, friendship and hospitality.

- The Irish are known for their special kind of friendliness, warmth and hospitality—qualities that are reflected in Irish Mist.

- Irish Mist is unique because of its high, genuine Irish Whiskey content blended with honey.

Introduction

Irish Mist's combination of strength, sweetness and rich mellow flavor make it perfect for sipping straight, over ice or as an essential ingredient in a variety of delicious mixed drinks.

Irish Mist can be enjoyed in a variety of ways: neat, as a shooter, after dinner, "on the rocks" or ice cold straight from the freezer.

A TALL TINKER

1¼ oz. IRISH MIST

3 oz. Ginger Ale

3 oz. Club Soda

Combine ingredients with lots of ice in a tall glass.

AUNT ROSE

1¼ oz. IRISH MIST

2 oz. Cranberry Juice

2 oz. Orange Juice

Combine all ingredients in a shaker and shake vigorously. Strain into a chilled cocktail glass. Garnish with lemon.

BALLSBRIDGE BRACER

¾ oz. IRISH MIST

1 oz. Tullamore Dew Irish Whiskey

3 oz. Orange Juice

1 Egg White (for two drinks)

Mix all ingredients with cracked ice in a shaker or blender. Shake or blend. Strain into a chilled whiskey sour glass.

BLACK MIST

1 oz. IRISH MIST

1 oz. Hiram Walker Dark Creme de Cacao

Serve in a rocks glass over ice.

BUNGI JUMPER

1¼ oz. IRISH MIST

4 oz. Orange Juice

½ oz. Cream

splash Hiram Walker Amaretto

Mix all but the Amaretto in highball glass. Float the Amaretto on top. Serve straight up or over ice.

BUNRATTY PEG

½ oz. IRISH MIST

1 oz. Tullamore Dew

¼ oz. Hiram Walker Amaretto or Drambuie

Stir with ice and strain into a chilled cocktail glass.

COLD IRISH

½ oz. IRISH MIST

1½ oz. Tullamore Dew Irish Whiskey

2-3 drops Hiram Walker Creme de Cacao

Whipped Cream

Coffee Soda

Pour Irish Mist and Irish Whiskey over ice. Fill with coffee soda and stir. Touch up the whipped cream with the Creme de Cacao and use it to top the drink.

COOL MIST

2 oz. IRISH MIST

Tonic Water

Combine in a tall glass with crushed ice. Add a shamrock for a garnish.

CUP OF GOLD

1 oz. IRISH MIST

3 oz. Apple Cider

Garnish with apple slice.

DUBLIN DRIVER

1 oz. IRISH MIST

3 oz. Orange Juice

Serve in a tall glass over ice.

ERIE TOUR

1 part IRISH MIST

1 part Carolans Irish Cream

1 part Tullamore Dew Irish Whiskey

Combine over ice.

EXTRA NUTTY IRISHMAN

1 part IRISH MIST

1 part Frangelico

1 part Carolans Irish Cream

Whipped Cream

Shake. Top with whipped cream. Serve in a goblet-style glass.

GINGER MIST

1 part IRISH MIST

3 parts Ginger Ale

Combine in a tall glass and serve with a lime wedge.

GYPSY'S KISS

1 part IRISH MIST

1 part Orange Juice

1 part Lemon Juice or Major Peters' Sweet & Sour Mix

Combine in a highball glass. You can also add a dash of grenadine.

HANNIBAL'S REVENGE

1 oz. IRISH MIST

2 oz. Milk

Serve on the rocks.

HOT MIST

2 parts IRISH MIST

1 part Boiling Water

Combine in the glass and garnish with a slice of lemon and some cloves.

IRISH CANADIAN

½ oz. IRISH MIST

1½ oz. Canadian Club
Whiskey

In a mixing glass half-filled with ice, combine both of the ingredients. Stir well. Strain into a cocktail glass.

IRISH-CANADIAN SANGAREE

2 tsp. IRISH MIST

1¼ oz. Canadian Club
Whiskey

1 tsp. Orange Juice

1 tsp. Lemon Juice

Combine and stir well. Add ice and dust with nutmeg.

IRISH FIX

½ oz. IRISH MIST

2 oz. Tullamore Dew Irish
Whiskey

1 oz. Pineapple Juice

½ oz. Lemon Juice

½ tsp. Sugar Syrup

Fill mixing glass with ice. Combine ingredients and stir.

IRISH LACE

2 oz. IRISH MIST

2 splashes Coco Lopez Cream
of Coconut

2 splashes Half & Half

3 splashes Pineapple Juice

2 scoops Ice

Blend and serve in a margarita glass. Garnish with an orange flag.

IRISH MIST ALEXANDER

1 oz. IRISH MIST

1 oz. Light Cream

1 oz. Hiram Walker Dark
Creme de Cacao

Shake ingredients with cracked ice and strain. Sprinkle with nutmeg.

IRISH MIST AND SODA

1½ oz. IRISH MIST

4 oz. Club Soda

Serve with ice and wedge of lime in tall glass.

IRISH MIST KISS

1 part IRISH MIST

dash Hiram Walker Blue Curacao

splash Soda

Serve in a rocks glass over ice.

IRISH MIST SODA

1 part IRISH MIST

3 parts Club Soda

Serve with ice and a wedge of lime or lemon in a tall glass.

IRISH MIST SOUR

2 parts IRISH MIST

1 part Lemon Juice

Shake well over ice. Serve in a tall glass.

IRISH SURFER

1¼ oz. IRISH MIST

3 oz. Orange Juice

Sugar

Club Soda

Shake Irish Mist, orange juice, and sugar. Pour into a glass and fill it with club soda.

KINSALE COOLER

1 oz. IRISH MIST

1½ oz. Tullamore Dew Irish Whiskey

1 oz. Lemon Juice

Club Soda

Ginger Ale

Mix the first three ingredients with cracked ice in a shaker or blender. Pour into a chilled collins glass. Fill with equal parts of club soda and ginger ale. Stir gently. Twist a lemon peel over the drink and drop it in.

MILK & HONEY

1 part IRISH MIST

1 part Carolans Irish Cream

Combine in a rocks glass on ice.

MINT OLD FASHIONED

1¼ oz. IRISH MIST

Orange Slice

Cherry Bitters

Sugar

Club Soda or Water

Muddle the orange, cherry bitters, and sugar. Add Irish Mist. Top with club soda or water.

MIST SOUR

2 oz. IRISH MIST

2 oz. Major Peters'
Sweet & Sour Mix

*Either over the rocks or
straight.*

MISTER MURPHY

1 part IRISH MIST

1 part Bacardi White Rum

1 part Orange Juice

dash Angostura Bitters

*Combine in a rocks glass over
ice with a dash of Angostura
Bitters.*

MISTY MIST

1¼ oz. IRISH MIST

Serve on shaved ice.

MS. TEA

1¼ oz. IRISH MIST

3 oz. Iced Tea

Mix with ice; serve over ice.

MISTLETOE

1½ oz. IRISH MIST

4 oz. Egg Nog

*On the rocks or chilled with
garnish of grated nutmeg.*

MURPHY'S DREAM

1 part IRISH MIST

1 part Beefeater Dry Gin

1 part Lemon Juice
Sugar

*Shake. Serve straight up or
over ice.*

NELLIE JANE

1¼ oz. IRISH MIST

¼ oz. Hiram Walker Peach
Schnapps

3 oz. Orange Juice

1 oz. Ginger Ale

*Mix all but the ginger ale.
Float the ginger ale on top.*

NUT 'n' HOLLI

1 part IRISH MIST

1 part Hiram Walker
Amaretto

1 part Carolans Irish Cream

1 part Hiram Walker
Hazelnut Liqueur

*Shake. Serve straight up in a
shot glass.*

O.J. MIST

2 oz. IRISH MIST

3 oz. Orange Juice

Combine in a tall glass over ice.

PADDY O'ROCCO

2 oz. IRISH MIST

3 oz. Orange Juice

splash Hiram Walker
Amaretto

*Mix Irish Mist and orange juice.
Top with a splash of Amaretto.*

POET'S PUNCH

2 oz. IRISH MIST

1 stick Cinnamon

twist Lemon

twist Orange

½ tsp. Vanilla

½ tsp. Milk

*Heat the milk, cinnamon stick,
and lemon and orange twist to
boiling point. Add vanilla and
Irish Mist. Strain. Sprinkle with
nutmeg.*

SHETLAND PONY

¾ oz. IRISH MIST

1½ oz. Cutty Sark

dash Orange Bitters
(optional)

*Mix all ingredients with
cracked ice in a mixing glass
and strain into a chilled cocktail glass.*

SPEARAMISTY

1 oz. IRISH MIST

¼ oz. Hiram Walker
Spearmint Schnapps

*Stir ingredients and serve
straight up or over ice.*

THE ULTIMATE TEA

2 oz. IRISH MIST

Hot Tea

*Pour Irish Mist in a warm glass.
Fill with hot tea. Garnish with
lemon slice.*

U-Z

¾ oz. IRISH MIST

¾ oz. Carolans Irish Cream

¾ oz. Kahlua

*Shake ingredients and strain
into shot glass.*

THE VIKING MISTRESS

IRISH MIST on the rocks with a twist of lemon.

ULTIMATE IRISH COFFEE

2 oz. IRISH MIST

Generous cup of steaming coffee. Top with whipped cream.

Add your favorite Irish Mist drink recipes here.

TULLAMORE DEW

History

The origins of Tullamore Dew Irish whiskey can be traced back to 1829 when the Tullamore Distillery was founded in Tullamore, County Offaly, situated in the heart of Ireland. The owner was a famed distiller, Michael Molloy.

The location was well chosen—a rich agricultural and grain growing region, providing both the fine barley and pure water essential to the creation of good whiskey.

Following the death of Mr. Molloy, the distillery passed into the hands of the Daly family with Captain Bernard Daly in charge of the business. A keen sportsman, Captain Daly left the routine running of the distillery to one of his colleagues, Daniel E. Williams, who eventually became general manager of Tullamore.

Daniel E. Williams was the major influence on the expansion and development of the distillery and his family became joint shareholders in Tullamore with Captain Daly.

His initials, D-E-W, inspired the whiskey to be named "Tullamore Dew" with its slogan "Give every man his Dew" which is still featured on every bottle today.

Not only was Tullamore famous for its Irish whiskey but, in 1947, it also became the birthplace of Irish Mist liqueur, based on an ancient Irish recipe rediscovered by Daniel E. Williams' grandson, Desmond.

Tullamore Dew whiskey was used in the preparation of Irish Mist for many years.

For nearly 50 years the whole Irish whiskey industry was badly affected by two international events that, together, caused a serious decline in the fortunes of all the leading brands.

The first event was the USA's Prohibition period (1919-1933) during which time a major export market disappeared completely. The second was a trade war with England in the 1930s which resulted in the loss of all Irish whiskey sales in England and the British Empire—including Canada, Australia, New Zealand and parts of the Caribbean and Far East.

With the majority of Irish whiskey markets removed, the distilleries decreased their production and lowered their stockholdings of maturing whiskeys.

The final consequence of this chain of events was felt when Prohibition laws in the United States were eventually repealed. Immediately, demand was renewed—but the Irish whiskey industry had insufficient stocks to satisfy it (allowing Scotch whisky to gain a substantial position in the market).

Tullamore Dew, like many Irish whiskeys, was unable to sustain itself successfully through this difficult period. In 1965, the business was sold to Powers.

Between 1966 and 1972, all the remaining Irish distillers came together to regenerate the industry—ultimately under the name of "The Irish Distillers Group."

Production was also consolidated into two distilleries—Midleton Distillery in County Cork (where Tullamore Dew is distilled today) and the Old Bushmills Distillery in County Antrim, Northern Ireland.

THE TULLAMORE DEW - PRODUCTION

Tullamore Dew is a premium Irish whiskey—distilled, matured and vatted (blended) at the Midleton Distillery in County Cork, Ireland.

Its fine quality and distinctive taste are unique among Irish whiskeys. Connoisseurs describe Tullamore Dew's taste as "subtle, smooth and with a pleasant maltiness combined with charred wood undertones and the natural flavor of golden barley."

Tullamore Dew is also considered to have "none of the overlaying smokiness of Scotch whisky nor the sweetness of the American bourbon."

This subtle, smooth flavor is derived from the unique way in which Irish whiskey is produced.

Natural Cereal Grains

One of the most important flavor components in Irish whiskey is unmalted barley—which is distilled with malted barley in a pot still.

The malted barley is created by allowing barley to start growing in moist conditions, then stopping the growth by drying it over coal fires. This "malting" process brings out the sugars in the grain—which will later be turned into alcohol.

(The malting process itself differs from that used in Scotch. There, the grains are dried over peaty fires, giving Scotch whiskies their peaty smokiness. The absence of this is one of the defining characteristics of Irish whiskey.)

Mashing & Fermenting

The first stage in Irish whiskey production mixes hot Irish spring water with the crushed grains (known as "mashing").

The resulting sugary liquid ("wort") is collected and "fermented" by adding yeast to produce an alcoholic "wash" (with about 8.5% alcohol by volume).

Distilling

The "wash" is boiled in large copper pot stills and the vapor cooled and collected. This process is repeated to remove the harsh elements of the spirit and improve the quality of the final whiskey.

The main point of difference between Irish whiskey and other whiskies/whiskeys is that both pot still and grain whiskies are distilled three times not twice, giving a more concentrated and purer distillate.

In addition, the Irish distill their whiskey in much larger pot stills than the Scots, providing further individuality.

It is important to recognize that the distinctive character of Irish whiskey is derived from the distilling, not the blending. This is why the Irish refer to "vatting" rather than blending, to emphasize that the skill lies in creating the distillates rather than blending them later.

Maturing

The distillates (the new spirits) are matured in oak casks that have previously been used for either sherry or bourbon production. They mature for a minimum of three years—although usually for much longer.

Vatting (Blending)

As with Scotch, the flavorful pot still whiskey is blended with a lighter, more neutral grain spirit which serves to lighten the body of the final whiskey.

Blend variations are also achieved through the use of differing ages of whiskey and of different barrel types maturation—in casks previously used for sherry, rum or bourbon, or in new oak casks.

THE TULLAMORE DEW BLEND

Tullamore Dew's particular taste character depends on the correct balance of mature whiskeys vatted together by the blender:

POT STILL WHISKEY is the most important feature and provides the foundation flavor. Starting with a mash of both malted and unmalted barley, it is distilled three times in a giant copper "still."

GRAIN WHISKEY has a simpler flavor than its pot still equivalent, being based on maize and a small proportion of malted barley. It is distilled in a continuous column still, again three times.

Add your favorite Irish drink recipes here.

BLACK AND TAN

A 10 to 14 oz. glass

1½ oz. TULLAMORE DEW

1 oz. Bacardi Dark Rum

½ oz. Major Peters' Lime Juice

½ oz. Orange Juice

½ tsp. Superfine Sugar

6-8 Ice Cubes

4 oz. Ginger Ale, chilled

Combine Tullamore Dew, rum, lime and orange juices, and sugar and shake vigorously. Strain mixture into glass and fill with ginger ale.

BLARNEY COCKTAIL

1½ oz. TULLAMORE DEW

1 oz. Martini & Rossi Sweet Vermouth

2 dashes Hiram Walker Green Creme de Menthe

Shake. Strain into cocktail glass. Serve with green cherry.

BLUE BLAZER

2 measures TULLAMORE DEW

1 measure Clear Honey

½ measure Lemon Juice

1-3 measures Water

Cinnamon Sticks (garnish)

Pour all ingredients into a pan and heat very gently until they honey has dissolved. Place a teaspoon into a short tumbler and pour drink carefully into the glass (the spoon prevents the glass from cracking). Serve with cinnamon sticks.

BOW STREET SPECIAL

1½ oz. TULLAMORE DEW

½ oz. Hiram Walker Triple Sec

1 oz. Lemon Juice

Shake or strain into a chilled cocktail glass.

BRAINSTORM

1¾ oz. TULLAMORE DEW

¼ oz. Martini & Rossi Dry Vermouth

dash Benedictine

Stir; strain into a cocktail glass. Decorate with a twist of orange peel.

BOW STREET SPECIAL

1½ oz. TULLAMORE DEW

½ oz. Hiram Walker
Triple Sec

1 oz. Lemon Juice

Mix with cracked ice in a shaker or blender and strain into a chilled cocktail glass.

BUCKING IRISH OR IRISH HIGHBALL

1¼ oz. TULLAMORE DEW

5 oz. Ginger Ale

Combine in ice cube-filled highball glass. Garnish with lemon twist.

BUNRATTY PEG

1½ oz. TULLAMORE DEW

¾ oz. Irish Mist

Stir with ice and strain into a chilled cocktail glass or with ice cubes in an old-fashioned glass.

DINGLE DRAM

1½ oz. TULLAMORE DEW

½ oz. Irish Mist
Coffee Soda

dash Hiram Walker Creme de Cacao
Whipped Cream

Pour Tullamore Dew and Irish Mist into a chilled highball glass along with several ice cubes. Fill with coffee soda. Stir gently. Add a float of Creme de Cacao. Top with dollop of whipped cream.

EMERALD ISLE

¾ shot TULLAMORE DEW

¾ shot Hiram Walker Green Creme de Menthe

2 scoops Vanilla Ice Cream
Soda Water

Blend first three ingredients then add soda water. Stir after adding soda water.

Add your favorite Irish drink recipes here.

GLENBEIGH FIZZ

1½ oz. TULLAMORE DEW
¼ oz. Medium Sherry
¼ oz. Creme de Noyaux
½ oz. Major Peters'
        Sweet & Sour Mix
        Club Soda

Pour all ingredients except club soda with several ice cubes in a chilled highball glass and stir. Fill with club soda.

GRIT COCKTAIL

½ jigger TULLAMORE DEW
½ jigger Martini & Rossi
          Sweet Vermouth

Shake then strain into a cocktail glass.

HAWAIIAN HIGHBALL

2 oz. TULLAMORE DEW
2 tsp. Pineapple Juice
1 tsp. Major Peters'
        Sweet & Sour Mix
        Club Soda

Combine the whiskey with the juices; add ice and fill with soda. Stir gently.

HOT IRISH

1¼ oz. TULLAMORE DEW
1-2 tsp. Sugar
1 slice Fresh Lemon
4 Cloves
pinch Cinnamon or
       Cinnamon Stick
3-4 oz. Boiling Water

Stud lemon slice with cloves. Put lemon slice, sugar and cinnamon into stemmed glass. Add boiling water and Tullamore Dew. Stir and serve.

DIRTY NELLY

1 oz. TULLAMORE DEW
1 oz. Carolans Irish Cream

Shake with crushed ice. Strain into cocktail glass.

IRISH COFFEE

1¼ oz. TULLAMORE DEW
        Hot Coffee

Pour into warm, stemmed glass. Sugar to taste. Stir well. Float Carolans Irish Cream.

IRISH COOLER

1¼ oz. TULLAMORE DEW
6 oz. Club Soda

Pour whiskey into a highball glass over ice cubes. Top with soda and stir. Garnish with a lemon peel spiral.

IRISH COW

1½ oz. TULLAMORE DEW

8 oz. Hot Milk

1 tsp. Sugar

Pour the milk into a glass; add the sugar and whiskey. Stir well.

IRISH CRESTA

1 oz. TULLAMORE DEW

2 tsp. Irish Mist

2 tsp. Orange Juice

1 Egg White

Combine with ice; shake well. Strain and add ice.

IRISH FIX

1½ oz. TULLAMORE DEW

½ oz. Irish Mist

1 oz. Pineapple Juice

½ oz. Major Peters' Sweet & Sour Mix

½ tsp. Sugar Syrup

Fill mixing glass with ice. Add Tullamore Dew, Irish Mist, pineapple juice, lemon juice and sugar syrup. Shake. Strain into a rocks glass filled with ice. Garnish with lemon slice.

IRISH FIZZ

2 oz. TULLAMORE DEW

1½ tsp. Lemon Juice

1 tsp. Hiram Walker Triple Sec

½ tsp. Sugar

Club Soda

Combine (except the soda) with ice; shake. Strain; add ice and club soda.

IRISH KISS

¾ oz. TULLAMORE DEW

½ oz. Hiram Walker Peach Schnapps

4 oz. Ginger Ale

2 oz. Orange Juice

Combine in an ice cube-filled Collins or specialty glass. Garnish with lime wheel.

IRISH RICKEY

1½ oz. TULLAMORE DEW

1 Ice Cube

Juice of ½ Lime

Fill 8 oz. highball glass with carbonated water and stir. Leave lime in glass.

IRISH SLING

In an old-fashioned glass mix:

1 jigger TULLAMORE DEW

1 jigger Beefeater Dry Gin

Crush one lump of sugar and two lumps of ice and add to glass.

IRISH WHISKEY COOLER

1 jigger TULLAMORE DEW

1 pint Club Soda

1 dash Angostura Bitters

1 Lemon Rind

Serve in tall glass.

IRISH WHISKEY SOUR

1 jigger TULLAMORE DEW

Juice of Lemon

1 barspoon Sugar

Shake. Strain into sour glass or serve on the rocks. Dress with fruit (orange slice and cherry).

KERRY COOLER

1 oz. TULLAMORE DEW

½ oz. Sherry

1¼ Tbs. Creme de Almond

1¼ Tbs. Major Peters' Sweet & Sour Mix

Club Soda

Combine (except the soda) with ice. Shake well. Strain, add ice and soda. Top with lemon slice.

LEPRECHAUN

1¼ oz. TULLAMORE DEW

Tonic Water

In an old-fashioned glass with ice, fill with tonic water. Twist lemon peel over drink and add.

LET'S DEW COFFEE

1½ oz. TULLAMORE DEW

6 oz. Coffee

Generous dollop of whipped cream on top.

LUCK OF THE IRISH

2 parts TULLAMORE DEW

2 parts Carolans Irish Cream

1 part Irish Mist

Shake with ice and serve on the rocks.

MICHAEL COLLINS

1¼ oz. TULLAMORE DEW

Juice of 1 Lemon

1 tsp. Sugar Syrup

Club Soda

Shake with ice. Top with club soda.

MISTY DEW

1 part TULLAMORE DEW

1 part Irish Mist

Serve over ice in rocks glass.

NEW CASTLE'S BEST

1¼ oz. TULLAMORE DEW

½ oz. Irish Mist

few drops Hiram Walker White
Creme de Cacao

Shake with ice. Serve up or on the rocks.

PADDY COCKTAIL

¾ oz. TULLAMORE DEW

¾ oz. Martini & Rossi
Rosso Vermouth

2 dashes Bitters

Combine with ice, shake. Strain into an old-fashioned glass with ice.

PADDY WHACK

Equal Parts:
TULLAMORE DEW
Carolans Irish Cream

Serve as a shooter.

RED DEVIL

2 oz. TULLAMORE DEW

1½ oz. Clam Juice

1½ oz. Tomato Juice

1 tsp. Major Peters'
Lime Juice

Few Drops Worchestershire
Sauce

Pinch Pepper

Combine with ice; shake gently. Strain straight up.

RING OF KERRY

1½ oz. TULLAMORE DEW

1 oz. Carolans Irish Cream

½ oz. Kahlua

1 tsp. Shaved Chocolate

Mix all ingredients, except shaved chocolate, with cracked ice in a shaker or blender. Strain into a chilled cocktail glass. Sprinkle with shaved chocolate.

SERPENT'S TOOTH

1 oz. TULLAMORE DEW

1 oz. Martini & Rossi
Sweet Vermouth

½ oz. Kummel

1 oz. Major Peters'
Sweet & Sour Mix

dash Angostura Bitters

Stir well; strain into small wine glass.

WILD IRISH ROSE

1½ oz. TULLAMORE DEW

1½ oz. Major Peters'
Grenadine

½ oz. Major Peters' Lime
Juice

Club Soda

Fill a highball glass with ice. Add Tullamore Dew, grenadine and lime juice. Stir well. Fill with club soda.

TIPPERARY

¾ oz. TULLAMORE DEW

¾ oz. Martini & Rossi
Rosso Vermouth

1 Tbs. Hiram Walker Green
Chartreuse

*Combine with ice; shake well.
Strain into an old-fashioned
glass with ice.*

TULLAMORE NEAT

*Generous portion of
TULLAMORE DEW IRISH
WHISKEY into a snifter glass.*

TULLAMORE
YANKEE DEW

*Generous portion of
TULLAMORE DEW IRISH
WHISKEY over ice.*

Add your favorite Tullamore Dew drink recipes here.

© Foley Publishing Corp

KROATZBEERE

The original "Wild and Pure" blackberry liqueur. Considered to be the world's best blackberry liqueur, Echte Kroatzbeere continues to be prepared according to the traditional family recipe, using wild-grown blackberries since 1908.

Only pure blackberry juice, alcohol, sugar, and some secret ingredients are carefully blended to produce Echte Kroatzbeere's rich, full blackberry flavor—each bottle contains more than 50% natural blackberry juice.

Enjoy Echte Kroatzbeere chilled and straight up, on the rocks, or in a variety of mixed drinks which call for either raspberry or blackberry brandy.

For additional recipes, visit our website at
http://www.ourniche.com

BERRIED TREASURE

1 oz. ECHTE KROATZBEERE

1 oz. Hiram Walker Amaretto

3 oz. Major Peters' Sweet & Sour Mix

Serve in highball glass over ice, shake and top with club soda. Happy hunting!

BLACK MAGIC

1½ oz. ECHTE KROATZBEERE

1 part Cranberry Juice

1 part Grapefruit Juice

Serve in a tall glass with ice.

CLUB E.K.

1½ oz. ECHTE KROATZBEERE

Pour into tall glass with ice; fill with club soda. Refreshing!

E.K. BLACK BELT

1 part ECHTE KROATZBEERE

2 parts Bourbon

Pour over ice into small highball glass.

E.K.G.

Get your heart started! Mix equal parts ECHTE KROATZBEERE and Orange Liqueur and serve over ice.

GRAPE CRUSH

1 part ECHTE KROATZBEERE

1 part Absolut Vodka

1 part Cranberry Juice

1 part Major Peters' Sweet & Sour Mix

Mix together, chill over ice and serve straight up.

JELLY BEAN

Float a dash of Ouzo on top of 1½ — 2 oz. ECHTE KROATZBEERE.

KIR ROYALE

2 parts ECHTE KROATZBEERE

Dry Champagne or Sparkling Wine

Garnish with a blackberry and enjoy.

LEMONBERRY COOLER

1 oz. ECHTE KROATZBEERE

6 oz. Schwepps Bitter Lemon

Fill an 8 oz. glass with ice.

PURPLE HAZE

A shot of ECHTE KROATZBEERE, chilled and straight up.

RED RUSSIAN

1½ oz. ECHTE KROATZBEERE

¼ oz. Absolut Vodka

¼ oz. Kahlua

Fill glass with cream, mix in highball glass over ice and shake.

THE NEWBURGH, NEW YORKER

Compliments of Gus's Tavern

2 parts ECHTE KROATZBEERE

1 part Dujardin Brandy

Mix in a snifter glass. Heat in microwave until nice and hot. Service with a warning!

VICE-GRIP

Add 1-1½ oz. ECHTE KROATZBEERE to a Weissbeer; add a slice of lemon. "Berry" delicious and thirst-quenching!

Add your favorite Echte Kroatzbeere recipes here.

© Foley Publishing Corp

MAJOR PETERS'

BLOODY MARY...FROM THE BEGINNING.

In the early 1940s, shortly after the repeal of prohibition, flavored cocktails such as Gimlets, Sidecars, Manhattans and Old Fashioneds began to gain popularity over straight liquors. The Martini followed suit in the late 40s and early 50s. It wasn't until the mid 1960s that the Bloody Mary, a zesty tomato-based beverage, gained recognition as a premier cocktail favorite.

In the fall of 1968, Major Peters—the quintessential Bloody Mary—was perfected and named after the man who, some say, may have invented it.

Over the years, many have tried to duplicate Major Peters' Bloody Mary mix—a unique blend of fresh vine-ripened tomatoes, over 40 distinctive spices and 100% natural ingredients—yet, none have succeeded. Only the Major delivers a signature Bloody Mary that's bursting with all natural flavor.

History dictates that the Bloody Mary originated somewhere in the British Isles...exactly when and where is unknown. Some speculate that it may have been during the reign of King Henry the 4th, while others insist Sir Winston Churchill had a hand in its creation. However, an inside source tells us that it was the one and only Major Peters, the fabled British noble, who developed the original Bloody Mary formula. The following entry was allegedly recovered from a journal kept by the Major during his legendary adventures in the British countryside—date unknown:

Under the warm summer sun, I came upon a man who's toil intrigued me so that I hastened my step and paused to reflect. He was a bartender by trade, mixing swill for the local dignitaries I had assumed. As the sweat began to trickle from underneath my turban, I stepped inside the tavern to cool my hide and tickle my fancy. To my amazement, bushels upon bushels of fruits and vegetables were abound.

The bartender, a weathered looking chap with coarse hands, took a swig from his cup and grimaced with disgust. "What's the matter?" I inquired, settling up to the bar. "This isn't right," he replied, reaching for a lime. "It just doesn't taste right!" Sampling a portion for myself, I agreed. "Why do you labor over it then, my good man?" I pondered. "'Tis the queen who summoned me to quench her thirst in this ungodly heat," he answered. "Although my lady prefers to drink only freshly squeezed juice, she also insists on a touch of the spirits now and again. If the taste is not to her liking, sir, it could mean my head."

The bartender mixed yet another round, this time using the juice that he had squeezed from a pear. We both wet our palates with this latest concoction. From his initial reaction, I could tell that he had come to his very wit's end. "By the by, what do you call this grog?" I asked, trying to keep his hopes high. "A bloody failure," he sighed.

The sun was beginning to set as my belly moaned of hunger. Instead of scouting for a morsel to dine on, I decided to purchase a bushel of tomatoes from my new acquaintance and be on my way. I was nearly to my mount when suddenly...it came to me!

Apparently, the Major's entry ended abruptly here. No one is exactly sure what happened next. But the rest, as they say, is history. Presently, the Bloody Mary is among the top three cocktail mixes sold in the entire United States and Major Peters' is the number one on-premise Bloody Mary mix. Although this amazing tale may or may not be historically correct, the quality and tradition of Major Peters still prevails.

The legendary origin of Lime Juice and Grenadine mixes. An excerpt from the journal of Major Peters...

We set sail for the new world on a merchant's vessel, not realizing the danger that approached from the southwest. A tropical storm had arisen, leaving a path of destruction in its wake. Lost at sea for what seemed to be eons, our water supply soon vanished. The ravenous thirst of the ship's crew and her passengers began to take its toll. I was sadly reminded of a verse from an old navigator's poem: "Water, water everywhere, but not a drop to drink."

Tempers soon flared as the captain struggled to right our course. Amidst his anxiety, a mutiny brewed. Sensing that reason would quickly give way to disparity, I attempted to squelch this bloody rebellion in its infancy. For my trouble, I was forced to walk the plank. Nearing its edge, with all hope abandoned, a miracle occurred. The first mate, perched high above the starboard bow, shouted "Land Ho" to the disbelief of the angry throng below him. Cheers erupted feverishly as a glorious island chain unfolded before our eyes. Scores of men jumped into the warm water and swam to the serenity of the nearest shore.

A bountiful harvest of limes, the finest I had ever tasted, engulfed the trees that blanketed the island. We took of the limes freely, their juices like a sweet nectar from the gods. I, being a connoisseur of fine fruits, graciously filled my sack with enough limes to survive our ship's passage to the new world.

Judging from the heat and the land's topography, the captain surmised that by some twist of fate we had reached the West Indies. He rerouted our course and we traveled on, stopping from time to time to replenish our supplies. One island in particular, named Grenada by its natives, bore a succulent fruit so rich in flavor and color that I could have only been dreaming. I vowed I would not leave this island paradise and its welcoming shores without claiming my new-found prize...

Mysteriously, the Major's entry ends here. However, according to certain lore, Major Peters went on to develop a variety of fruit-flavored mixes in the new world. Although it was possible to amass a fortune from these high caliber offerings, the Major felt that charging the King's ransom for the quality of juice was not such a "Rosy" idea! It seems like times never change. Today, Major Peters' Lime Juice and Grenadine bring out the finest flavors of any beverage at a fraction of the competitor's cost.

For additional recipes, visit our website at
http://www.majorpeters.com

MAJOR MARGARITA

½ oz. MAJOR PETERS' LIME JUICE

4 oz. MAJOR PETERS' MARGARITA MIX

1½ oz. Cuervo Tequila

1½ cups Ice

Blend until slushy. Pour into salt-rimmed glass. Garnish with lime slice.

MAJOR PETERS' BLOODY MARY

6 oz. MAJOR PETERS' BLOODY MARY MIX

1¼ oz. Absolut Vodka

Combine in a highball glass filled with ice cubes; stir. Garnish with a stalk of celery.

MAJOR PETERS' FROZEN VIRGIN MARY

4 oz. MAJOR PETERS' BLOODY MARY MIX (Regular or Hot & Spicy)

5 oz. Orange Juice

¼ oz. MAJOR PETERS' LIME JUICE

1½ cups Ice

Blend until smooth and pour into a 16 oz. glass. Garnish with lime slice, celery stalk, and cherry tomato.

MAJOR PETERS' GIN & TONIC

½ oz. MAJOR PETERS' LIME JUICE

1¼ oz. Beefeater Dry Gin

6 oz. Tonic Water

Pour Major Peters' Lime Juice and gin into highball glass filled with ice. Fill glass with tonic; stir.

MAJOR PETERS' GINZA MARY

2 oz. MAJOR PETERS' BLOODY MARY MIX

2 oz. Absolut Vodka

1½ oz. Sake

½ oz. Fresh Lemon Juice

2 dashes Soy Sauce

Freshly ground black pepper to taste

Combine all ingredients with cracked ice in a mixing glass. Stir well and pour into chilled old-fashioned glass.

MAJOR PETERS' SALSA MARY

6 oz. MAJOR PETERS' SALSA BLOODY MARY MIX

1¼ oz. Absolut Vodka

Combine in a highball glass filled with ice cubes; stir. Garnish with a stalk of celery or jalapeño pepper.

MAJOR PETERS' TEQUILA MARIA

4 oz. MAJOR PETERS' BLOODY MARY MIX

½ oz. MAJOR PETERS' LIME JUICE

2 oz. Cuervo White Tequila

Freshly ground black pepper to taste

pinch Cilantro

Lime wedge

Combine all ingredients, except lime wedge, with cracked ice in a mixing glass. Pour into a chilled old-fashioned glass and garnish with lime wedge.

MAJOR STRAWBERRY MARGARITA

½ oz. MAJOR PETERS' LIME JUICE

1½ oz. Cuervo Tequila

½ cup Strawberries (fresh or frozen)

OR

4 oz. Major Peters' Strawberry Margarita Mix

1½ cups Ice

Blend until slushy. Pour into salt-rimmed glass.

THE MAIDEN MARGARITA

4 oz. MAJOR PETERS' MARGARITA MIX

1½ cups small cube ice

2 oz. Lemon Lime Soda

Blend and serve in a salt-rimmed glass and garnish with a wedge of lime. Garnish with strawberry.

Add your favorite Major Peters' recipes here.

© Foley Publishing Corp

MARTINI & ROSSI

In 1863 three partners, Alessandro Martini, Teofilo Sola and Luigi Rossi, joined together to found a company which today is the market leader in the Vermouth industry. They took over an established 18th century firm that had been producing Vermouth in Torino, Italy, and by the end of the same year, were exporting the first Martini Vermouth for sale in the United States. As the firm sought to penetrate every market in the world, the main production plant was moved from Torino to Pessione, closer to the Port of Genoa for better world-wide export. The first shipment went to Brazil in 1864, to Argentina in 1866, to Greece, Portugal, Belgium, Switzerland, Egypt and Turkey in 1868.

In 1879, Rossi bought Sola's shares and the company's name became Martini & Rossi. The new enterprise was representative of the emerging technology in the 19th century—the period of the industrial Revolution. Ernesto Trevisani, author of the "Industrial and Commercial Review of Turin and the Provinces" in 1897 wrote:

"The first thing one notices in the factory of Pessione is the perfect order that reigns everywhere, the technical distribution of the various departments, the types of distilleries...the great size of the space, the distribution of numerous pieces of machinery, the appearance of light, which all together induce a total response in every one of the demands of modern industrial technology and hygiene."

The men who founded Martini & Rossi were exceptional in many ways, yet characteristic of their times. Ernesto Trevisani described them as "men of steel quick to bring to fruition their intelligence, their practicality and their will."

Luigi Rossi's sons, Ernesto, Cesare, Enrico and Teofilo took over management of the company in the year 1900. It was their plan to further increase the exports by establishing plants abroad in addition to Europe and South America. Biographers of Teofilo Rossi consider him to have been one of the greatest mayors of Torino. He was a man of a thousand interests, a senator of the kingdom and ministry, a man of culture, a scholar of Dante and a historian.

Perhaps because of the influence of Rossi, the company has always been involved with the community and its development. An active patron of the arts, M&R sponsored both instrumental and vocal concerts, especially "Belcanto," or "beautiful song," a vocal technique developed in Italy during the 18th century, emphasizing vocal flexibility and ease of singing especially for Italian opera. Also a supporter of fine art, Martini & Rossi has sponsored exhibitions of the works of Picasso in Venice, De Chirico in New York and Caravaggio in London, among others.

The company began its well-known association with sports in 1924 with the Grand Cup of Bicycling. The company name is probably best known for its association with auto racing: Porsche in the World Championship for manufactures; Tecno, Brabham, Lotus in F1; Lancia in Endurance and Rally championships. Martini & Rossi has also sponsored the offshore and F1 in speed boating, as well as world cup skiing, fencing, golf, sailing and polo. Finally in 1960, Martini & Rossi's greatest contribution to the preservation of culture, the wine museum of Torino was created. With the assistance of the Department of Culture, it exhibits more than 500 artifacts from winemaking activities dating from as early as the 7th century, B.C.

Over the course of the years, other product lines have been developed. Martini & Rossi Asti Spumante is the largest exported fruity, sparkling wine in the world. Riserva Montelera authentic brut "Champenoise," and a Riesling are others available worldwide. Liquors include Chinamartini, Fernet Martini, Bosford Gin, Vodka Eristow, Menta Sacco, just to mention a few.

Today, Martini & Rossi plants around the world are engaged in the production of Vermouth under the direction of Bacardi-Martini.

Alberto Viriglio, author of "Turin and the Turinese" wrote in 1898:

"it is said that one cannot go to a region of the world so remote that one cannot detect the passage of a missionary, a scoundrel from Lucca, or a traveling salesman. That salesman will certainly offer something from the cosmopolitan house of Martini & Rossi."

Now, more than a century after the first export, the same is true—there is hardly a place in the world where Martini & Rossi products are not available.

An Ancient Tradition

Vermouth is a true aperitif—that is a wine incorporating aromatic substances and bitter plants. It is differentiated from other aromatized wines by the presence of bitter plants which stimulate digestive juices.

It is said that Hippocrates of ancient Greece invented Vermouth over 2,000 years ago when he made a grog by blending almonds, herbs and gray amber with wine, a concoction to become known as a "Hippocras." Whether it started with him or not, the tradition of flavoring wines arose for two very practical reasons in ancient times, wine often tasted bad and was partly spoiled due to its primitive winemaking techniques and containers. Plants and herbs covered up and improved the flavor as well as helped to resist spoilage. Additions of seawater and pine resin were also common.

The second reason for combining herbs and spices with wine was medical and mystical. Medicines, narcotics and live potions were mostly botanical and wine was the solvent of choice for the ancient pharmacist. It served as both the vehicle to imbibe desirable herbal flavors and preserve them. Many of the botanical medicines of real value are bitter such as those containing quinine, for example. As a result, a bitter taste came to be desired and preferred. The alcohol of the wine preserved the medicine, tonic or potion while the antibacterial and preservative value of the oils extracted from herbal medicines kept the wine from spoiling.

Additives commonly used in Vermouth are put into two categories: carminatives and bitters. Bitters are the principal active agents which, through their chemical effect increase the secretion of gastric juices, stimulating the appetite and facilitating the working of the digestive system. Rhubarb root relieves congestion of the liver; ginger activates the circulation; cola beans and benzoin improve digestion; and coriander, cardamom and aloes are considered intestinal regulators. Quinquina bark and thistle reduce fever.

The Mediterranean abounds in aromatic plants. From Crete comes dittany and arthemisia absinthium (wormwood), which possesses tonic and digestive properties. The Romans introduced other aromatic plants and herbs such as thyme, rosemary, myrtle and celery. During the Middle Ages, the Venetians brought aromatic plants and spices from the East such as ginger, nutmeg and cloves.

The word Vermouth comes from the German "Wermut" which means wormwood—a shrub whose flowers were often added to wine. Piedmont, the region surrounding Torino in the northwest corner of Italy, favored the production of Vermouth. Aromatic plants were plentiful in the nearby Alps and the dry and sweet wines, mostly Muscat Canelli, were suited to making aromatized wines.

From the time of the Renaissance, Torino became one of

the major centers of Hippocratic wines and liqueurs. There are two classes of Vermouths recognized in the trade, the sweet or Italian-type Vermouth and the dry or French-type. Each evolved because of regional tastes and nearby vineyards. While the Muscat Canelli grapes were available to Italian winemakers, a drier Vermouth was developed by a French winemaker in 1800 using the thin semi-sweet Herault grapes of the Midi, more akin to French taste. Today, both countries produce dry and sweet vermouths.

Vermouth is principally served "straight" in European countries. In the United States, it is used most often in mixed drinks such as the Martini and Manhattan cocktails. In Argentina, the consumption of a glass of Vermouth or "copetin" is such a wide-spread custom that the time of day between 5 and 6 p.m. is known as the "Vermouth Hour" and the movie shown at that time of day is called the "Vermouth feature." Around the world, drinking Vermouth is the continuance of a very ancient tradition.

Vermouth Production

Inside the whitewashed walls of the Martini & Rossi estate in the village of Pessione just over the hills from Torino are the original cellars now housing an extensive wine museum, a villa used for entertainment, numerous warehouses, separate winemaking facilities for both Asti Spumante and Vermouth, and a small, exotic garden where guests can see a selection of the herbs that make Vermouth unique.

Three main types of Vermouth are made: a sweet white called Bianco, a dry white called Extra Dry, and a sweet red labeled Rosso. All are created by adding herbs, spices, distillates and sugar to a light base wine, with the main differences arising from the grape varieties used, the herb flavorings selected, and the final sugar and alcohol levels.

Fine wine grapes are selected from numerous vineyards throughout the region, vinified under the supervision of

Martini & Rossi technicians, and the base wines brought to Pessione where the Vermouth making process begins.

The blend of herbs and spices are different for each Vermouth and a carefully guarded secret. The essence infusions for Martini & Rossi's 15 world-wide facilities are all made in Pessione. The list of herbs available is long: bitter-tasting plants include aloe, angelica, blessed thistle, cinchoma, European centaury, germander, lungwort, lungmoss, quassia and rhubarb. Aromatic plants are anise, bitter almond, cardamom, cinnamon, clove, coriander, dittany of Crete, galingale, marjoram, nutmeg, Roman camomile, rosemary, summer savory, thyme, tonka bean, and vanilla bean. The bitter aromatic plants include allspice, elder, elecampane, gentian, juniper, bitter orange, sweet orange, saffron, sage, sweet flag, speedwell, wormwood, and yarrow.

The quality of herbs and spices is extremely important. Thus, only the best wild herbs and imported spices are purchased from reliable suppliers to ensure their freshness and full flavor. An "infusion" is then made from the herbs and spices either through distillation or maceration.

Distillation of herbs takes place in a mixture of alcohol and water heated to 80°C. Volatile aromas are recovered at the same time as the alcohol in which they are dissolved. The distilled extract is then drawn off, herbs pressed, washed to recover the alcohol, pressed again, removed and burned. The resulting liquid is amber in color with a strong bouquet but has practically no taste.

Aromatic and bitter plants are introduced to the wine in the form of an extract created by maceration. This part of the infusion both fortifies the wine and gives it a distinctive rich, bitter flavor. Fixed stainless steel pipelines lead through the immaculate cellars into large blending tanks where the various ingredients are added to the base wines. Martini & Rossi's world-wide reputation for quality is no doubt based on their commitment to using only the finest ingredients. Absolutely no artificial flavors or extracts are used. To the base wine is added cane sugar, the distilled aromatic alcohol, the bitter tasting maceration extract, and finally to the Rosso only, caramel. Made from sugar heated and cooked until it becomes a brown, viscous mass, caramel is the only coloring allowed by government laws. It gives Rosso its deep amber hue and imports a special flavor, extra body, and smoothness to the red Vermouth.

The blend is mixed thoroughly then aged for three to six months. After aging, the Vermouth is cold stabilized to remove natural impurities, tartrates and salts. A final sterilizing filtration ensures the wine's purity and stability after it reaches the more than 200 export markets of Martini & Rossi.

In taste and style, each Vermouth is distinctive as the result of variations during its creation. The quality of herbs and spices used for dry Vermouth is lighter and much different than for sweet. The portions of base wine used in the blends are 70% for the Extra Dry and 75% for the sweet types, Rosso and Bianco. The final sugar and alcohol levels also vary. Rosso and Bianco have an average residual sugar of 16% and alcohol of 16%; Extra Dry has an average of 2% residual sugar and 18% alcohol.

Martini & Rossi's success is based upon its reputation as the finest Vermouth in the world—one well earned and carefully preserved. The entire facility at Pessione reflects their preoccupation with quality. Although it has grown from an old company, it has been modernized into a model of organization and efficiency. Martini & Rossi produces wines and spirits of outstanding quality and value and have been recognized throughout the world with numerous medals and recognition by leading wine and spirits critics. The Martini & Rossi name is synonymous with the very best and has achieved worldwide notoriety.

For additional recipes, visit our website at
http://www.bacardi.com

10 R 10

¾ oz. MARTINI & ROSSI EXTRA DRY VERMOUTH

¾ oz. Dry Sherry

dash Bitters

Stir. Add lemon twist.

ACCURATE

¼ oz. MARTINI & ROSSI ROSSO VERMOUTH

¼ oz. Saki

1¼ oz. Cognac

Stir. Serve on the rocks.

AMERICANO

¾ oz. MARTINI & ROSSI ROSSO VERMOUTH

¾ oz. Campari

Club Soda

Build Campari and Martini & Rossi Rosso Vermouth in tall glass. Fill with club soda. Add twist.

ASTI MARTINI

½ oz. MARTINI & ROSSI EXTRA DRY VERMOUTH

4 oz. MARTINI & ROSSI ASTI

dash Chambord

Add well chilled Asti to the remaining ingredients and serve in a champagne flute. Garnish with a fresh raspberry.

B&B MANHATTAN

1 part MARTINI & ROSSI SWEET VERMOUTH

2 parts B&B Liqueur

dash Angostura Bitters

Shake and serve up. Garnish with a cherry.

BITCH ON WHEELS

½ oz. MARTINI & ROSSI EXTRA DRY VERMOUTH

1½ oz. Beefeater Dry Gin

½ oz. Pernod

1½ oz. Hiram Walker White Creme de Menthe

Shake all ingredients with ice and strain into a chilled martini glass.

BLUE EYES

1 oz. MARTINI & ROSSI EXTRA DRY VERMOUTH

2 oz. Bacardi Limón

5 drops Hiram Walker Blue Curacao

Stir in a mixing glass. Pour into martini glass and garnish with a twist of lemon.

BOUNTY

1 oz. MARTINI & ROSSI ROSSO VERMOUTH

1¼ oz. Canadian Club

3 dashes B&B Liqueur

Stir with cracked ice. Strain into cocktail glass. Serve with twist of lemon peel.

CARDINALE

⅖ oz. MARTINI & ROSSI EXTRA DRY VERMOUTH

⅖ oz. Beefeater Dry Gin

⅕ oz. Bitters

Add ice and serve.

CARUSO

½ oz. MARTINI & ROSSI EXTRA DRY VERMOUTH

½ oz. Beefeater Dry Gin

¼ oz. Hiram Walker Green Creme de Menthe

Stir. Serve on the rocks.

CLASSIC MARTINI

½ oz. MARTINI & ROSSI EXTRA DRY VERMOUTH

1½ oz. Beefeater Dry Gin

Shake with ice. Strain into chilled martini glass. Garnish with a twist or an olive.

CONTINENTAL COOLER

2 oz. MARTINI & ROSSI ROSSO VERMOUTH

4 oz. Soda

splash Major Peters' Grenadine

Stir. Serve on the rocks.

FAITHFUL JACK

½ oz. MARTINI & ROSSI EXTRA DRY VERMOUTH

½ oz. Beefeater Dry Gin

¼ oz. Hiram Walker Triple Sec

¼ oz. Brandy

Shake. Serve on the rocks with a cherry.

FRENCH KISS

1 part MARTINI & ROSSI ROSSO VERMOUTH

1 part MARTINI & ROSSI EXTRA DRY VERMOUTH

Serve over ice in rocks glass.

EL PRESIDENTE

¾ oz. MARTINI & ROSSI EXTRA DRY VERMOUTH

1½ oz. Bacardi Light Rum

dash Angostura Bitters

Stir with ice and strain into martini glass. Serve with twist of lemon.

FORMULA 1

1½ oz. MARTINI & ROSSI EXTRA DRY VERMOUTH

1½ oz. MARTINI & ROSSI ROSSO VERMOUTH

½ slice Orange

Mix. Serve with a squeeze of lemon peel.

FORMULA 2

1½ oz. MARTINI & ROSSI ROSSO VERMOUTH

1½ oz. MARTINI & ROSSI EXTRA DRY VERMOUTH

¾ oz. Grapefruit Juice

¾ oz. Tonic

Prepare directly in a tumbler with ice cubes and decorate with a slice of grapefruit.

GOLDEN BOY

½ oz. MARTINI & ROSSI EXTRA DRY VERMOUTH

½ oz. Beefeater Dry Gin

¼ oz. Grand Marnier

Stir. Serve on the rocks.

GRAPE ESCAPE

1 part MARTINI & ROSSI EXTRA DRY VERMOUTH

1 part Beefeater Dry Gin

1 part Brandy

1 part Bacardi Rum

splash Major Peters' Lime Juice

Stir well on the rocks.

HARVARD COCKTAIL

¾ oz. MARTINI & ROSSI ROSSO VERMOUTH

1½ oz. Brandy

2 tsp. Lemon Juice

1 tsp. Major Peters' Grenadine

dash Angostura Bitters

Shake ingredients with ice. Strain into cocktail glass.

INTERLUDE

¼ oz. MARTINI & ROSSI EXTRA DRY VERMOUTH

½ oz. Cutty Sark Scotch

¼ oz. Grand Marnier

Prepare in a mixing glass with ice cubes. Pour into double cocktail glass and decorate with slice of orange.

INVERTED MARTINI

3 oz. MARTINI & ROSSI EXTRA DRY VERMOUTH

1 oz. Beefeater Dry Gin

Add an olive or lemon twist.

ITALIAN ICED TEA

1 part MARTINI & ROSSI ROSSO VERMOUTH

2 parts Ginger Ale

Serve on the rocks with a slice of lemon.

LEMONTINI

2 oz. MARTINI & ROSSI EXTRA DRY VERMOUTH

Lemonade

Fill with lemonade, add a slice of lemon.

LIMÓN NEGRONI

2 parts MARTINI & ROSSI SWEET VERMOUTH

2 parts Bacardi Limón

1 part Campari

Serve on the rocks and stir well. Can also be served up. Garnish with twist of orange.

LIMÓN SCREWTINI

splash MARTINI & ROSSI EXTRA DRY VERMOUTH

1½ oz. Bacardi Limón

splash Orange Juice

Shake ingredients with ice and strain into a chilled martini glass. Garnish with orange twist.

LIMÓN TOPAZ MARTINI

½ oz. MARTINI & ROSSI EXTRA DRY VERMOUTH

1½ oz. Bacardi Limón

splash Hiram Walker Blue Curacao

Shake with ice and serve in a martini glass.

LUCIEN

1 part MARTINI & ROSSI
         ROSSO VERMOUTH

1 part MARTINI & ROSSI
         EXTRA DRY
         VERMOUTH

2 parts Cognac

2 parts Cutty Sark Scotch

In a tall glass with ice.

MANUELA

⅓ oz. MARTINI & ROSSI
        EXTRA DRY
        VERMOUTH

⅓ oz. MARTINI & ROSSI
        ROSSO VERMOUTH

⅓ oz. Beefeater Dry Gin

2-3 drops Cognac

2 drops Bitters

Prepare in a mixing glass. Pour into cocktail glass.

MARTINI & ROSSI "007" COCKTAIL

2 parts MARTINI & ROSSI
         EXTRA DRY
         VERMOUTH

2 parts Orange Juice

splash Major Peters'
        Grenadine

Stir. Serve on the rocks.

MARTINI SWEET

⅓ oz. MARTINI & ROSSI
        ROSSO VERMOUTH

⅔ oz. Beefeater Dry Gin

Prepare in a mixing glass with 4-5 ice cubes. Serve in a cocktail glass.

NEGRONI

½ oz. MARTINI & ROSSI
        EXTRA DRY
        VERMOUTH

½ oz. Beefeater Dry Gin

½ oz. Campari

Serve in rocks glass over ice.

PARADISE

¼ oz. MARTINI & ROSSI
        ROSSO VERMOUTH

1½ oz. Bacardi Limón

1 oz. Orange Juice

1 oz. Pineapple Juice

splash Major Peters'
        Grenadine

Serve in a tall cocktail glass with ice. Garnish with a slice of pineapple.

PERFECT MANHATTAN

¼ oz.   MARTINI & ROSSI
        ROSSO VERMOUTH

¼ oz.   MARTINI & ROSSI
        EXTRA DRY
        VERMOUTH

1½ oz. Bourbon

1-2 dshs. Bitters

Stir. Serve straight up or on the rocks.

PIE-IN-THE-SKY

1 part   MARTINI & ROSSI
         ROSSO VERMOUTH

1 part   Bacardi Rum

4 dashes Brandy

1 part   Major Peters'
         Lime Juice

2 dashes Major Peters'
         Grenadine

Shake. Serve on the rocks.

RAY'S BEST

¾ oz.   MARTINI & ROSSI
        ROSSO VERMOUTH

¾ oz.   Brandy

dash   Bitters

dash   Major Peters'
        Grenadine

Stir over the rocks.

RED RABBIT

¼ oz.   MARTINI & ROSSI
        EXTRA DRY
        VERMOUTH

½ oz.   Beefeater Dry Gin

¼ oz.   Hiram Walker Cherry
        Flavored Brandy

dash   Campari

Shake with ice. Serve over rocks.

RED ROSE

1 part   MARTINI & ROSSI
         ROSSO VERMOUTH

1 part   Hiram Walker
         Sloe Gin

2 dashes Bitters

         Club Soda

Stir. Add club soda.

RIVERSIDE

½ oz.   MARTINI & ROSSI
        EXTRA DRY
        VERMOUTH

½ oz.   MARTINI & ROSSI
        ROSSO VERMOUTH

½ oz.   Beefeater Dry Gin

½ oz.   Orange Juice

Shake. Serve over ice.

ROSSO SUNSET

1½ oz.   MARTINI & ROSSI ROSSO VERMOUTH

½ oz.   Hiram Walker Triple Sec

3 oz.   Orange Juice

splash   Master Peters' Grenadine

Shake. Serve over ice.

ROYAL ROSSI

¼ oz.   MARTINI & ROSSI ROSSO VERMOUTH

1 oz.   Beefeater Dry Gin

¼ oz.   Liquore Galliano

½ oz.   Campari

Shake. Serve on the rocks.

RUM MARTINI

dash   MARTINI & ROSSI EXTRA DRY VERMOUTH

1¼ oz.   Bacardi Rum

Stir on the rocks or strain into cocktail glass. Add olive or lemon twist.

SELECT MANHATTAN

¼ oz.   MARTINI & ROSSI ROSSO VERMOUTH

½ oz.   MARTINI & ROSSI EXTRA DRY VERMOUTH

1½ oz.   Bacardi Select Rum

1-2 dashes Angostura Bitters

Stir with ice and strain into martini glass. Garnish with cherry or lemon twist.

SHINING APPLE

½ oz.   MARTINI & ROSSI ROSSO VERMOUTH

½ oz.   Brandy

¼ oz.   Hiram Walker Cider Mill Schnapps

Shake. Serve over crushed ice.

SIRIO

½ oz.   MARTINI & ROSSI EXTRA DRY VERMOUTH

1½ oz.   MARTINI & ROSSI ASTI

½ oz.   Absolut Vodka

½ oz.   Hiram Walker Peach Schnapps

Add chilled Asti to ingredients. Serve in champagne flute. Garnish with slice of peach and squeeze of lemon peel.

SWEET & DRY

¾ oz. MARTINI & ROSSI ROSSO VERMOUTH

¾ oz. Bacardi Rum

3 dashes Brandy

1 dash Major Peters' Grenadine

1 oz. Lemon Juice

Shake. Serve on the rocks.

SWEET ROCKS

2 oz. MARTINI & ROSSI ROSSO VERMOUTH

Serve on the rocks with a lemon twist.

TEN TON COCKTAIL

1 Tbs. MARTINI & ROSSI EXTRA DRY VERMOUTH

1¼ oz. Canadian Club

1 Tbs. Grapefruit Juice

Combine with ice. Shake well. Strain and add ice. Add a cherry.

THE PRINCESS

1 part MARTINI & ROSSI ROSSO VERMOUTH

1 part Bacardi Rum

Stir over ice.

THE SWING COCKTAIL

1 oz. MARTINI & ROSSI ROSSO VERMOUTH

1 oz. MARTINI & ROSSI EXTRA DRY VERMOUTH

3 oz. Orange Juice

1 tsp Powdered Sugar

Shake well with ice. Serve on the rocks.

THE TONIC TWIST

2 oz. MARTINI & ROSSI EXTRA DRY VERMOUTH

4 oz. Tonic

Add a twist of lime.

UNDER THE VOLCANO MARTINI

1½ oz. MARTINI & ROSSI EXTRA DRY VERMOUTH

½ oz. Cuervo Tequila

1 Jalapeño Stuffed Olive

Shake ingredients with ice and stain into a chilled martini glass.

VERMOUTH CASSIS

2 oz. MARTINI & ROSSI
EXTRA DRY
VERMOUTH

½ oz. Hiram Walker Creme
de Cassis

Club Soda

*Fill with club soda, ice and add
lemon twist or wedge.*

VERMOUTH COCKTAIL

2 oz. MARTINI & ROSSI
ROSSO VERMOUTH

1 dash Bitters

1 dash Cherry Juice

Stir well. Serve on the rocks.

VERMOUTH COOLER

2 oz. MARTINI & ROSSI
EXTRA DRY
VERMOUTH

dash Major Peters'
Grenadine

Club Soda

*Serve in large glass with ice.
Fill with club soda.*

VERY DRY

2 ½ oz. MARTINI & ROSSI
EXTRA DRY
VERMOUTH

*Serve over ice. Add lemon
twist.*

WESTERN ROSE

¼ oz. MARTINI & ROSSI
EXTRA DRY
VERMOUTH

1¼ oz. Beefeater Dry Gin

¼ oz. Brandy

*Shake. Serve in rocks glass
with ice.*

Add your favorite Martini & Rossi recipes here.

© Foley Publishing Corp

MOZART
CHOCOLATE LIQUEUR

Mozart Liqueur is a delicious melody of creamy chocolate and hazelnut-nougat, finely blended with a touch of kirschwasser. Connoisseurs all over the world love the creaminess of the nougat-chocolate and its discreet sweetness. Mozart is the only chocolate liqueur made from all-natural ingredients and loaded with chocolate taste. On the rocks, with coffee, or just poured over ice cream, Mozart Chocolate Liqueur is a delight for chocolate lovers.

For additional recipes, visit our website at
http://www.ourniche.com

DON GIOVANNI

3 parts MOZART
CHOCOLATE
LIQUEUR

1 part Hiram Walker
Amaretto

Top with whipped cream.

M-PRESSO

1½ oz. MOZART
CHOCOLATE
LIQUEUR, chilled

*Pour chilled Mozart into glass
M-Presso cup. Run Espresso
into cup. Espresso and foam
will layer on top of Mozart.
Serve with a short straw.*

MOZART COLA

1 part MOZART
CHOCOLATE
LIQUEUR

3 parts Chilled Cola

*Mix well and pour over a
scoop of vanilla ice cream.*

MOZART CUP

1½ oz. MOZART
CHOCOLATE
LIQUEUR

2 scoops Ice Cream
or Frozen Yogurt

Whipped Cream

*Pour the Mozart Chocolate
Liqueur over the whipped cream
and ice cream or yogurt.*

MOZART ICE COFFEE

1 part MOZART
CHOCOLATE
LIQUEUR

2 parts Coffee, chilled

1 scoop Vanilla Ice cream

*Mix well and pour over a
scoop of vanilla ice cream.
Top with whipped cream and
chocolate flakes.*

MOZART MILKSHAKE

4 parts MOZART
CHOCOLATE
LIQUEUR

3 tsp. Coffee

1 tsp. Cocoa

1 Tbsp. Sugar

½ cup Cold Milk

*Mix for a couple of seconds in
a blender.*

MOZART MINT

3 parts MOZART
CHOCOLATE
LIQUEUR

1 part Hiram Walker White
Creme de Menthe

Serve on the rocks.

MOZART ON
THE ROCKS

1½ oz. MOZART
CHOCOLATE
LIQUEUR

*Serve with one or two ice
cubes.*

MOZART ORANGE

1 part MOZART
CHOCOLATE
LIQUEUR

1½ parts Orange Juice

*Mix well with bar spoon, pour
over ice cubes and serve with
a straw.*

MOZART ROYAL

¾ oz. MOZART
CHOCOLATE
LIQUEUR

¾ oz. Echte Kroatzbeere
Blackberry Liqueur

6 oz. Soda

*Combine Mozart and Echte
Kroatzbeere over ice in a
12 oz. tumbler; top with soda.
Garnish with an orange wheel.*

MOZART SONATINE

1 part MOZART
CHOCOLATE
LIQUEUR

⅓ tsp. Hiram Walker
Triple Sec

*On the rocks. Decorate with
slice of orange.*

NEOPOLITAN
ICE CREAM SHOT

⅓ part MOZART
CHOCOLATE
LIQUEUR

⅓ part Vanilla-flavored
Cream Liqueur

⅓ part Hiram Walker
Strawberry Liqueur

*Layer chilled liqueurs in shot
glass and enjoy. Yummy!*

Add your favorite Mozart recipes here.

© Foley Publishing Corp

NON-ALCOHOLIC RECIPES

BANANA LOPEZ

2 oz. Coco Lopez® Cream
of Coconut

1 med. Banana

1 tsp. Lemon Juice

1 cup Ice

Mix in blender until smooth.

COCO LOPEZ SHAKE

2½ oz. Coco Lopez® Cream
of Coconut

1 scoop Vanilla Ice Cream

1 cup Ice

Mix in blender until smooth.

COCO MOCHA LOPEZ

4 oz. Coco Lopez® Cream
of Coconut

2 oz. Cold Black Coffee

½ tsp. Brandy Flavor

1½ cups Ice

Mix in blender until smooth.
Sprinkle with nutmeg.

FLORIDA BANANA LOPEZ

2 oz. Coco Lopez® Cream
of Coconut

4 oz. Orange Juice

1 med. Banana

1 cup Ice

Mix in blender until smooth.

FROZEN APRICOT ORANGE LOPEZ

2 oz. Coco Lopez® Cream
of Coconut

1½ oz. Orange Juice

2 oz. Apricot Nectar

1½ cups Ice

Mix in blender until smooth.

GRAPE LOPEZ

3 oz. Coco Lopez® Cream
of Coconut

4 oz. Grape Juice

1½ cups Ice

Mix in blender until smooth.

LIME SORBET LOPEZ

2½ oz. Coco Lopez® Cream
of Coconut

½ oz. Major Peters'
Lime Juice

1 scoop Lime Sherbet

½ cup Ice

Mix in blender until smooth.

NADA COLADA

1 oz. Coco Lopez® Cream
of Coconut

2 oz. Pineapple Juice

1 cup Ice

Mix in blender until smooth.

NEW ORLEANS DAY

2 oz. Coco Lopez® Cream of Coconut

1 oz. Butterscotch Topping

1 oz. Half & Half

1 cup Ice

Mix in blender until smooth.

ORANGE SMOOTHIE

2½ oz. Coco Lopez® Cream of Coconut

3 oz. Orange Juice

1 scoop Vanilla Ice Cream

1 cup Ice

Nutmeg

Mix in blender until smooth.
Sprinkle with nutmeg.

ORANGE SORBET LOPEZ

2 oz. Coco Lopez® Cream of Coconut

1 oz. Orange Juice

1 scoop Orange Sherbet

½ cup Ice

Mix in blender until smooth.

PINEAPPLE LOPEZ

2 oz. Coco Lopez® Cream of Coconut

1½ oz. Pineapple Juice

½ Banana

1 cup Ice

Mix in blender until smooth.

PINEAPPLE SORBET LOPEZ

1½ oz. Coco Lopez® Cream of Coconut

2 oz. Pineapple Juice

1 scoop Pineapple Sherbet

1 cup Ice

Mix in blender until smooth.

STRAWBERRY BANANA LOPEZ

2 oz. Coco Lopez® Cream of Coconut

2 oz. Strawberries

½ med. Banana

1 cup Ice

Mix in blender until smooth.

TROPICAL FREEZE LOPEZ

2 oz. Coco Lopez® Cream of Coconut

1½ oz. Orange Juice

1½ oz. Pineapple Juice

1 cup Ice

Mix in blender until smooth.

Add your favorite non-alcoholic drink recipes here.

For additional recipes, visit our website at
http://www.cocolopez.com

© Foley Publishing Corp

ROMANA SAMBUCA

THE ULTIMATE ANISE FLAVORED LIQUEUR

Romana Sambuca is the authentic Italian liqueur which embodies the Italian passion for life and good times. Romana Sambuca denotes the sophistication and impeccable taste of its connoisseurs which are cultured, confident social drinkers who all share the same "Passione de la Vita!" Though versatile to be used in many delicious cocktails and mixed with specialty coffees, many believe its unique flavor is best served in the traditional manner. It is traditionally cherished "Con Mosca," where three roasted coffee beans float on top of the clear liqueur. Romana's proud Italian heritage carries a mythical tradition that adds to the cordial's mystique and allure. Legend has it that anyone enjoying Romana served "Con Mosca" is granted one wish, and good fortune will surely follow! The celebrated beans are meant to signify Health, Wealth and Happiness.

Perfect after dinner, Romana encourages conversation and lends itself as a convivial way to keep the evening going. Romana Sambuca is the perfect complement to the current coffee craze where it is mixed in coffee, cappuccino, espresso and latte. Its bold flavor can also stand up to any full-bodied meal and as experts of the "best things in life," more and more people are proud to drink the original and classic sambuca of Italy...Romana Sambuca.

The attraction of sambuca historically revolves around its strong association with anise, long exalted for its medicinal and therapeutic properties. An early form of sambuca can be traced to the Arab invasion of Sicily around the year 1000. Modern day sambuca combines the best properties of anise in an alcoholic beverage that has become firmly established in the minds, hearts, and traditions of the Italian people.

Romana's bold, velvety, smooth flavor contains quality all natural ingredients without any artificial flavors or preservatives. Its fennel and anise seed nose has many elaborate high notes which are not found in many other sambucas. In the finish there are hints of spice combined with a beautiful core of fresh fennel, green anise seed and star anise.

Romana is the definitive sambuca produced with care, expertise, and a respect for tradition second to none in the industry. The first bottles of Romana were produced by the Pallini family at their facility in the shadow of the Pantheon in the heart of old Rome, the perfect setting for the liqueur that embodies the style and fashion of contemporary Italy combined with the romance and intrigue of age-old tradition.

Add your favorite Romana Sambuca recipes here.

HOT RECIPES

BUCA-CINO

1 oz. ROMANA SAMBUCA

4 oz. Hot Cappuccino

Mix ROMANA SAMBUCA with hot cappuccino. Top with whipped cream.

CAPE CODDER

1½ oz. ROMANA SAMBUCA

Half & Half

Coffee

Pour coffee over ice, add ROMANA SAMBUCA, Half & Half and brown sugar to taste.

HOT SHOT

½ oz. ROMANA SAMBUCA

½ oz. Hot Coffee

Whipped Cream

Pour the Sambuca and coffee into a pony glass. Layer freshly whipped cream on top.

ROMAN CHOCOLATE

1½ oz. ROMANA SAMBUCA

5 oz. Hot Chocolate

Pour ROMANA SAMBUCA into large mug with hot chocolate. Top with whipped cream and chocolate shavings.

ROMANA CAFE

1 oz. ROMANA SAMBUCA

5 oz. Espresso

Add ROMANA SAMBUCA to espresso; top with sweetened whipped cream.

THERMOSTAT

1 oz. ROMANA SAMBUCA

½ oz. Hiram Walker
Hazelnut Liqueur

Hot Coffee

Pour ROMANA SAMBUCA and Hiram Walker Hazelnut Liqueur into hot coffee. Add nutmeg to taste.

COLD RECIPES

B-53

1 part ROMANA SAMBUCA

1 part Kahlua

1 part Hiram Walker
Triple Sec

Serve in shot glass.

BAILEYS COMET

¼ oz. ROMANA SAMBUCA

1 oz. Baileys Irish Cream

¼ oz. Goldwasser

¼ oz. Hiram Walker
Butterscotch
Schnapps

Shake. Serve over ice.

BLACKOUT

1 part ROMANA SAMBUCA

1 part Romana Black

1 part Kahlua

Mix in a shot glass.

BOCA ROMANA

1½ oz. ROMANA SAMBUCA

3 oz. Orange Juice

Serve over ice in a tall glass.

BOOTLEGGER

½ oz. ROMANA SAMBUCA

1 oz. Jack Daniel's

½ oz. Southern Comfort

Serve over ice in a rocks glass.

COLOSSEUM COOLER

1 oz. ROMANA SAMBUCA

3 oz. Cranberry Juice

In a tall glass, fill with soda and garnish with lime wedge.

EMPEROR'S DELIGHT

1 oz. ROMANA SAMBUCA

½ oz. Hiram Walker Amaretto

1 oz. Cream

Serve in a lowball glass over ice.

FERRIS WHEEL

1½ oz. ROMANA SAMBUCA

1 oz. Brandy

1 Lemon Twist

In a mixing glass half-filled with ice cubes, combine the Sambuca and brandy. Stir well. Strain into a cocktail glass. Garnish with the lemon twist.

FLAMING LAMBORGHINI

½ oz. ROMANA SAMBUCA

1 oz. Kahlua

½ oz. Carolans Irish Cream

dash Hiram Walker Blue Curacao

FLATLINER (aka Fireball)

1 oz. ROMANA SAMBUCA

½ oz. Cuervo Tequila

dash Tabasco Sauce

Shake. Serve in shot glass.

FOREIGN AFFAIR

1 part ROMANA SAMBUCA

1 part Metaxa Brandy

Mix in snifter.

FOX TAIL

1 oz. ROMANA SAMBUCA

½ oz. Heavy Cream

pinch Instant Coffee
Powder

Pour the Sambuca into a pony glass. Using the back of a spoon, slowly pour the cream in so that it floats on top. Finally, dust the drink with the coffee powder.

FREDDY KRUGER

½ oz. ROMANA SAMBUCA

½ oz. Jagermeister

½ oz. Absolut Vodka

Shake. Serve in shot glass.

ITALIAN AMERICAN

1 part ROMANA SAMBUCA

3 parts Lemonade

splash Major Peters'
Grenadine

Mix, serve over ice.

ITALIAN SUNSET

1½ oz. ROMANA SAMBUCA

3 oz. Orange Juice

splash Major Peters'
Grenadine

Serve over ice in a tall glass.

JELLY BEAN

1 part ROMANA SAMBUCA

1 part Hiram Walker
Blackberry Brandy

Mix; strain over ice.

LIQUID NITROGEN

Equal Parts:

ROMANA SAMBUCA

#12 Ouzo

Mix; strain over ice.

NERO'S DELIGHT

In a shot glass, layer equal parts:

ROMANA SAMBUCA

Carolan's Irish Cream

Absolut Vodka

ROMA

½ oz. ROMANA SAMBUCA

¾ oz. Beefeater Dry Gin

¾ oz. Grappa

½ oz. Martini & Rossi
Dry Vermouth

1 scoop Crushed Ice
Green Olive

Mix all the ingredients, except the olive, in a shaker or blender. Strain the mixture into a chilled cocktail glass and garnish with the olive.

ROMAN ANGEL

1 oz. ROMANA SAMBUCA

5 oz. Eggnog

Mix; add nutmeg to taste.

ROMAN SNOWBALL

1 scoop Crushed Ice

2-3 oz. ROMANA SAMBUCA

5 Coffee Beans

Fill a tulip glass with crushed ice, pour in the Sambuca. Drop the coffee beans into the glass and serve with a straw.

ROMANA CON MOSCA

1½ oz. ROMANA SAMBUCA

3 Roasted Coffee Beans

Pour 1½ oz. ROMANA SAMBUCA into a tall, slender liqueur glass. Float coffee beans on top.

RUSSIAN ROULETTE

½ oz. ROMANA SAMBUCA

½ oz. Kahlua

½ oz. Absolut Vodka

½ oz. Orange Juice

Shake. Serve on the rocks or as a shot.

SAMBUCA SLIDE

½ shot ROMANA SAMBUCA

¼ shot Absolut Vodka

¼ shot Cream

Chill.

SAMSON

½ oz. ROMANA SAMBUCA

½ oz. Hiram Walker Blackberry Brandy

½ oz. Hiram Walker Amaretto

1½ oz. Light Cream

In a shaker half-filled with ice cubes, combine all of the ingredients. Shake well. Strain into a cocktail glass.

SICILIAN TEA

1½ oz. ROMANA SAMBUCA

Iced Tea

Pour over ice in highball glass.

SILVER SPLINTER

½ oz. ROMANA SAMBUCA

1 oz. Bacardi Dark Rum

2 oz. Heavy Cream

Stir over ice and strain into a cocktail glass.

SLIPPERY NIPPLE

In a shot glass, layer equal parts:

> ROMANA SAMBUCA
> Carolan's Irish Cream

SNOW MELTER

¾ oz. ROMANA SAMBUCA

½ oz. Bacardi Rum

½ oz. Hiram Walker Light
           Creme de Cacao

Pour into a large shot glass.

THE IRISH-ITALIAN SPIRIT

¾ oz. ROMANA SAMBUCA

¾ oz. Carolan's Irish Cream

Mix in a lowball glass over ice.

WHITE CLOUD

1½ oz. ROMANA SAMBUCA

5 oz. Club Soda

Serve over ice in a tall glass.

WHITE HEART

1½ oz. ROMANA SAMBUCA

½ oz. Hiram Walker White
           Creme de Cacao

½ oz. Cream

Shake with ice. Serve up.

ZIMBEER

1½ oz. ROMANA SAMBUCA

2 oz. Root Beer

Serve in tall glass with ice.

Add your favorite Romana Sambuca recipes here.

© Foley Publishing Corp

SCHOENAUER APFEL SCHNAPPS

Refreshingly crisp and delicious, Schoenauer combines the aromatic juices of apples from Germany's best-known fruit and vegetable growing area ("Altes Land," located only a few miles east of Hamburg), with the highest quality wheat and rye distillates, for the production of an outstanding grain spirit, referred to as "Apfelkorn."

At 42 proof, Schoenauer can easily be enjoyed chilled and straight up, or on the rocks. In addition to being a good shot drink, Schoenauer's pronounced apple flavor lends itself well as a versatile ingredient in a variety of mixed drinks.

For additional recipes, visit our website at
http://www.ourniche.com

APPLE BREEZE

1½ oz. SCHOENAUER
        APFEL SCHNAPPS

splash Cranberry Juice

        Soda Water

Pour in a chilled collins glass over ice; garnish with lemon slice.

BEER AND SCHOENAUER

Enjoy 1½ oz. chilled SCHOE-NAUER APFEL SCHNAPPS with your favorite beer on the side.

BIG APPLE

3 parts SCHOENAUER
         APFEL SCHNAPPS

4-6 parts Club Soda

         Lemon Wedge

Pour Schoenauer over ice in an old-fashioned glass; squeeze in lemon juice, add wedge and stir well. Pour in soda and stir.

CARMEL APPLE

Put 1 carmel candy in a shot glass and fill with SCHOE-NAUER APFEL SCHNAPPS. Shoot and chew candy!

DIANE'S APPLE PIE

Equal parts:

        SCHOENAUER
        APFEL SCHNAPPS

        Basilica Hazelnut

dash Cinnamon

Guaranteed to whet your whistle and warm your belly!

HAPPY APPLE

2½ oz. SCHOENAUER
        APFEL SCHNAPPS

1 oz. Absolut Vodka

Light splash Club Soda

Over ice in tall glass, pour Schoenauer and vodka, stir well and add club soda. WILL MAKE YOU GLOW!

HOT APPLE TODDY

1½ oz. SCHOENAUER
APFEL SCHNAPPS

*Fill mug with hot apple cider,
garnish with cinnamon stick.*

SINFUL APPLE

¼ part SCHOENAUER
APFEL SCHNAPPS

1½ parts Absolut Vodka

*Shake and serve on the rocks
or in a shot glass.*

SKIER'S DELIGHT

1½ oz. SCHOENAUER
APFEL SCHNAPPS

*Fill mug with hot cinnamon
tea.*

Add your favorite Schoenauer Apfel Schnapps recipes here.

© Foley Publishing Corp

SINGLE MALTS

Defenders of the Malt

Romans, Vikings, English and Germans—a series of breaches, battles, boundaries broken and restored. This land, so jealously defended and joyously celebrated, holds over a hundred distilleries, each distinct by virtue of its exact location on Scottish earth. Many began as lone pot-stills, hidden in caves, defying the bounty-hunting tax men. These maverick distillers protected and preserved their precious recipes—their treasure, their right.

A Defender of the Malt has this rebel spirit in every dram. Add a mysterious chemistry that captures the malt and the essence of its birthplace, and you've distilled a Defender. Defenders of the Malt fight for the right to bring their history, their land, their magic, across centuries, seas and continents—to you.

The Single Malts

Generations of Scots have worked in distilleries; whole villages are built around the creation of the "water of life." Every hamlet that is home to a single malt conspires to meld the earth and air and water of their specific space into a substance that carries its character. Each distiller guards its lore and superstitions as if following a recipe handed down from ancient sorcerers.

It is modern day alchemy. The character of a single malt depends on many variables; when the barley is harvested, how much water from a local brook covers the seedlings, how long the grains dry over a peat fire—how big a fire, how much peat is taken from a neighboring field. Then the mystery of the pot-still; no one understands how the shape of the pot and the height of the still affect the taste of a single malt. What they do know is not to change it once they've found the perfect vessel for their particular elixir.

Distillery workers defend every detail of their traditional whisky, taking fierce pride in its personality. The spirit of the single malt; a signature of people and place.

Single Malt Essentials

STEP 1: Fully ripened barley is soaked in water in steeps for up to 3 days.

STEP 2: The barley is drained and spread to germinate on the floor of the malting house for up to 12 days.

STEP 3: The green malt is spread on the kiln floor to dry, fired by slow burning peat.

STEP 4: After a month, the grain is crushed in mills to produce malt grist.

STEP 5: The grist is mixed with hot water in the mash tun to make wort, a sugary water.

STEP 6: The wort is poured into a wash tun and yeast is added. Fermenting creates a low alcohol beer or wash.

STEP 7: The wash now passes through a wash still and a spirit still and condenser emerging water white and about 120° proof.

STEP 8: Spring water is added to reduce the spirit to about 110° proof.

STEP 9: Whisky is stored in sherry oak casks, or Bourbon oak casks, to mature.

The Glendronach

15 Year Old

Description: Glendronach is matured 100% sherry in casks from Spain. The Unsurpassed 100% Sherry Cask Malt.

Color: Deep ruby-red gold

Nose: Big sherry, followed by spicy-smoke, deep whisky

Body: Big, velvety and luscious

Palate: Burst of sherry, malty, lightly peated, lingering oak and smoke

Finish: Deep, rich, warmly lingering

Laphroaig

10 Year Old

The smokiest and peatiest of all whiskies, stored in white oak casks in "the beautiful hollow by the broad bay." The Definitive Islay Malt.

Color: Full-refractive-gold

Nose: Very peaty with the tangy sweetness of the sea

Body: Full and hardy

Palate: Richly smoky—fully peated, with still a hint of sweetness—salty

Finish: Lingering and unique

The Laphroaig 15 Year Old is even richer, smoother and more complex than its younger cousin. Maturity has added spice to the bold peatiness, creating a silky, oily elegance that cannot be surpassed. The Quintessential Single Malt.

Scapa 12 Year Old

From the isles of ancient adventure. Aged in Bourbon casks warehoused by the sea. The Ultimate Orkney Malt.

Color: Brilliant honeyed gold

Nose: Sweet, creamy vanilla, honeyed notes, floral aroma, slight salt

Body: Silky-smooth and rounded

Palate: Spicy, heather honey mixed with oat sweetness, mild salty aftertaste

Finish: Smooth and warming, airy and light

Laphroaig

The western isle of Islay is covered with deep and ancient peat bogs that provide fuel for the island and the essential character of its whiskies. Laphroaig, "the beautiful hollow by the broad bay," burns peat from its own peat beds in the drying of the malt in its floor maltings. The white oak casks full of aging whisky are stored in a warehouse on the sea, where the wood breathes in the briny sea-mist, air of salt and seaweed, as waves lap against the warehouse at high tide.

Laphroaig is the most challenging and individual of malt whiskies, the smokiest and peatiest of all. The taste is uncompromising and as unexpected as its history: the distillery whose founder, Dugald Johnston, drowned in a vat of his own whisky. The first distillery to be run by a woman, Bessie Williamson, in the late 1950s. The single malt awarded a royal warrant by Prince Charles.

The taste is unmistakably Islay: bold and peaty, golden topaz, sea-salt and a hint of sweetness, with a big round finish that lingers like a ring of smoke. Laphroaig is the

Definitive Islay Malt.

Glendronach

The heart of the Highlands, bordered by granite mountains and lines of rivers crossing barley-green valleys, is home to half of Scotland's whiskies. Water takes hundreds of years to seep out of granite, form springs and streams; each sip of scotch follows this journey from rock to river.

Glendronach, "valley of blackberries," is on the eastern edge of Speyside, nestled against the hills of Aberdeenshire farming country. Matured 100% in sherry casks from Spain, the whisky sleeps in stone warehouses for at least fifteen years before it becomes pure sherry pleasure in a bottle. Rooks, symbols of good fortune and prosperity, return there each year to nest.

No wonder; the taste of Glendronach invites return visits. Deep ruby-red gold, with a burst of sherry, oak and smoke, rich and warmly lingering. Glendronach is the Unsurpassed 100% Sherry Cask Malt.

Scapa

White cliffs, wild North Sea surf, and a wind-shifting sky that colors and shapes the light, moment by moment. The Ring of Brodgar, a circle of enormous standing stones, carefully placed in enigmatic order over two thousand years ago. The Orkney Isles, ancient land of misty secrets and mystic adventure—the land where time began.

Scapa is one of only two distilleries on the Orkney isles. Scapa's water supply is flavored by distinctive Orkney peat, yet the distillery uses only unpeated malt. Aged in Bourbon casks warehoused by the sea, Scapa breathes in the salt air and exhales the time-honored "share for the angels." The distillery is still, in part, powered by the waterwheel built there in 1885, preserving the craft that makes this malt an effortless beauty.

Scapa's honeyed, clean, yet spicy taste embodies the intriguing spirit of the Orkney Isles. Sweet spice, tangy salt of the open sea, amber silk texture—Scapa is The Ultimate Orkney Malt.

Are You a Defender?

A Defender celebrates difference, appreciates the truly unique, loves the mystery of genuine quality. Defenders are not afraid to strike out alone, confident in their own taste and certain they'll find others who share their insight.

Defenders search for the flavor of excellence, and find it in the challenging uniqueness of these single malts. They share the same qualities as the whiskies: strength of character, pride in their own beliefs...subtly rebellious. From the peaty Islay boldness of Laphroaig, through the Highland sherried elegance of Glendronach, to the spicy, honeyed Scapa of the Orkneys, Defenders of the Malt have discovered a taste for adventure.

SINGLE MALT TASTING SHEET
Guide to Tasting Notes:

"Don't worry about using expert language or terminology. The most important thing to remember is that enjoying single malt whisky is a personal experience. When it is shared with other people each one of them will use their own words, based on their individual experiences."

STEP 1: Look at the COLOR of the single malt in the glass. We begin tasting with our eyes. The color can tell you a lot about the taste and the character of a whisky (e.g. honeyed gold, ruby-red, amber, bronze). Color can vary from very pale, to a rich caramel brown or even red, depending whether oak or sherry barrels are used. Hold the scotch up to the light to check the color.

STEP 2: Check out the NOSE, or the aroma of the malt before you add water. The nose provides further clues on the whisky. It especially tells you a lot about its taste, as 80% of what you taste is actually through the nose (e.g. sweet, spicy-smoke, fully peated, big, sherry).

STEP 3: Add the same amount of water to the glass as whisky. Remember to give it a good swirl.

STEP 4: Nose the single malt again. You will notice a real difference and significantly more intense aromas than prior to adding water.

STEP 5: Take a sip of the whisky. Look for the following:

- The BODY, or the texture. Simply put, it is the way the whisky feels in your mouth (e.g. oily, silky-smooth, rounded, velvety, hardy).

- The PALATE, or the flavor. In other words, the taste of the whisky (e.g. spicy, lingering oak, fully peated, grassy, malty).

- The FINISH, or the aftertaste. The flavor that remains in your mouth (e.g. rich, warmly lingering, light, dry, restrained).

STEP 6: Have a drink of water to cleanse your palate.

STEP 7: Go on to the next number on your tasting mat.

STEP 8: Repeat the process.

MALT WHISKY
FLAVOR DESCRIPTIONS
BLAND

Lack of distinctive characteristics.

BODY: Describes the sensation created in the mouth. Usually qualified by terms such as "full bodied" or "lacks body."

COARSE: Indifferent quality. Certain flavors and aromas are intense and are strongly felt in the mouth and on the nose.

DRY: A general sensation of astringency; a lack of sweet aromas or sweetness in the mouth.

FLAT: Dull and flavorless.

FRESH: The opposite of flat. Product is in ideal condition.

HARD: The opposite of soft. Strong metallic, flinty and nasal astringency.

HEAVY: Flavors and aromas are easily distinguished; not necessarily a criterion of quality.

LIGHT: Good balance in intensity of flavor and aroma. Tends to be delicate in type: e.g. fragrant.

MELLOW: Describes a whisky which has reached maturity, the pungency of the alcohol has been reduced.

ROBUST: A whisky which is rich in taste and aroma.

ROUND: A good balance between flavor and aroma.

SHARP: Imparts nose and mouth prickle.

SOFT: Does not contain any alcoholic pungency.

SWEETNESS: Sugary taste from malted barley.

THIN: Lack of aroma and flavor, giving rise to the terms "diluted" or "watery."

For additional recipes, visit our website at
http://www.laphroaig.com

ANHEUSER-BUSCH, INC

At Anheuser-Busch, Inc., the phrase "Somebody Still Cares About Quality" accurately depicts the philosophy of the world's largest and most successful brewing operation.

With 34 domestic brands and five imports, Anheuser-Busch, Inc. offers consumers the most diverse, high quality family of beers in the brewing industry.

Since its establishment as a small South St. Louis brewery in 1860, the company has maintained key commitments to product quality, tradition and leadership. Through the years, the beer brands of Anheuser-Busch have become part of the American scene, quality products consumed responsibly by an overwhelming majority of American beer consumers.

HISTORY OF BEER

The origins of beer are older than recorded history, extending into the mythology of ancient civilizations. Beer, the oldest alcoholic beverage, was discovered independently by most ancient cultures—the Babylonians, Assyrians, Egyptians, Hebrews, Africans, Chinese, Incas, Teutons, Saxons and the various wandering tribes that were found in Eurasia.

In recorded history, Babylonian clay tablets more than 6,000 years old depict the brewing of beer and give detailed recipes. An extract from an ancient Chinese manuscript states that beer, or "kiu" as it was called, was known to the Chinese in the 23rd century B.C.

With the rise of commerce and the growth of cities during the Middle Ages, brewing became more than a household activity. Municipal brew houses were established, which eventually led to the formation of the brewing guilds. Commercial brewing on a significantly larger scale began around the 12th century in Germany.

Although native Americans had developed a form of beer, Europeans brought their own version with them to the New World. Beer enjoys the distinction of having come over on the Mayflower and, in fact, seems to have played a part in the Pilgrims' decision to land at Plymouth Rock instead of farther south, as intended. A journal kept by one of the passengers—and now in the Library of Congress—states, in an entry from 1620, that the Mayflower landed at Plymouth because "we could not now take time for further search, our victuals being much spent, especially our beer..."

The first commercial brewery in America was founded in New Amsterdam (New York) in 1623. Many patriots owned their own breweries, among them Samuel Adams and William Penn. George Washington even had his own brew house on the grounds of Mount Vernon, and his handwritten recipe for beer—dated 1757 and taken from his diary—is still preserved.

BREWING AT ANHEUSER-BUSCH

In 1876, Adolphus Busch created a beer that would become known for its uncompromising quality. The original Budweiser label guaranteed a beer brewed by a unique process, using only the highest quality ingredients.

Today Budweiser's label gives the same assurance of quality. On the label for all to see are the words: "This is the famous Budweiser beer. We know of no brand produced by any other brewer which costs so much to brew and age. Our exclusive beechwood aging produces a taste, a smoothness and a drinkability you will find in no other beer at any price." Today more than a century later, the quality is still there, still uncompromised.

The secret of fine, traditional brewing is really no secret at all—take the choicest, most costly ingredients, skillfully brew them allowing plenty of time for nature to work its wonders, age the beer slowly and naturally, and take intense pride and care in every step along the way. That's the way Anheuser-Busch has always brewed beer.

INGREDIENTS

Beer is a food product made from barley malt, hops, grain adjuncts, yeast and water. The alcohol in beer results from the fermentation by yeast of an extract from barley malt and other cereal grains. In addition to alcohol, beer commonly contains carbohydrates, proteins, amino acids, vitamins (such as riboflavin and niacin) and minerals (such as calcium and potassium) derived from the original food materials.

All Anheuser-Busch beers vary in the type and mix of ingredients and in certain refinements in the brewing process to achieve their distinctive and unique characteristics. But all are like in one respect—every Anheuser-Busch beer is completely natural without any artificial ingredients, additives or preservatives.

Superior ingredients are basic in the brewing of truly great beers. Anheuser-Busch uses only the finest, choicest, most costly ingredients available, selected through the most exacting requirements and specifications in the brewing industry. Again, nothing secret or mysterious, just the same basic ingredients that have been known for centuries as the way to make fine beers—barley malt, hops, rice or corn, yeast and water.

Malt - Malt is the soul of all great beers and Anheuser-Busch uses more malt per barrel than any other major brewer in the country. The malt it uses begins with the choicest golden barley selected from the finest fields in America— from the sweeping plains of Minnesota and the Dakotas and from the Western states of Idaho, Washington, Wyoming, Colorado, Oregon, Montana and California.

There are two basic types of malting barleys. One produces two rows of kernels on each stalk, the other, six rows.

The flavor of the two varieties differs, with two-row barley malt being a choicer ingredient because it produces a smoother-tasting beer. Anheuser-Busch beers contain a varying percentage of two-row barley malt. Michelob contains the highest percentage.

In a carefully controlled malting procedure, the barley is cleaned, steeped, germinated and kilned. Malt is a natural source of carbohydrates, enzymes and flavor compounds. Most of the enzymes are developed during the malting process. During brewing, the complex malt carbohydrates are broken apart by the enzymes. As a result, simple sugars are formed. These sugars are used by the yeast as an energy source during fermentation.

Hops - Hops, the cone-shaped clusters of blossoms from the vine-like hop plant, are the spice of beer, adding their own special aroma, flavor and character. Anheuser-Busch uses only the choicest imported and domestic hops, hand-selected by company agents from the world's finest fields in Europe and Washington, Oregon and Idaho.

Rice - Rice adds lightness and crispness to Budweiser and Michelob brands, while some of our other brands are made with corn to produce a milder flavor.

Yeast - The brewer's yeast used in all Anheuser-Busch beers has been perfected and protected over decades, and all of the company's breweries are supplied from one carefully maintained pure-culture system.

Water - Pure water is also a key ingredient in brewing great beer. Water is checked just as rigidly as other ingredients and, when necessary, the water is treated to ensure conformity to Anheuser-Busch's exacting standards.

BREWING PROCESS

Next comes the brewing process. Here, too, there is no secret—visitors have always been welcome to tour Anheuser-Busch breweries and witness the painstaking and exacting care it takes to produce its beers. As an example, following are the steps in the Budweiser brewing process.

Brewing at Anheuser-Busch is a long, natural process taking up to 30 days or longer. It may appear old-fashioned to brew beer principally the way they have been brewing it for more than 100 years but Anheuser-Busch has never found a better way to brew than by combining the finest ingredients with slow, precise steps which give nature the time it needs to create great beer. There are modern shortcuts such as forcing fermentation by mechanical agitation, using enzyme preparations for chillproofing or artificially injecting CO_2 into the beer for carbonation—but they don't create great beers.

MODERN TECHNOLOGY AND QUALITY ASSURANCE

While it chooses not to use chemical advances to cut corners in brewing, Anheuser-Busch has always been innovative in the use of science to promote quality. The company pioneered in the application of pasteurization in the brewing industry and developed the use of refrigeration railcars and a nationwide system of rail delivery.

Today, the Anheuser-Busch traditional brewing process is strictly maintained using modern technology in a rigorous program of quality assurance. Scientists and technicians use every skill available to ensure that each bottle, can or keg of beer is the very finest that can be produced, and to ensure that each Anheuser-Busch beer has its own great taste glass after glass, year after year.

Quality assurance at Anheuser-Busch begins with the testing of ingredients before brewing ever begins. Perfection is sought through close scrutiny extending down to the smallest detail of the packaging operation, including bottle crowns and can lids.

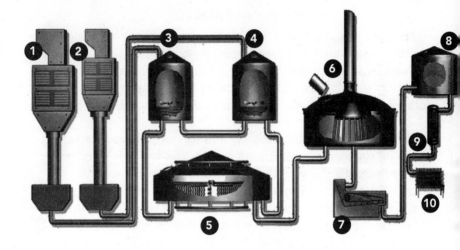

Anheuser-Busch Brewing Process

The Budweiser brewing process begins at the:

1. malt mill and

2. rice mill, where both ingredients are ground and precisely weighed. Using a double mash system, the ground malt is then combined with water in the

3. mash vessel, where it is agitated and heated. The rice is combined with water and a small portion of the malt mash in the

4. cereal cooker, where it is brought to a boil. This cooked cereal is then transferred to the mash vessel and combined with the malt mash. After a prescribed heating period, the entire mash mixture is transferred to the

5. lauter tub, where the sugar-rich liquid, called "wort," is separated from the spent grains and transferred to the

6. brewkettle, where it is boiled and hops are added. The spent hops are removed in the

7. hop jack. Before fermentation, wort is pumped to the

8. hot wort receiver, where some of the malt protein flakes, called "trub," are removed by swirling the wort in this tank. It is then passed through the

9. wort aerator, where sterile air will help drive off volatile compounds, and then cooled in the

10. wort cooler. In the

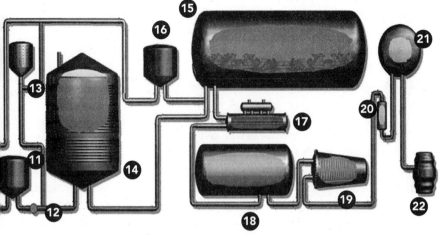

11. cold wort settler, additional trub is settled out, and the wort is pumped to the fermentor. On the way to the fermentor,

12. sterile air and

13. yeast are added to the wort. The yeast begins its work in the

14. fermentor where CO_2 and alcohol are produced. The beer is then transferred to the

15. lager tank, where

16. kraeusen (freshly yeasted wort) is added for a secondary fermentation stage. Beechwood chips are also present in this tank to increase the surface area for the yeast. After this aging cycle, the resulting product is called "chip" beer. It is then moved through the

17. chillproofing cooler, where the beer is cooled and transferred to the

18. chillproofing tank, where the beer is stabilized prior to filtration. The

19. filter operation removes insoluble material (including yeast) to clarify the beer. The beer then passes through the

20. polishing filter into the

21. filtered beer tank. At this point quality is assured by our brewmasters before beer is released for packaging into

22. bottles, cans, or draft kegs.

No scientific test, however, can replace tasting as the final judgment of quality. Numerous flavor panels meet daily at company headquarters and at each brewery to judge the aroma, appearance and taste of packaged, filtered and unfiltered beer. In addition, samples are flown into St. Louis from each brewery for taste evaluation.

Control of quality does not cease at the brewery. Anheuser-Busch's wholesalers play a key role in seeing that the quality that begins with the ingredients and continues through the brewing and packaging processes is preserved until it reaches the consumers. Anheuser-Busch wholesalers, at their expense, provide controlled environment warehouse systems that maintain beer freshness during storage.

In the marketplace, quality standards and beer freshness are maintained through Anheuser-Busch's unique "Born On" Freshness Dating program. Initiated in September of 1996, the program tells consumers the exact day, month and year the beer was packaged so they know how fresh it is. All Anheuser-Busch domestic brands feature "Born On" dates, with an alpha-numeric code that is easy for consumers to read and understand. The "Born On" date is accompanied by a "Brewery Fresh Taste Guaranteed" seal and a "Freshest Taste Within 110 Days" tag.

The final result of all these efforts is a family of naturally brewed beers that the company believes is the freshest in the industry. And millions of consumers agree.

Anheuser-Busch remains firmly committed to quality, which it believes is, and has always been, the fundamental, irreplaceable ingredient in its successful performance.

Anheuser-Busch further believes that the consuming public will increasingly come to recognize and appreciate the natural quality and value that it has been brewing into its beers for more than a century.

BUDWEISER MOBILE BEER SCHOOL

The Budweiser Mobile Beer School is a classroom on wheels that enables Anheuser-Busch to bring its brewmasters anywhere in the United States to teach people who serve and sell beer—such as bartenders, bar managers and wholesaler personnel—as well as beer drinkers, about the art, science and tradition of brewing beer. There are currently four Budweiser Mobile Beer Schools traveling the country.

The Budweiser Mobile Beer School program includes a brief look at the history of beer around the world, a description of the all-natural ingredients Anheuser-Busch uses to brew its beers and an overview of the principles of brewing, allowing participants to see the step-by-step process by which barley malt, brewer's rice, hops, yeast and water are crafted into fresh Budweiser. Brewmasters then introduce guests to the wide variety of beer styles that are popular today and discuss the benefits of drinking brewery-fresh beer.

The Budweiser Mobile Beer School is an extension of the Budweiser Beer School, a program also taught by Anheuser-Busch brewmasters that began in early 1995. Budweiser Beer School is taught primarily at Anheuser-Busch brewery sites, along with a few off-site locations, and in 1996 more than 2,700 attendees completed the program. With the addition of the mobile exhibits, Anheuser-Busch has been able to make the popular Beer School program available to the public.

HISTORY OF ANHEUSER-BUSCH

It was 1852 and a tiny brewery on St. Louis' south side operated by George Schneider, opened for business. From 1857 to 1860, ownership of that brewery changed hands—three times. But it wasn't until 1860 that a great tradition of beer would begin.

His name was Eberhard Anheuser, a successful manufacturer turned brewery owner. And, in 1860, an expanded brewery reopened its doors under the name of E. Anheuser & Co.

The following year, Eberhard's daughter, Lily, married a young St. Louis brewery supplier named Adolphus Busch. Enticed by his father-in-law's offer, Adolphus joined the brewery in 1864 as a salesman. In 1865, E. Anheuser & Co. produced 8,000 barrels of beer, featuring St. Louis Lager, the company's original flagship beer.

By 1873, Adolphus was a full partner in the brewery, serving as the company's secretary. And in 1876, with his close friend, Carl Conrad, Adolphus created a new beer—Budweiser Lager—which became the brewery's new flagship beer, and 120 years later, still owns that title.

Upon the death of Eberhard in 1880, Adolphus became president and production of beer was up to 141,163 barrels, largely representative of an increase in the popularity of Budweiser Lager.

Michelob was introduced in 1896, and by 1901, production of Anheuser-Busch beer broke the million-barrel mark.

Adolphus Busch died in 1913 and August A. Busch, Sr., was named president—entering an era in which Anheuser-Busch was to face a variety of social and political changes: The First World War...Prohibition...and the Great Depression.

Intent on the survival of the company and protecting the jobs of its many hundreds of loyal employees during Prohibition, August focused the company's expertise and energies in new directions —including the production of corn products, baker's yeast, ice cream, soft drinks, commercial refrigeration units and truck bodies.

During this period, the company also introduced Bevo, a non-alcohol malt-based beverage, as well as a number of carbonated soft drinks including chocolate-flavored Carcho;

coffee-flavored Kaffo; Buschtee, flavored with imported tea leaves; Grape Bouquet grape drink; and Busch Ginger Ale. Each enjoyed various levels of success, but all were eventually discontinued when Prohibition ended and Anheuser-Busch could return to its core business—beer.

Baker's yeast proved to be another story—a long-term success story. This product, first manufactured in St. Louis in 1927, made great gains under the watchful eye of Adolphus Busch III, who became the company's president in 1934. Anheuser-Busch eventually became the nation's leading producer of compressed baker's yeast, a position it held until its Busch Industrial products subsidiary was sold in 1988.

August A. Busch, Jr., succeeded his brother as president in 1946 and served as the company's chief executive officer until 1975. He continued to serve as chairman of the board until 1977, when he was named honorary chairman. During his tenure, eight branch breweries were constructed; annual sales increased from three million barrels in 1946 to more than 34 million in 1974; Busch beer was introduced; and corporate diversification was extended to include family entertainment, real estate, can manufacturing, transportation and major league baseball. August Busch, Jr., died in 1989.

August A. Busch III became president in 1974 and was named chief executive office in 1975, becoming the fourth generation of his family to serve the company in that capacity. In 1977, he was elected chairman of the board.

Under his leadership, the company has: opened two breweries; introduced more than 20 new beer brands; launched the Anheuser-Busch Specialty Brewing Group; acquired a 25 percent stake in the Redhook Brewery of Seattle, WA; acquired a minority equity interest in Widmer Brothers Brewing Co. of Portland, OR; opened new family entertainment attractions through its Busch Entertainment Corp. subsidiary; launched the largest brewers expansion projects in company history; increased vertical integration capabilities with the addition of new can manufacturing and malt production facilities; and diversified into container recovery, metalized label printing, international marketing and creative services.

BEER BRANDS

Anheuser-Busch has developed products to meet a wide range of consumer tastes and price preferences. And, although each brand is produced according to a time-honored Old World brewing method, using only the finest natural ingredients, all Anheuser-Busch beers have their own unique characteristics.

Budweiser, the company's flagship brand, reigns as the top-selling beer brand in the world. Budweiser was introduced in 1876 when company founder Adolphus Busch set out to create the nation's first truly national beer brand—a beer that would be universally popular and transcend regional tastes.

Today, Budweiser leads the premium beer category. In fact, it outsells all other domestic premium beers combined. With broad appeal among virtually all demographic consumer groups, the brand truly lives up to its reputation as the "King of Beers."

Bud Light is the company's premium entry in the light beer category and continues to be the industry's fastest growing light beer. Introduced in 1982, Bud Light became the best-selling light beer in America in 1994 and the No.2 brand overall, trailing only Budweiser.

Introduced in 1993 as Ice Draft from Budweiser, **Bud Ice** is ice brewed to create a taste that is rich, smooth and remarkably easy to drink.

Bud Ice Light, introduced in 1994, incorporates advanced, state-of-the-art brewing methods to deliver a smooth taste at only 96 calories per serving.

Anheuser-Busch launched **Bud Dry** in 1989. An American Dry Lager, Bud Dry is not as sweet as Budweiser and has little aftertaste.

In 1896, Anheuser-Busch developed another beer brand, **Michelob**. Considered a "beer for connoisseurs," Michelob was served only on draught in the finest retail establishments. Michelob became available in bottles—with the distinctive hourglass shape and red ribbon—in 1961 and in cans in 1966.

In recent years, Michelob and the Michelob Family of beers have experienced a sales and awareness resurgence never before seen in American brewing—all the result of a combination of integrated marketing campaigns, renewed wholesaler confidence in the brands, strong retailer support and renewed value for the Michelob name in the consumer's eye.

In 1978, **Michelob Light** was introduced as the industry's first super premium light beer, for consumers who prefer a full-bodied, rich tasting beer with reduced calories. Michelob Light's growing popularity in recent years—its sales volume was up 6 percent in 1996—has sparked the Michelob Family's strong performance.

Three years later, in 1981, **Michelob Classic Dark** was introduced, offering consumers Michelob's smooth taste in a rich, dark beer. A two-time Great American beer festival gold medal winner in the dark lager category, Michelob Classic Dark is brewed using black malt, which gives the brand its deep color and a pleasant, malty character.

Michelob Dry was introduced nationally in 1988 as America's first super premium dry beer. It derives its distinct, clean taste from the use of the exclusive DryBrew method of brewing. The longer brewing process produced a less sweet beer with no aftertaste.

Michelob Golden Draft was introduced in 1991 as Anheuser-Busch's first entry into the clear bottle, packaged draft market. Its smooth, full taste is packaged in unique bottles and cans that feature exclusive faceted edges.

Michelob Golden Draft Light, also introduced in 1991, offers the same brewing and packaging features as Michelob Golden Draft, but with significantly fewer calories.

Busch, a popular priced beer, has achieved strong growth in many key markets. Introduced in 1955, the brand is now available in 48 states and the District of Columbia, and it ranks as one of the nation's 10 largest selling beers.

In 1989, Anheuser-Busch introduced **Busch Light**, the low calorie partner of the successful Busch brand.

Popular priced **Busch Ice**, introduced in 1995, combines the smooth refreshing taste of Busch beer with Anheuser-Busch's exclusive ice brewing process to produce a very drinkable beer.

Natural Light, the sub-premium priced beer unveiled in 1977, offers an excellent price/value for light beer drinkers seeking a quality product at an attractive price.

Introduced in 1995, sub-premium priced **Natural Ice** was developed in response to continued consumer interest in ice-brewed beers.

Michelob Malt was introduced in 1995 and is Anheuser-Busch's premium brand in the malt liquor category. It offers a smooth, full-bodied taste to consumers looking for a step up from their normal malt liquor brand.

Hurricane Malt Liquor, with a slightly sweet, robust taste, was introduced in 1996.

King Cobra was the first Anheuser-Busch entry into the malt liquor category. First available in 1984, the brand is now sold in more than 300 markets across the United States, offering a smooth, high quality malt liquor taste.

O'Doul's non-alcohol brew was introduced in 1989. It contains less than 0.5 percent alcohol by volume—about the same amount of alcohol found in some soft drinks and fruit juices. O'Doul's is marketed to consumers who want the great taste of an Anheuser-Busch beer, but without the alcohol.

Busch N/A, Anheuser-Busch's first sub-premium priced non-alcohol brew, was introduced in 1994 to help meet the demands of the growing non-alcohol segment. It contains less than 0.5 percent alcohol by volume.

Anheuser-Busch Specialty Brewing Group

In the 1990s, "The Specialty Brewing Group of Anheuser-Busch" was launched. The group was created by selecting some of the most independent-minded, creative brewmasters and beer enthusiasts within Anheuser-Busch and the industry. The result is a team of autonomous, self-driven beer lovers committed to nothing short of excellence.

The family of beers that has been born out of the Specialty Brewing Group has already garnered tremendous support from the beer drinking community. Although some of the beers are currently available only in selected markets, some, such as the Michelob Specialty Ales & Lagers and the

American Originals and Red Wolf are available nationwide. Each of the beers constitutes an important part of the Anheuser-Busch family.

Michelob Specialty Ales & Lagers

When Adolphus Busch first brewed Michelob in 1896, he had just one goal in mind—to create a specialty beer, the finest in the world. Today, Anheuser-Busch continues the spirit and quality brewing heritage inspired by Michelob for over a century with the next generation of specialty beers—the Michelob Specialty Ales & Lagers.

Anheuser-Busch's top-selling specialty beer, **Michelob Amber Bock** is an American-style bock beer that debuted in 1995. It is brewed with the finest dark roasted malts to produce a rich, malty flavor, amber color and full body, while its unique blend of hops and a touch of brewers rice give Amber Bock its characteristic smooth, clean finish.

Michelob Golden Pilsner is a classic European-style pilsner. Full-bodied and deep golden in color, Golden Pilsner has a rich malty flavor and a spicy aroma. It was introduced in early 1997.

An unfiltered American wheat ale, **Michelob Hefeweizen** (pronounced hay-fuh-vise-un) was introduced in Oregon in late 1995, and after expanding throughout the Northwest in 1996, Hefeweizen was released nationally in 1997. It is brewed with 50-percent wheat malt to produce a beer with a smooth, refreshing taste and cloudy golden color.

Michelob Honey Lager is brewed with natural wildflower honey to enhance the naturally sweet, creamy flavor of the beer. Also introduced in early 1997, Honey Lager is a very drinkable specialty beer, with a balanced taste and a uniquely soft, slightly sweet finish.

Michelob Pale Ale is a full-bodied golden pale ale. In addition to being brewed with the finest, all-natural barley malt and hops, Pale Ale is dry-hopped, adding a pronounced hop character to its malty aroma.

Michelob Porter, available in several select Northwestern markets, is brewed with a distinct blend of chocolate, black, caramel and pale malts and roasted barley, producing a hearty, full-bodied and robust dark ale.

American Originals

The three beers in the American Originals family were originally introduced by Adolphus Busch at the turn of the century. Close to the style, taste and look of the 5 original beers, today's American Originals were created from a variety of handwritten notes and sales literature from the late 1800s, found in the Anheuser-Busch archives. They are available nationally on draught and in bottles in select markets.

Originally brewed in 1895, **American Hop Ale** was Anheuser Busch's first mail-order beer. Customers could order cases of the brand and have it shipped directly to their homes. Today's American Hop Ale is a full-bodied amber ale, brewed with only American Fuggles and Cluster hops.

First brewed in 1885, **Faust** is an all-malt lager that is aged in lager tanks with beechwood chips for 25 days. Its deep golden color complements its complex malt, hoppy flavor.

Black & Tan porter was particularly popular on draught in saloons when it was first brewed in 1899. This full-bodied, porter-style ale has extra malt to soften the flavor. Its taste is slightly fruity, with chocolate notes, and a roasted and hearty flavor. First introduced on the East Coast in October 1994, **Red Wolf Lager** met with immediate consumer support, and became available nationally in January of the next year. Red Wolf is a very drinkable, smooth and subtly sweet red lager made from 100 percent all natural ingredients, including choice hops, select grains, water, yeast and specially roasted barley malt.

Currently available only in Texas, **Ziegenbock** is rich and dark in color with a rich, smooth, full-bodied taste. The beer was first introduced in selected cities in Texas in March 1995, and became available statewide in June 1995.

Pacific Ridge Pale Ale is an intensely hopped, full-bodied pale ale, brewed in Northern California exclusively for beer drinkers in Northern California. This regional beer, released in November of 1996, was created by the brewmasters at Anheuser-Busch's brewery in Fairfield, California.

Special Winter Brew, Anheuser-Busch's first seasonal beer, is a hearty, flavorful lager, reminiscent of traditional German-style holiday beers. Adolphus Busch first created a Christmas beer in the 1890s and in 1995, Anheuser-Busch brought back that tradition.

Imports

In addition to the wide variety of recently introduced domestic brews from the Specialty Brewing Group, several other beers in the family are imported into the United States by Anheuser-Busch.

Brewed under license from Denmark's Carlsberg A/S by Labatt Brewing Company in Canada, **Elephant Red** is distributed in the U.S. by Anheuser-Busch, Inc. Its dark red color is complemented by a drinkable, yet very full-bodied taste.

Brewed in Denmark by Carlsberg A/S since 1959, **Elephant Malt Liquor** has been available stateside since Anheuser-Busch began importing it in 1985. Very much in the European style, this malt liquor has a very strong, bold and distinctive taste.

The full-bodied character, and smooth and pleasing flavor of **Carlsberg** has been available in Europe since Carlsberg began brewing it in 1847. Americans have been enjoying the classic lager since it was first imported by Anheuser-Busch in 1985.

Nearly a century and a half after Carlsberg Beer was first brewed in Europe, its lighter calorie version was introduced to consumers. **Carlsberg Light** was made available to Europeans in 1985 and was first imported into the United States the next year. Using the same fine ingredients as its namesake, Carlsberg Light offers the flavor of Europe without all of the calories.

Rio Cristal is brewed in Brazil by Companhia Antarctica Paulista and imported by Anheuser-Busch. Originally test-marketed in Norfolk, Virginia, and Key West, Florida, Rio Cristal is now available in Miami, Fort Lauderdale and West Palm Beach as well. A smooth, refreshing golden lager, Rio Cristal captures the mystery and allure of Rio de Janeiro and its famous Carnaval celebration.

Anheuser-Busch - dedication, quality and tradition—trademarks that have dictated the growth of the company and positioned it as the largest and most successful brewer in the world.

BEER CLEAN GLASSES

Anheuser-Busch, the world's largest brewer, assures excellence in its draught beer from the brewery to the wholesaler. Likewise, Anheuser-Busch wholesalers take the necessary steps to make certain that the product is delivered to retail establishments in first-class condition. However, it's up to the bartender to draw the best possible glass of draught beer for the consumer.

The first step is to serve the draught beer in a clean glass...a Beer Clean Glass. A glass may look clean, but is it near clean or beer clean?

Following are a few tips for obtaining a "Beer Clean Glass," the eye-appealing glass filled with one of Anheuser-Busch's great beers with a clear, golden color and a good tight collar of foam.

A three or four-sink setup is ideal for getting glasses beer clean; a three-tank setup is most common. The first tank is for washing followed by two rinsing compartments.

A beer glass should be washed each time it is used—unless the customer requests that his glass be refilled. Proper cleaning and drying can be accomplished in four simple steps.

1. Used glasses should be emptied and rinsed with clear water to remove any foam or remaining beer which will cause dilution of the cleaning solution.

2. Each glass should be brushed in water containing a solution of odor-free and non-fat cleaning compound that will thoroughly clean the surface of the glass, and rinse away easily in clear water.

3. The glass must then be rinsed twice in fresh, clean, cool water—with the proper sanitizer in the last tank. Proper and complete rinsing is most important for a "beer clean" glass.

4. Dry glasses upside down on a deeply corrugated surface or stainless steel glass rack. Never towel dry glasses. Store air-dried glasses away from sources of unpleasant odors, grease or smoke that are emitted from kitchens, restrooms or ashtrays.

And, another secret to serving a perfect glass of beer...rinse the "beer clean" glass with cold, fresh water just before filling with Anheuser-Busch draught beer.

DISPENSING DRAUGHT BEER

Obtaining a "beer clean" glass is just one step involved in the proper dispensing of perfect "brewery fresh" draught beer. Equally important are proper refrigeration, cleanliness of dispensing equipment and proper pressures.

Since draught beer is perishable, it must not be exposed to warm temperatures. The retailer must preserve it by providing equipment that will maintain the temperature of the beer in the barrel between 38 - 42 degrees Fahrenheit. These temperatures should be maintained throughout the dispensing equipment so the beer in the glass as it is served to the consumer will also be 38 - 42 degrees Fahrenheit. This range of temperature seems to satisfy the majority of tastes and is too small a variation to affect its flavor or quality.

Cleanliness is a most vital consideration. The beer faucets, tubing, hose, coils, taps and vents, including direct draw systems, must be thoroughly cleaned regularly. Glasses should be "beer clean," and no effort should be spared to keep the bar clean and bright.

Finally, proper pressure in the barrel is very important. To maintain the brewery fresh taste in the beer, its natural or normal carbonation must be preserved. The dispensing equipment through which the beer flows must have a pressure that corresponds to the normal carbonation of the beer at the temperature of the beer in the barrel. The size and length of the coil in the dispensing equipment will determine the pressure to be used.

With the dispensing equipment properly set up, you are ready to serve fresh draught beer.

The right head of foam is important to giving a glass of beer that essential eye appeal. The size of the head is controlled by the angle at which the glass is held at the beginning of the draw. If the glass is held straight, so that the beer drops into the bottom, a deep head will result. If the glass is tilted sharply so that the beer flows down the side, the head of foam will be minimized.

For most beer glasses—and to please most customers—the head should be allowed to rise just above the top of the glass without spilling over, then settle down to a ¾" or 1" head of frothy white foam.

Remember, there are two key steps for serving a truly perfect glass of draught beer:—Use a "beer clean" glass, and before filling, rinse the glass in cold, running water.

© Foley Publishing Corp

SIGNATURE DRINKS
FROM ACROSS AMERICA

"440" DRINK

½ oz. Amaretto

½ oz. Chambord

½ oz. Midori

½ oz. Peach Schnapps

½ oz. Cranberry Juice

½ oz. Orange Juice

splash 7-Up

Shaken not stirred (all but 7-Up). Serve up in rocks glass.

Curtis Leroy
Doc Masters
San Diego, CA

$RICHIE RICH$

½ Dom Perignon

½ Grand Marnier

Over crushed ice; slice of orange.

Rich Linderman
Elenor Rigby's
Mineola, NY

ABSOLUTELY WILD

1½ oz. Absolut Vodka

½ oz. Wild Spirit Liqueur

Serve on the rocks. Garnish with cinnamon stick.

Rocky Horan
Howard's Cafe
Waterbury, CT

ALEXANDER'S COCKTAIL

1 oz. Dry Gin

1 oz. Green Creme de Menthe

Whipped Cream

Ice

Blend until smooth. Serve in tulip glass. Top with whipped cream. Drizzle Creme de Menthe over whipped cream swirls. Serve with soda straw.

Sue Newman
Alexander's
Feeding Hills, MA

ALTA VISTA FORE!-PLAY

1 oz. Bacardi Limón

1 oz. Tia Maria

Fill with hot coffee. Top with whipped cream. Put in two long sipper-straws.

Michael J. Jones
Alta Vista Country Club
Placentia, CA

ATLANTIC WAVE

1 oz. Vodka

½ oz. Peach Schnapps

½ oz. Blue Curacao

splash Sour Mix

Rub Rim of cocktail glass with lemon rind and dip in green Creme de Menthe and sugar. Blend ingredients with ice for short time and strain into sugar-rimmed glass.

Juan Castillo & Franklin Cruz
Mariscos del Atlantico
Bronx, NY

BABY GUINNESS
(Shot)

Fill 1½ oz. shot glass with:

1 oz. Coffee Liqueur

½ oz. Baileys Irish Cream

Float the Baileys on top of the liqueur. It looks like a small glass of Guinness.

Brian Kennedy
O'Connor's Pub
Liberty, NY

BAYOU BREEZE

1½ oz. Stoli Razberi

¾ fill Cranberry Juice

fill Pineapple Juice

Lime Wedge

Shake well. Serve over ice.

Christine Perl
French Quarter Daiquiris
Baton Rouge, LA

FRENCH QUARTER
Daiquiris

BEACH BUM BLUES

1 oz. Jose Cuervo Gold

1½ oz. Peach Schnapps

1½ oz. Blue Curacao

3 oz. Pineapple Juice

Wipe the rim of glass with a lime wheel and dip into sugar. Shake ingredients with ice, strain and serve with lime wheel garnish.

Andrew G. Chan
Kwong Ming Restaurant
Wantagh, NY

BEAU-JONNY

½ glass Beaujolais Nouveau

½ glass Brut Champagne

Jonathan Caws-Elwit
Sans Blague
Cafe Fauviste
Friendsville, PA

BLUE MOONRISE

1 oz. Malibu Coconut Rum

1 oz. Blue Curacao

2 oz. Ice Cream

Blend with two scoops of ice until smooth. Pour into an 8 oz. tulip glass. Top with whipped cream sprinkled with toasted coconut and garnish with a cherry.

Felicia Cote
Crow's Nest Restaurant
Palm Bay, FL

BOAT DRINK

2 oz. Captain Morgan
      Spiced Rum

Top with ginger ale. Squeeze two limes into it. Garnish with lime.

Dana Lawrence Forrar
Harry Denton's Bar & Grill
San Francisco, CA

Harry Denton's

CAFE ENRIQUE

1 oz. Tia Maria
½ oz. Coco Lopez
      Hot Coffee

Top with whipped cream and sprinkle with cinnamon and sugar.

Orlando Villarreal
Henry's Diner & Cantina
San Angelo, TX

CANTINARITA

1¼ oz. Cuervo Gold
¼ oz. Cointreau
¼ oz. Grand Marnier
¾ oz. Sweet & Sour
¼ oz. Rose's Lime Juice
2 oz. Orange Juice

Garnish with a wedge of lime and a little Mexican flag.

Charlie Harrison
The Cantina
Oakland, CA

CAPTAINS BUBBLEGUM BREEZER

1½ oz. Captain Morgan
      Original Spiced Rum
8 oz. Oceanspray Ruby
      Red Grapefruit Drink

Mix above with crushed ice and shake or place in a blender with crushed ice for a daiquiri.

David E. Pouliot
American Legion Jutras Post #43
Manchester, NH

CHECK MATE (CZECH MATE)

½ pint Pilsner Urquell
½ pint Guinness

Fill ½ of a pint glass with the Pilsner Urquell then layer Guinness on top.

Darren Cumminhs
MacGregors'
Fairport, NY

CHOCOLATE HAZELNUT TORTE

½ oz. Truffles

½ oz. Frangelico

⅓ oz. Chambord

Serve on rocks or in freshly brewed coffee!

Pete Tselious
Christos' Restaurant & Lounge
Bellingham, WA

COCONOT CREAM PIE

1 oz. Malibu Rum

1 oz. Buttershots Schnapps

     Ice Cream

     Ice

     Half & Half

Blend until smooth. Top with whipped cream and shaved coconut.

Joyce Hunt
Maxwell Inn
Maxwell, CA

COLADA BLUES

1 oz. Bacardi Añejo Rum

1 oz. Blueberry Schnapps

1 oz. Pineapple Juice

1 oz. Cream of Coconut

or 2 oz. Pina Colada mix in lieu of pineapple juice and coconut cream

This is a frozen drink. Fill blender with the ingredients listed above. Add ice and blend until smooth. Garnish with a few blueberries on top in a brandy snifter.

Mary-Antonia Lombardi
Adobe Blues
Staten Island, NY

COSY COVE

½ oz. Myers's Rum

½ oz. Tia Maria

½ oz. Chambord

Serve in glass mug. Top with coffee. Garnish with whipped cream and shaved chocolate.

Wendy Winford
Timber Cove Lodge South
Lake Tahoe, CA

DANCIN' COWBOY

⅓ oz. Kahlua

⅓ oz. Bols Creme de
Banana

⅓ oz. Baileys

Layer in shot glass in above order.

Nyla Pitts
Rock 'N' Rodeo
Medford, OR

DO YOU LOVE ME

"Now that I can dance..."

A refreshing blast of

Jack Daniel's

Triple Sec

Sweet & Sour

Top with splash of 7-Up.

Christopher Cunningham
MOTOWN Cafe
New York, NY

EL PATRON RITA GRAND

Patron Tequila

Cointreau

**The County Line on the Lake
Austin, TX**

ELK REFUGE

This is what the elk bugle for!

Myers's Rum

Orange Juice

Pineapple Juice

Cream of Coconut

Joseph DiPrisco
Lame Duck Restaurant
Jackson, WY

FIRE CIDER

1½ oz. Fire Hot Cinnamon Schnapps

1 packet Apple Cider Mix

7 oz. Hot Water

Preheat glass. Add apple cider mix hot water and Fire Hot Cinnamon Schnapps. Stir and garnish with lemon twist and dash of cinnamon.

Karen & Jay Graham
The River Haven Restaurant & Lounge
Hoquiam, WA

FRISCO QUAKE

½ oz. Southern Comfort

½ oz. Amaretto

½ oz. Sloe Gin

½ oz. Vodka

½ oz. Grenadine

Orange Juice

Sour Mix

Combine in a poco grande glass and garnish with a flag.

Frisco's Lounge
Days Inn
Butler, PA

FRICK COOLER

½ oz. Castillo Rum

½ oz. Barton Vodka

½ oz. McCormick Gin

½ oz. LaSalle Triple Sec

Sour Mix

Cranberry Juice

Sprite

Fill 16 oz. Mason Ball Jar with ice and combine liquor ingredients. Fill the rest of the jar with sour mix and cranberry juice. Shake well top off with Sprite and serve with a slice of lemon.

Ray and Teresa Frick
Fricker's
Perrysburg, OH

FROZEN PEACH FROST

1 part Captain Morgan Original Spiced Rum

1 part Peachtree Schnapps

2 parts Peach Puree

Blend with ice until thick and frosty. Serve with orange slice and cherry.

Dawn Busse
The Shore Club Restaurant
Bass Lake, Knox, IN

FUZZY MUSHROOM

- 1 oz. Vodka
- 1½ oz. Kahlua
- 1½ oz. Captain Morgan Spiced Rum
- 2 oz. Heavy Cream
- 2 oz. Cola

Blend ingredients with one barscoop of ice. Makes approximately 8 oz. to be served in tulip glass. Top with whipped cream and nutmeg.

Victoria L. Plonski
Rustic Ridge Inn
Clymer, NY

GREEN RIVER

- ¾ oz. Absolut Citron
- ½ oz. Midori
- 5 oz. Sunkist Lemonade
- float Sprite

Serve in poco glass with stem. Garnish with lime wedge.

Newport Bay Restaurant
Portland, OR

GTO

In 16 oz. glass filled ¾ full ice:

- ¼ oz. Vodka
- ¼ oz. Rum
- ¼ oz. Triple Sec
- ¼ oz. Amaretto
- ¼ oz. Yukon Jack
- ¼ oz. Southern Comfort
- ¼ oz. Grenadine

Fill with equal parts orange juice pineapple juice and sour mix. Shake.

Terry Oelschlager
Getaway Cafe
Pittsburgh, PA

HARRY DENTON'S STARLIGHT MARTINI

Beefeater Gin

Spray of Dry Vermouth

Burnt Lemon

Harry Denton's Starlight Room
Atop the Sir Francis Drake Hotel
San Francisco, CA

HENNESSEY'S HAMMER

1 oz. Midori Melon
      Liqueur

1 oz. Baileys Irish Cream

Float Baileys over Midori
      in a pony glass.

Jim "Hambone" Hennessey
Hennessey's
Morristown, NJ

HOW 'BOUT THEM APPLES

Hot Cider

1 oz. Chambord

½ oz. Malibu Rum

splash Godiva Chocolate

Pour into mug. Fill with hot
cider. Top with whipped cream.

Ken DePietro
Farmington Woods, C.C.
Farmington, CT

ISLAND MIST

½ oz. White Creme de
      Cacao

¼ oz. Frangelico

½ oz. Baileys

Sprinkle ground cinnamon on
top. Layer in shot glass.

Robbie J. Acoba
Steck's Restaurant & Bar
Honolulu, HI

JAMMER SLAMMER

2 oz. Bacardi Black Rum

2 oz. Pineapple Juice

1 oz. Orange Juice

1 oz. Coconut Milk

Shake well, serve over ice. Top
with cherry and orange slice.

Kathy Sebastiano
Jammers Grill & Party Pub
Islamorada, FL Keys

JANETINI

3 oz.	Stoli Ohranj chilled
½ oz.	Chambord
1 tsp.	Sugar
½	Fresh Lemon squeezed

Shake until very cold. Serve straight-up with lemon twist garnish.

Mixed by Marti
Perfected by Janet
Baja Mexican Cantina
Boston, MA

KEY WEST OYSTER SHOOTER

1 oz.	Bloody Mary Mix
1 oz.	Peach Schnapps
	Oyster
	Tabasco
	Black Pepper

Thomas W. Burnham
Key West Cafe
St. Louis Union Station
St. Louis, MO

LEMON DELIGHT

1½ oz.	Malibu Rum
1 oz.	Lemon
	Sour Mix
2 scoops	Lemon Sherbert
6 oz.	Ice

Fill the blender with ice add the above ingredients blend, pour into a hurricane glass and garnish with a wedge of fresh lemon and a cherry. Enjoy!

David R. Bouffard
Unk's on the Bay Restaurant
Waterford, CT

LIMELIGHT CREATOR

¾ oz.	Midori Melon Liqueur
¾ oz.	Light Rum
½ oz.	Sweet & Sour Mix
splash	Soda

Shake/strain over ice.

Stephen Michael Jaramillo
Older Buttwiser
Yuma, AZ

LIMERICK BITCH

1½ oz. Jameson Irish Whisky

1½ oz. Baileys Irish Cream

splash Kahlua

Fill rocks glass with ice; pour ingredients as listed.

Karen M. Carrig
O'Connor's Pub
Liberty, NY

LIMERICKS IRISH FLAG

1 oz. Green Creme de Menthe

1 oz. Baileys Irish Cream

1 oz. Brandy

Layer, with a spoon in a pousse cafe or stem martini glass or as a shooter.

Trudy Nelson
Limericks Pub & Grille
Fitzgeralds Hotel/Casino
Reno, NV
Submitted by: Jon Butterbaugh
Assoc. Prop.

LIQUID MARTINI

2 parts Absolut Vodka

splash Pineapple Juice

splash Blue Curacao

Shake gently over ice. Pour into chilled martini glass. Garnish with a lemon wedge.

Cassandra Schmidt
Liquid
Chicago, IL

Liquid

LONG ISLAND MARGERITA

¾ oz. Tequila

¾ oz. Rum

¾ oz. Gin

¾ oz. Vodka

¾ oz. Triple Sec

Pour into a Margerita glass with salt around the rim. Add half Rose's Lime Juice, half Sweet & Sour, splash of Coke and Sprite. Garnish with a lime or lemon wedge.

Natasha Yarbrough
Martin's Steak & Seafood
Lakeland, FL

MELON (WATER) COCKTAIL

½ oz. Vodka

½ oz. Rum

½ oz. Southern Comfort

½ oz. Amaretto

4 oz. Pineapple Juice

¾ oz. Grenadine

Shake with ice. Serve in a collins glass.

John Trksak
Bernie's Holiday Restaurant
Rock Hill, NY

MONKEY MARTINI

1¼ oz. Ketel One Vodka

¼ oz. Dark Creme de Cacao

¼ oz. Banana Liqueur

Shake well over ice. Strain into a martini glass and garnish with dark chocolate chips.

Denise Feiler
General Manager
The Iron Monkey Restaurant & Bar
Jersey City, NJ

THE IRON MONKEY
RESTAURANT & BAR

MOTOWN SMASH

Ridiculous mixture of:

Absolut Vodka

Captain Morgan Rum

Gin

Sauza Tequila

Triple Sec

Chambord

splash 7-Up

dash Pineapple Juice

WARNING: This drink is outrageous, proceed with caution.

Christopher Cunningham
MOTOWN Cafe
New York, NY

NORTHWEST RAINBOW

1¼ oz. Smirnoff Vodka

1½ oz. Sweet & Sour

1½ oz. Pineapple Juice

2 oz. Cranberry Juice

Splash Myers's Rum on top. Garnish with orange/cherry. Tall glass on the rocks. Pour in above order.

Alberto Meza
Fitzgerald's on 5th
The Westin Hotel
Seattle, WA

PARROT HEAD PUNCH

¼ oz. Strawberry Liqueur

¼ oz. Sloe Gin

¼ oz. Midori

¼ oz. Amaretto

¼ oz. Southern Comfort

Fill with orange juice and cranberry juice.

Brad Gallant
Acadien Social Club
Gardner, MA

PASSION PIT

In an ice-filled shaker:

½ oz. Key Largo Schnapps

½ oz. Wilderberry
        Schnapps

1 oz. Crantasia Schnapps

¼ oz. Frangelico

Shake and strain into a sugar-rimmed cocktail glass.

Sheryl J. Ridenour
Colters Lodge
Afton, WY

PIER MILKSHAKE

1 oz. Godiva Liqueur

½ oz. Baileys Irish Cream

½ oz. Buttershot Schnapps

1 scoop Vanilla Ice Cream

splash Half & Half

Blend with ice until creamy. Pour into a brandy snifter. Top off with whipped cream and chocolate powder.

Veronica Novack
Pier de Orleans
Phoenix, AZ

PIG TAIL

1½ oz. Absolut Vodka

½ oz. Blue Curacao

1 oz. Sour Mix

½ oz. Grenadine

Shake well; serve over ice. Fill with 7-Up cherry and orange peel twist.

Jon Greene
Purple Pig Pub
Alamosa, CO

PURPLE PACHYDERM SQUIRM MASTODON

1½ oz. Absolut Kurant
¼ oz. Chambord
¼ oz. Triple Sec
½ oz. Pineapple Juice
2 oz. Welch's Frozen Grape Concentrate

Blend with a scoop of ice. No garnish.

The Elephant Walk Lounge
Holiday Inn
Hotel Tanglewood
Roanoke, VA

PURPLE PISSANT or PURPLE ANTEATER

1½ oz. Blue Maui Hawaiian Schnapps
1 oz. Vodka
splash Grenadine (add to color)

In 12 oz. glass, plenty of ice pour, flash blend, or stir until purple color. Top with cherry.

Dennis D.J. Johnson
My Buddy's Place
Sheridan, WY

RASPBERRY TRUFFLE

1 oz. Stoli Razberi Vodka
1 oz. Godet White Chocolate
4 oz. Coffee
Whipped Cream

In a mug, top with whipped cream.

Mitchell
O'Casey's
New York, NY

RED LEMON

1 oz. Lemon Blitzur
1 oz. Absolut Citron
4 oz. Cranberry Juice

Top with soda.

Leonard J. Phillips
Lenny's
Toledo, OH

Lenny's

RED WHITE & MALIBLUE

1 oz. Light Rum
½ oz. Malibu
¼ oz. Blue Curacao
1 packet Sugar
Coco Lopez
Pineapple Juice

Blend. Pour over ladle of strawberries at bottom of glass.

Bill Davis
Peppers
Lancaster, PA

ROCKIN' RASPBERRY

1 oz. Absolut Vodka
1 oz. Gaetano Black
Raspberry Liqueur
2 oz. Sweet & Sour Mix

Pour into blender with ice, blend until frozen.

Marisa Santacroce
Santacroces'
Hood River, OR

ROSE PETAL

1 oz. Amaretto
½ oz. Baileys Irish Cream
2 oz. Strawberry Puree
1 oz. Half & Half
dash Grenadine
large dollop Whipped
Cream

Blend and serve in a snifter. Garnish with whipped cream, a sliced strawberry and green sprinkles.

Json Nakagawa
Tony Roma's
Westridge, HI

SEEING DOUBLE

1½ oz. Absolut Citron
½ oz. Chambord
splash Lime Juice

Straight up in a martini glass garnished with twin (two) raspberries.

Debra & Lisa Ganz
(The Ganz Twins)
Twins Restaurant
New York, NY

SEXUAL TRANCE

1 oz.   Absolut Citron

½ oz.   Midori

½ oz.   Chambord

½ oz.   Orange Juice

½ oz.   Pineapple Juice

splash Sweet & Sour

Cherry garnish

Tyri Squyres
Voo Doo Cafe & Lounge
Rio Suite Hotel & Casino
Las Vegas, NV

SIBERIAN SUNRISE

1½ oz. Stolichnaya Ohranj

5 oz.   Fresh Squeezed
Orange Juice

splash Cranberry Juice

Shake well with ice.

Mike Hrazanek
La Fontana Ristorante
New Brunswick, NJ

SLICK WILLIE

2 oz.   Stolichnaya Ohranj

1 oz.   Orange Juice

Top with soda. Garnish with orange wheel.

Rick Benedetti
DeFlippo's Restaurant
Lockport, NY

SMILE OF THE ORIENT

1 oz.   Gin

½ oz.   Lime Juice

½ oz.   Simple Syrup (Sugar)

⅓ oz.   Grenadine

1 oz.   Orange Juice

½   Fresh Papaya (Cut fruit
in half remove seeds
with a spoon cut one
half in handy wedges
and peel the green skin
off with a barknife.)

Blend all ingredients in Hamilton Beach blender with one barscoop of ice. Makes approximately 6 oz. to be served in a Martini glass garnished with a lime wedge.

Pierre Bonnet
L'Uraku Restaurant
Honolulu, HI

SOFIA

½ oz. Gordon's Vodka

½ oz. Kahlua

½ oz. Ouzo

1 oz. Light Cream

¼ oz. Green Creme de Menthe

Fill tall glass with ice and combine the ingredients. Stir well. Top with whipped cream and splash of green Creme de Menthe.

**Margarita & Bozidar Janakiev
Cafe Sofia Restaurant
Winchester, VA**

SPENCER SPICED COOLER

(Named for customer Barry Spencer)

1½ oz. Captain Morgan Spiced Rum

½ oz. Absolut Citron

2 oz. Orange Juice

Orange Sherbet

Blend with ice and serve this refresher on a hot day in a tall glass.

**Tom Hess
The Churchville Inn
Churchville, PA**

SPIKED WATERMELON MARGHERITA

1 shot Cuervo Gold

1 shot DeKuyper Mad Melon Watermelon Schnapps

2 cubes Seedless Watermelon (optional)

7-Up to fill

Blend with ice to make frozen. Garnish with a wedge of watermelon and a lime wheel.

**Sean Krebs
Studio Cafe
MGM Grand Hotel
Las Vegas, NV**

STEELE BREEZE

¼ oz. DeKuyper Bluesberry
        Schnapps

¼ oz. DeKuyper
        Wilderberry
        Schnapps

¼ oz. DeKuyper Key Largo
        Tropical Schnapps

¼ oz. Hiram Walker
        Raspberry Schnapps

¼ oz. Crown Royal

8 oz. Orange Juice

*Shake and serve over ice in
hurricane glass. Garnish with
umbrella and fruit wedge.*

John Steele, Jr.
The Steele Pier
Altoona, PA

 THE STEELE PIER

THE "BEAR DROPPING"

(collected fresh nightly)

In a chilled shot glass with
miniature chocolate chips on
the bottom:

⅓ Coffee Brandy

⅓ Irish Cream

⅓ Butterscotch
    Schnapps
    (a little less than ⅓)

*"Watch out for the Surprise on
the Bottom!"*

Eve Brancato
The Black Bear Tavern
Tahoe City, CA

Black Bear
Tavern

THE "WAY" ORANGE RITA

1¼ oz. Distinqt Orangy
         Tequila

¾ oz. Grand Marnier

2 oz. Sweet & Sour

*Pour into blender over ice,
blend until frozen. Garnish with
an orange slice.*

Rhonda Jung
Newport's Seafood
Dallas, TX

NEWPORT'S
SEAFOOD

THE CINNAMON STICK

½ oz. Godiva Chocolate
       Liqueur

½ oz. Baileys Irish Cream

½ oz. Kahlua

pinch Ground Cinnamon

*Ice and blend, serve in tulip
glass. To make a coffee drink,
just add coffee and top with
whipped cream and cinnamon
stick.*

Andrew Tosetti
The Inn at Chester
Chester, CT

THE COMPASS

½ oz. Myers's Rum

½ oz. Absolut Citron

½ oz. Grand Marnier

1 oz. Sweet & Sour

1 oz. Cranberry Juice

*Shake over ice and strain.
Serve in a double martini glass.*

Tom Godfrey
North by Northwest
Gig Harbor, WA

THE CREEKSIDE BREEZE

1 shot Bacardi Light Rum

1 shot Peach Schnapps

1 shot Amaretto

2 parts Cranberry Juice

1 part Sweet & Sour

splash 7-Up

*Combine with ice in blender.
Top with whipped cream and
garnish with lime & cherry.
(Makes 2-3 drinks)*

Valerie Hunt
Deadwood Gulch Resort
Creekside Restaurant
Deadwood, SD

THE GOLDEN GATE

In a Collins glass:

½ oz. DiSaronno Amaretto

½ oz. Malibu Rum

½ oz. Captain Morgan

½ oz. Stolichnaya 80 proof

1¼ oz. Pineapple Juice

1¼ oz. Orange Juice

*Shake it up. Top with ½ oz.
cranberry juice. No garnish.*

Scott McIntosh
T.G.I. Friday's, Fisherman's Wharf
San Francisco, CA

THE GRAND FLORIDIAN

1 oz. Grand Marnier

½ oz. Absolut Citron

1 oz. Orange Curacao

3 oz. Orange Juice

½ oz. Half & Half

Build in blender over ice and freeze. Serve in specialty glass. Garnish with lime, lemon or orange wheel.

Roberto De Jesus
Disney's Grand Floridian
Beach Resort
Orlando, FL

THE KING BRUCE

Fill bottom third of flute-style shot glass with Kahlua Liqueur. Add 1-2 drops B&B Liqueur and float ice cold Baileys Irish Cream on top.

Janet E. Morann
The Killingworth Cafe
Killingworth, CT

THE HARBORMASTER

1 oz. Carolans Irish Cream Liqueur

splash DeKuyper Hazelnut Liqueur

splash Hiram Walker Chocolate Mint Liqueur

½ oz. DeKuyper Butterscotch Schnapps

splash Grand Marnier Liqueur

Serve in snifter with 2 oz. Hot Coffee (whipped cream optional) or on the rocks.

Casey Maule
Diamond Jim's Restaurant and Lounge
Vancouver, WA

THE ORGAN DONOR

Absolut

Light Rum

Gin

Triple Sec

Tia Maria

Kahlua

Sour Mix

splash Cranberry Juice

Jekyll & Hyde Club
New York, NY

THE PAUPACK PUNCH

2 oz. Captain Morgan Spiced Rum

2 oz. Myers's Rum

2 oz. Boggs Cranberry Liqueur

fill Tropicana Twister - Cranberry Orange

Combine all ingredients into a 31 oz. snifter with ice. Garnish with palm tree stir sticks two gummy sharks speared with swords and two straws.

Stephen Ehrhardt
The Silver Birches Inn and Motel
Ehrhardt's Lakeside, Hawley, PA

THE PLUM

½ oz. Bacardi

½ oz. Bacardi 151

½ oz. Peach Schnapps

½ oz. Blue Curacao

2½ oz. Sour Mix

1 oz. Grenadine

splash Lime Juice

Shake and pour over ice. Float Grand Marnier. Garnish with cherry and lime.

Vyncent Larsen
Neighbours, Seattle, WA

THE STATION BLUES

Absolut

Malibu Rum

Blue Curacao

Orange Juice

Cranberry Juice

Kevin Heinold
The Station
Bernardsville, NJ

THE TROPICAL LOUIE

Fill 12 oz. glass with crushed ice:

1 oz. Bacardi Limón

¼ oz. Triple Sec

¼ oz. Peach Schnapps

¼ oz. Sloe Gin

Fill remainder of glass with cranberry and pineapple juice.

Shake and serve with wedge of pineapple or orange.

Louie Salvino
Lake Ontario Playhouse
Comedy Club
Sackets Harbor, NY

LAUGH
or DIE
AT
LAKE ONTARIO PLAYHOUSE
SACKETS HARBOR, N.Y.

TOMOKO

½ oz.   Vodka

¼ oz.   Peach Schnapps

¼ oz.   Triple Sec

¼ oz.   Midori

¼ oz.   Grenadine

¼ oz.   Lime Juice

¼ oz.   Chardonnay

splash   Orange Juice

splash   Pineapple Juice

splash   Cranberry Juice

squeeze   One Lemon Wedge

Shake and pour into hurricane glass. Garnish with orange wheel.

Jeff Lokey
Cherry Blossom Japanese Restaurant
Novi, MI

TSUNAMI

¼ oz.   Captain Morgan Spiced Rum

¼ oz.   DiSaronno Amaretto

¼ oz.   Peach Schnapps

splash   Orange Juice

splash   Pineapple Juice

Chill over ice; strain into shot glass.

Chris McCullough
Cha Cha Cha Salsaria
Waikiki, Honolulu, HI

TUNA TICKLER

Bacardi Light Rum

Absolut Vodka

Tanqueray Gin

Chambord

Sweet & Sour Mix

splash   Lemon-Lime Soda (Sprite)

Shake contents with ice and serve in original shaker glass.

The Tuna Crew
Aceitunas* Beer Garden
El Paso, TX
*olives in Spanish

Beer Garden

WILD COFFEE

½ oz. Wild Spirit

½ oz. Butterscotch Schnapps

½ oz. Baileys Irish Cream

Balance coffee. Sprinkle with nutmeg.

**Michael J. Carpenter
Springfield Inn
Springfield, PA**

WIPE OUT

1 oz. Rum

1 oz. Tequila

2 oz. Pineapple Juice

1 oz. Orange Juice

splash Sour Mix

Shake, strain over ice in salted rim glass. Garnish with pineapple and cherry.

**Steve DiSantos
Martins Restaurant & Lounge
Flagler Beach, FL**

WOODY'S LAFAYETTE

1 shot Chambord

½ shot Dailey's Pina Colada Mix

½ oz. Jacquin Rum

Whipped Cream

In a blender combine liquor and Dailey's mix. Add ice and fill blender half way with aerosol whipped cream. Blend until liquid. Pour into glass.

**James Lombardo
Crimson Rose Restaurant
Pittston, PA**

ZAMBONI

Red Wine

1½ oz. Stoli Persik Vodka (Peach)

splash Chambord

7-Up

In a tall glass fill ¾ with red wine. Top with Stoli Persik and Chambord.

**Marideth Post and Sara Ledoux
Puccini & Pinetti
San Francisco, CA**

PUCCINI & Pinetti

All Recipes published as submitted.

© Foley Publishing Corp

POUSSE-CAFES

Pousse-Cafe, French for "after coffee," was and is the quintessential test of a Bartender's ability as a mixologist. Pousse-Cafes are French in origin and are layered specialty drinks. Bartenders in New Orleans first popularized Pousse-Cafes in the late 1840s and the drinks became a fad in bars and restaurants throughout the United States in the early 1900s.

A Bartender is really put to the "test" when making a Pousse-Cafe. One needs a steady hand and the knowledge of specific gravities of cordials, syrups and brandies. From three to twelve different types of the above-mentioned are poured over the back of a spoon into a cordial glass. The spoon brakes the fall of the liquids, enabling them to layer more easily. By adding the ingredients in order of their specific gravities, they remain separate and the result is a colorful rainbow effect. Pousse-Cafes can be prepared ahead of time for use at a party or to end a special dinner. They will keep for at least an hour in the refrigerator before the layers start to blend. If brandy is your last ingredient, the "show" would go on further by flaming it when served or even squeezing an orange peel on the lit brandy would heighten the effect.

THE ULTIMATE COCKTAIL BOOK is happy to present a listing of the Hiram Walker cordial line and their specific gravities. So grab your spoons and cordial glasses and "Pousse-Cafe the night away!!"

The Hiram Walker cordials, liqueurs and products shown below can be used in Pousse-Cafes. Be sure to pour slowly over the back of a spoon. For best results allow at least five units between each liqueur starting with the type having the highest number.

HIRAM WALKER
POUSSE-CAFE SPECIFIC GRAVITY INDEX*

No.	Proof	Product	Specific Gravity	Color
1	40	Creme de Cassis	1.1833	Lt. Brown
2	25	Grenadine Liqueur	1.1720	Red
3	54	Creme de Cacao	1.1561	Brown
4	48	Hazelnut Schnapps	1.1532	Tawny
5	40	Praline	1.1514	Brown
6	54	Creme de Cacao, Wht.	1.1434	Clear
7	56	Creme de Noyaux	1.1342	Red
8	48	Licorice Schnapps	1.1300	Clear
9	54	Chocolate Cherry	1.1247	Brown
10	56	Creme de Banana	1.1233	Yellow
11	54	Chocolate Mint	1.1230	Brown
12	48	Blue Curacao	1.1215	Blue
13	54	Swiss Choc. Almond	1.1181	Brown
14	60	Creme de Menthe, Wht.	1.1088	Clear
15	60	Creme de Menthe, Gr.	1.1088	Green

16	60	Orange Curacao	1.1086	Tawny
17	60	Anisette, White and Red	1.0987	Clear/Red
18	48	Creme de Strawberry	1.0968	Red
19	48	Wild Strawberry Schnapps	1.0966	Clear
20	48	Red Hot Schnapps	1.0927	Red
21	60	Triple Sec	1.0922	Clear
22	60	Rock & Rye	1.0887	Yellow
23	40	Cranberry Cordial	1.0872	Red
24	50	Amaretto	1.0842	Tawny
25	48	Old Fashioned Root Beer Schnapps	1.0828	Tawny
26	84	Sambuca	1.0813	Clear
27	40	Country Melon Schnapps	1.0796	Pink
28	70	Coffee Flavored Brandy	1.0794	Brown
29	48	Red Raspberry Schnapps	1.0752	Clear
30	48	Snappy Apricot Schnapps	1.0733	Tawny
31	48	Cinnamon Schnapps	1.0732	Red
32	48	Spearmint Schnapps	1.0727	Clear

33	60	Shamrock Schnapps	1.0617	Green
34	60	Peppermint Schnapps	1.0615	Clear
35	48	Jubilee Peach Schnapps	1.0595	Clear
36	70	Raspberry Flavored Brandy	1.0566	Red
37	70	Apricot Flavored Brandy	1.0548	Tawny
38	70	Peach Flavored Brandy	1.0547	Tawny
39	70	Cherry Flavored Brandy	1.0542	Red
40	70	Blackberry Flavored Brandy	1.0536	Purple
41	90	Peach Schnapps	1.0534	Clear
42	90	Root Beer Schnapps	1.0441	Brown
43	50	Amaretto and Cognac	1.0394	Tawny
44	90	Cinnamon Spice Schnapps	1.0358	Red
45	60	Sloe Gin	1.0241	Red
46	70	Ginger Flavored Brandy	0.9979	Light Br.
47	90	Kirschwasser	0.9410	Clear

*If you use other brands, the specific gravity will vary from one manufacturer to another.

SOME SIMPLE RECIPES

ANGEL'S KISS

1 oz. Hiram Walker Dark
Creme de Cacao

1 oz. Cream

It's an Angel's Tit when you garnish with a cherry on a toothpick centered across the top.

FIFTH AVENUE

Equal parts:

Hiram Walker Dark
Creme de Cacao - Brown

Hiram Walker Apricot
Brandy - Gold

Cream - White

FOURTH OF JULY

⅓ shot Major Peters'
Grenadine

⅓ shot Absolut Vodka

⅓ shot Hiram Walker
Blue Curacao

GRAVURE

Equal parts:

Major Peters'
Grenadine - Red

Hiram Walker Dark
Creme de Cacao - Brown

Hiram Walker
Triple Sec - Clear

IRISH FLAG

⅓ shot Hiram Walker Green
Creme de Menthe

⅓ shot Carolans Irish Cream

⅓ shot Hiram Walker
Triple Sec

SAVOY HOTEL

½ oz. Hiram Walker White
Creme de Cacao

½ oz. Benedictine

½ oz. Brandy

TRAFFIC LIGHT

⅓ oz. Hiram Walker Green
Creme de Menthe

⅓ oz. Hiram Walker Creme
de Banana

⅓ oz. Hiram Walker
Sloe Gin

YELLOW MORNING

1 part Hiram Walker Creme
de Banana

1 part Cherry Herring

1 part Cognac

© Foley Publishing Corp

INDEX

428

429

430

D

T

U, V

W, X

#

© Foley Publishing Corp

F.X. McRory's
Whiskey Bar — Seattle
22 ⅛" x 38"

Club House at Old St.
Andrews
21" x 28"

Polo Lounge
17 ¾" x 39 ½"

LeRoy Neiman Unlimited, Numbered Color Silk Screens Signed in the Plate: "Wine, Women and Cigar; Club House at Old St. Andrews; and California Cuisine $250.00 each; Posters: F.X. McRory's Whiskey Bar—Seattle; Polo Lounge $35.00 each. Add $15.00 for shipping & handling. NJ residents add 6% sales tax. Send check or money order to Foley Publishing, P.O. Box 158, Liberty Corner, NJ 07938. Tel: 908-766-6006; FAX: 908-766-6607. Credit cards only telephone: 1-800-463-7465 (9:00 am - 9:00 pm EST, M-F, only). Allow 2-4 weeks for delivery.
For more information on LeRoy Neiman Art call 908-766-6006

Contains just about
every shooter imaginable.
$7.95 (plus $2 shipping)

Over 150 X-Rated
drink recipes.
$6.90 (plus $2 shipping)

Over 300 quotes and advice
from one of the greatest
sources: Anonymous!
$7.95 (plus $2 shipping)

Travel to Ireland via your tastebuds
and experience the many Spirits of Irish
Whisky, Malts, Stouts, and Cream
Liqueurs. $10.95 (plus $2 shipping)

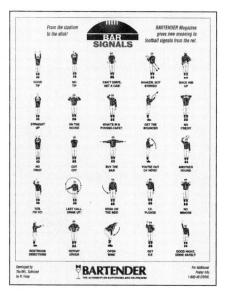

Bar Signals Poster
23" x 29"
$15.00 (plus $5 shipping)

Bartending for Dummies
$14.99 (plus $3 shipping)

The one and only
"BEARTENDER"
(11" tall) $20.00
(includes shipping)

Credit card orders phone: 1-800-GO-DRINK (9:00am – 9:00pm M-F, EST only) Or send, check or money order to: BARTENDER, PO Box 158, Liberty Corner, NJ 07938-9986

The 10 Best Reasons for Being A Bartender T-Shirt

Large or XLarge: $20.00
XXLarge: $25.00
(Shipping Included)

THE 10 BEST REASONS FOR BEING A BARTENDER

1. You get to stay out late.
2. You give "Last Call" and still drink.
3. No kids allowed.
4. You never go home alone.
5. You know where the restrooms are.
6. Only one Happy Hour a day.
7. You know Hymie Lipshitz personally.
8. You get to reject the songs on the jukebox.
9. You don't have to ask - "Do you want fries with that?"
10. Tips.

Back

Front

Credit card orders phone: 1-800-GO-DRINK (9:00am - 9:00pm M-F, EST only)
Or send check or money order to: BARTENDER Magazine
PO Box 158, Liberty Corner, NJ 07938-9986

YOUR FAVORITE RECIPE

YOUR FAVORITE RECIPE

YOUR FAVORITE RECIPE

YOUR FAVORITE RECIPE

YOUR FAVORITE RECIPE

YOUR FAVORITE RECIPE

YOUR FAVORITE RECIPE

YOUR FAVORITE RECIPE

YOUR FAVORITE RECIPE

YOUR FAVORITE RECIPE

YOUR FAVORITE RECIPE